Parent Power/Child Power

Parent Power/ Child Power

A New and Tested Method for Parenting
Without Guilt

by

HELEN DE ROSIS, M.D.

THE BOBBS-MERRILL COMPANY, INC.
Indianapolis / New York

ISBN 0–672–51915–1
Library of Congress catalog card number 73-11806
Designed by Jacques Chazaud
Manufactured in the United States of America

First printing

To my children

All   my   fondnesses
                    crash
                        into   one   drop
                                of   morning   dew.

ACKNOWLEDGMENTS

THERE ARE so very many persons who have made it possible for me to collect data and to work in the context of the parent discussion groups that I can name them only collectively. I am grateful to the superintendents of several New York City school districts (before decentralization) who listened to me, encouraged my plans, and then so graciously introduced me to school administrators in their districts. Through these men and women I was able to work with members of the Bureau of Vocational and Educational Guidance and with individual school personnel who made all arrangements for the group discussions. Other schools that provided me with opportunities to work with parent groups were public schools outside of New York City, as well as private schools and community agencies, principally the Riverdale Mental Health Clinic in New York City.

Perhaps my greatest single debt is to Dr. Stuart Keill, who, as Director of Community Mental Health Services some years ago, at The Roosevelt Hospital in New York, was consistently enthusiastic in his support of my ideas regarding problem prevention and parent education. And finally to my family, who, by their minimal demands, made it possible for me to get down to the actual task of preparing the manuscript.

Contents

Preface

This book has been written for three groups of parents:

1) Those who have small children (1–5) and who find themselves harried, irritated, or crushingly bored with all the nitty-gritties of child rearing, who want to be loving, effective parents, and who feel guilty because they react the way they do;

2) Those who have older children (6–12) and who find themselves harried, irritated, or crushingly bored with all the nitty-gritties of child rearing, who want to be loving, effective parents, and who feel guilty because they react the way they do; and

3) Those who have teen-age children, and feel the same as above, but who in addition find themselves disappointed in their youngsters and disliking them for making them react the way they do.

What makes it so difficult these days to live in harmony with a child? On the one hand, parents have brainwashed themselves into believing that they must not impose their expectations on their children (resulting in so-called permissiveness), and on the other, they are unaware of the many expectations they do impose. Caught in the middle, they are furious at their many failures to rear their children with the attitudes and values they feel the children should have, and furious also that they themselves have not lived up to their self-images of benevolent, nonintrusive parents. Their rage is then visited on the child, whom they do not "blame" intellectually. They cannot, however, control the feelings of blame, frustration, and rage which lurk within and which often lead to destructive equivocation and dissension.

In a quest for relief from such feelings, parents often seek help from experts. In doing so, however, they try to use the experts' suggestions as *the* way for them, without evaluating the compatibility of those suggestions with their own backgrounds, personalities, and family needs. To be useful, a suggestion must be filtered through your own evaluating system. It is for you then to accept or reject it. Only then can it have meaning and value within the context of your own family.

Introduction

Over ten years ago I began to work with groups of parents in schools and community centers, parents who were concerned about the quality of their parenting and who wanted to do as much as they could to help their children learn and grow. As I worked with them, many expressed feelings of inadequacy about their functioning as parents. Not only that, but they usually felt guilty because of their limitations.

Often their guilt was two-sided. Where children had even a small problem, parents felt that they had done something specific to cause the problem; furthermore, they felt neglectful in not having prevented it. So they were blaming themselves for doing too much—in causing the difficulty—and too little—in not preventing it. Such feelings lead to self-recrimination, which contributes to a form of circular thinking, escape from which parents often find extremely difficult if not impossible.

What I would like to do here is to revise the focus of parenting. Rather than focus on the "parent trap" of guilt and self-recrimination, I propose a two-step shift: First, a shift away from the guilt feelings through greater awareness of what brings them about in the first place; and second, a shift toward the use of parent power applied to tested ways of preventing destructive reactions to parent-child tension.

As the parent, you are in the best position to be the *primary agent* for preventing your child's discontent and his learning or behavior disorders. No one else is so available, so intimate, so committed, so powerful as you. This is true not only in the early years, but throughout adolescence and young adulthood. If you can appreciate this, you will be more interested in your parenting.

What I propose is a real understanding of your power and of your child's power; how to direct that power into constructive channels; how to use parent power to help bring satisfaction in rearing your children. If you can rid yourself of traditional worrisome stances, guilt-ridden self-views, and anxiety-laden attitudes toward children's venturing, as they must, into their worlds, then you approach the possibility of an uncluttered joy in viewing the unfolding of your child's unique potential.

In the parents' discussion groups, we discussed and explored our own roles as parents—at times severely limited, ineffectual, inexperienced, inarticulate, afraid—at times wise, patient, relaxed, and able to participate joyfully with our youngsters and smile at their natural childishness. Group members urged me to "write about" the many insights we had come upon so that "other parents could share them."

I thought I could best do this by using the many vignettes included in this book. These demonstrate what parents really do, think, and say, and in some cases why. Through them, I shall attempt to strip away your need to see yourself as a *superparent,* knowing and being all things to your child, and to accept yourself when you find out (over and over and over) that you are not.

Just let yourself go with this material. Read it easily, in as relaxed a fashion as you can. Don't search for answers. I'll describe a three-step method for you to follow—a method that will help you raise your own questions, find your own alternatives, and then put your findings into action. After you have read the book, if you feel that any of the material reflects what goes on in your family, try the three-step method I suggest. With it, you may be better able to look at what you are doing, and to begin, like charity, at home with the process of change.

Satisfactory parenthood has to be worked at. Having a child and seeing it through babyhood is only one small step, usually the easiest. It's like planting flowers. Once they are in the ground, they need attention, or the blossoms will be skimpy. Sun and water aren't enough. For children, food, shelter, clothing, and other objects aren't enough. They need mothers and fathers who are working at their parenting. Growing children need *growing parents;* it is difficult to imagine the satisfactory evolution of a child without the parallel evolution of a parent. Ideally, they develop and grow together.

I hope this book will afford you some relief from the tensions that accompany your parental attitudes and that it will supply some clues that will help you to grow, using your parent power and your child's power constructively.

Part One

CHAPTER I

Parent Education and Problem Prevention

WE ALREADY KNOW that the ultimate mental health of any individual is related to the nature of early relationships in the home. We also know that parents are subject to strong cultural and environmental pressures which influence family relationships to a greater or lesser degree. Nevertheless, *parents remain primarily responsible* for establishing feelings, moods, attitudes, values, and practices that will most influence youngsters' physical, emotional, and intellectual growth. Therefore, as the most significant link between a child and the quality of his entire future life, parents need and deserve the best available assistance in order to fulfill their responsibility.

Yet most people reach parenthood with little or no previous experience. They then expect to take on this most arduous task with boundless good cheer and optimism. They expect to be good parents without training or even without awareness that continuous effort must be made if they are to become knowledgeable as parents. We can imagine the dilemma of the untrained person who is thrust into a special technician's job, without any previous knowledge of the job, and who is expected to be a good technician immediately. Yet society tends to take for granted that young people thrust into parenthood can perform adequately, if not well. The contention is held that most of us have had experience by watching a parent of our own. What people often overlook, however, is that in terms of mental health our own parents' approaches may have left something to be desired.

As members of this society young parents are usually very hard on themselves, expecting as if by magic to know just how to make the parental pathway smooth. Take for example the young mother, with her first child, who read somewhere that newborn babies sleep about twenty hours a day. (The book actually said: A very few babies may sleep as many as twenty hours a day.) What a holiday that would be —all the time in the world to get laundry, formula, housekeeping, and even hair done. But apparently most newborns aren't aware of that possibility, and so prefer to sleep in small snatches whenever they happen to feel sleepy. A young mother fears that something may be wrong with her child, herself, or both. Edgy because of her doubts and self-critical feelings, pressured and fatigued by her new duties and responsibilities, she is now in a position to start a reciprocally antagonistic parent-child relationship. Parent-child tension has begun!

I consider parenthood the single most important job in the world. Yet until very recent years, little has been done in the field of education to lighten the burden of the uninformed parent. I often hear: "Doctor, we did our very best. We don't know how this happened. We didn't know what else to do." I might hear this at 3 A.M. in an emergency room where parents are devastated by the spectacle of a retching son or daughter who has tried suicide. I might hear it in my office when some parent is beside himself with worry over an adolescent who is a truant or who cannot become involved in any worthwhile activity. Little has been done to *prevent* such occurrences, to diminish the abysmal ignorance which somehow contributes to such sad outcomes. Little has been done in tangible, specific terms to convey to parents how they might proceed, at times despite overwhelming odds, to enhance the quality of their influence so that optimal growth is at least approached. So much has been left to chance. That is one reason why many parents, advantaged or not, experience only minimal satisfaction with their children's development, as with their own.

The way a child approaches learning, relating to peers, and encountering a wider world is determined before he ever leaves the home to spend a large part of his day in school. A child impoverished in these respects may be enriched or crushed by school experiences. Conversely, school experiences may either impair or strengthen the confidence of the child who comes from a home where the parents have a stable sense of self.

If school experiences cannot be relied upon to enhance and strengthen, should both parents then be educated to assist in the development of their children? Some institutions have already taken steps in the direction of parent education. But I believe that *all* appropriate educational facilities must undertake this task. Parents must be helped to make contact with their own resources, their talents, or whatever skills they can bring to rearing a child.

Does a father know that his aptitude at repairing a door or painting a room is an extraordinarily important feature of his fathering? If not, who is to convey this information to him? How can he know that he can include in a repair job any member of his family who shows interest in it; that he can make each small project a memorable moment of family harmony; that he needn't rush to finish the job (unless it's an emergency) but permit an interested child to relish the experience of finding the right tools, shopping for materials, measuring and preparing them, seeing the work accomplished, experiencing the satisfaction and thanks when the job is done? (Mind you, I leave out *well,* because it might not be done so "well" if the child has had a real hand in it beyond the planning and preparation.) However, it will be done well later on as he becomes older and more experienced. It is worthwhile for a father to learn this and hundreds of other things he needs to know to enjoy and fulfill his job as parent.

Parents are quick to point out their shortcomings, to wallow in guilt, and to hate themselves for their limitations. These preoccupations, together with the energy and time they take, can be redirected by parents toward an appreciation of their strengths and toward a search for ways to restore interest and confidence in themselves. My experience has shown me that people are often stronger than they realize, wiser than they believe, and more effective than they ever imagined. The problem is to make them aware of and to connect them with their many *untapped reservoirs of mental health.* For it is an unfortunate truth that parents who think ill of themselves are not able to inspire true self-confidence and well-being in their children.

The views and approaches described here have been developed in the context of *mental health,* not mental illness. Health and wellness, in terms of reservoirs of strength, resourcefulness, and untapped skills are repeatedly underscored. Parents need to feel optimistic about this potential mental health and to make efforts to let it serve them. Self-doubt and pessimism are so prevalent among parents that good common sense is often corroded, accessibility to experience is lost, and hard-earned wisdom is deeply undermined. Too many parents cry, "I can always tell someone else what to do in a similar situation. But I turn off when it's my own child!"

Prevention

This book has been prepared essentially for parents who have relatively good mental health. The focus of the book is on the maintenance of the wellness just mentioned, on the eliciting of strengths, and on the prevention of common stresses and problems which too often intrude upon moments of potential happiness within families.

Parents who can be helped to understand some of the underlying causes for parent-child tension may serve as *primary preventive agents* in overcoming 1) common communication gaps within the family, 2) behavioral disorders in school or at home, and 3) learning disorders. In other words, we intend to prevent the development of any form of destructive disturbance in children. If a member of a family already faces one of these problems, this approach may be used to help alleviate or partially overcome that problem. Here as elsewhere, the adage that an ounce of prevention is worth a pound of cure is especially applicable. Stating it more emphatically, and surely more exactly, I say that in parent-child relations an ounce of prevention may relieve parents of tons of future anguish.

The principle of prevention as applied here parallels that of preventing physical diseases. Although not every child will be exposed to smallpox, polio, or diphtheria, a concerted, large-scale effort must be made to protect *all* children. The effort is well worthwhile if thousands of youngsters are protected—youngsters who might otherwise have contracted these diseases.

Considering the many youngsters who are exposed to psychological damage, unwittingly imposed by family or society, the task of preventing emotional, learning, and behavioral disorders assumes its proper significance. Even minor disorders or undue parent-child tensions may blunt the child's ability to reach, touch, explore, and satisfy those inner wellsprings of curiosity, spontaneity, creativity, and joy. Part of this blunting might be prevented in the context of the early child-parent relationship. Furthermore, this might be accomplished with less difficulty, less time, and less expense than would be required to treat the disorders once they become established.

One key to success in preventive work is the constructive use of the parent's mental health. In order to tap this wellness, however, the parent must be shown how to identify and appreciate his areas of health and how to put them into service. The parent can then develop a sense of autonomy and approach his youngster with less inner conflict and therefore with less anxiety. Thus he can put his previously unrecognized resources to work and expand upon them.

I want to tell you in some detail how preventive moves may be initiated and what results may follow. In a parents' discussion group, a young mother described her disobedient ten-year-old son. Then, rising to leave, she remarked, "And I've got a girl who's just the opposite. She's so good. She does everything I say, and she never gives me any trouble." One of the other women remarked, "Well, maybe that could be a problem too." The first woman asked, "You mean, maybe it's not such a good thing to be good all the time?"

The following week, she reported that her "good" daughter had come home one day visibly disturbed, telling her mother that she had disobeyed her teacher. The mother replied, "Oh, that's all right. You can't be good all the time." She told the group that she had made this remark because of the final few words at the meeting the previous week. She hadn't actually thought of these words, but she knew retrospectively that her comment to the child was directly influenced by those words.

This same eight-year-old girl had been wetting her bed every night for several years. She did not wet her bed the night following the above conversation, nor for five consecutive nights. This is a somewhat dramatic outcome and not a common one. But it demonstrates how parents, given a little assistance, can help their children in very important ways.

Another woman expressed her worry about her four-year-old

daughter. This woman's father had died some weeks before, and she had not told the child of her grandfather's death because she expected her to be frightened of the idea of death. Some group members agreed with her. Others assured her that this information would probably not harm the child. One group member ventured to say that perhaps the parent had anxieties about death, and that she was assuming her daughter shared them. Later discussion revealed that many of the women felt that children are naturally frightened by anything having to do with death. Some suggested that the child be told of her grandfather's death and no more than that unless she asked. At the next meeting, it was reported that the child had been told, and that there seemed to be no untoward reaction. The child had responded with a seeming indifference which had puzzled her mother.

Another woman told the group that when her four-year-old had learned of her grandmother's death, the child had remarked, "Oh, that's good. Now we won't have to be so careful at the table when we visit."

In the following discussion, it was emphasized that very young children may not have the fears that their parents believe they have. On the other hand, as they grow older, children may develop anxieties similar to those of their parents—even though the parent may try to protect the child against the anxieties. Such efforts frequently take the form of an anxiety-shrouded protectiveness which serves to convey the very fears that the parent is trying to hide. If infected by strong parental fears and anxieties, a child may often become debilitated and helpless. If a parent can succeed in preventing this, witnessing the child's freedom from fear proves that the parent's anxiety existed only for herself and not for the child.

I cannot offer you an easy program for prevention of potential stress situations. I can only offer general principles of relating, which, if understood and appropriately applied, can be useful in your relations with youngsters of any age. And since youngsters are people like anyone else, an understanding of these principles offers you a *lifelong bonus*—simply because you will find that they apply to any human situation, be it parent-child, husband-wife, teacher-pupil, employee-employer, etc.

Guilt

Parents who cannot prevent problems from arising and who fail to achieve an acceptable mode of relating to their children are not only deprived of a happy family experience; they usually suffer from guilt and self-recrimination for what they consider their failures. A cycle of guilt and self-recrimination can reach intense proportions. The cycle can also be found in much less intense forms among parents who achieve a large measure of success in parenthood. I have rarely spoken with a parent who hasn't had some personal experience with it.

We know that guilt is one of the most corrosively destructive feelings with which human beings have to cope. Generated by inner conflicts, it is a feeling which inhibits, interferes with judgment, gives rise to fear and anger, and completes the cycle back to conflict and anxiety. We also know that augmented feelings of anxiety lead to renewed entrenchment in old patterns. A child may then be exposed to a more intense form of the behavior which led to the adult's feelings of guilt in the first place. And so the child is drawn into a cycle against which he will have to construct elaborate defenses in order to withstand its inherent destructive power.

Guilt often arises from an unconscious need or wish to be a *superparent*. Although superparents may say that they don't expect to be perfect, that is what they really want, and they can settle for nothing less. They are busy trying to maintain not just high standards, but certain extravagantly high standards, and they cannot tolerate shortcomings related to these standards in themselves, and frequently not in others. These standards may not be testable on any common absolute scale. But they are absolute unto themselves, in the context of the superparent's neurotic character structure. In other words, a superparent can chide you for wanting always to keep your child clean. That just doesn't happen to be one of that superparent's "things." But superparents have their own list of inviolates, toward which they drive themselves with relentless intensity.

A sure indication of the superparent syndrome is the sudden flare of anger, utterly out of keeping with the issue at hand. I saw such an incident in the supermarket recently when a child began to cry because he was tired. The mother flew into a rage and struck the boy, urging him to be quiet. The real reason for her anger was probably that she felt she *should have* known better than to keep her child so long in the market. If she were a "decent" mother—that is, a perfect mother, in her view—she would have left much earlier, or not taken him along. She had suited her own convenience, though, and could not forgive herself for that. "Decent" mothers don't suit their own convenience, she holds. Where does one go from there? Every child a crown prince or princess? Can you just imagine all the fuel for guilt this poor mother generates?

Whenever you encounter the concept of *should have,* you can expect that certain extravagantly high standards are being held. When failure occurs, as it is bound to do repeatedly, small explosions of rage tell us that unreasonable demands are being made.

In parents' discussion groups, some mothers acknowledged the blame they felt on many issues. Dissatisfaction with self made them chronically angry and impatient with their families. They were not able to "talk" with their children. They snapped at them and made repeated demands which they really didn't care about very much. They couldn't seem to keep a pervasive irritability from touching almost every parent-child exchange. Venting their anger on the children made these parents feel even greater guilt and self-blame. They were caught in the vicious *parent trap* of guilt and self-recrimination and seemed unable to extricate themselves from the cycle.

As this point came up repeatedly, I wanted to find an uncomplicated way of bringing what they were doing to their attention *without arousing further guilt and anger.* I wanted them to be able to see and accept their limitations without feeling contempt for themselves. I wanted them to be easier on themselves, not to have such high expectations for themselves.

The purpose of our group discussions was to look at the group members in the context of their daily lives; to help them identify and grasp one single parent-child exchange that troubled them; to think about it; to consider what could be done; and then to make the necessary efforts to apply an alternative approach. As their efforts bore fruit in a more relaxed approach toward their children—in widening their view of possibilities and in reducing family tension—some found broader interests for themselves as well as benefits accruing for their marital relationships.

If you feel that you are among the parents who seem to be caught in a web of guilt feelings and sense of failure, you need not despair. There are ways of achieving some sense of well-being regarding your parenting. One step is to accept the fact of your influence. Then it is necessary to appreciate the power you can exert.

Your guilt may make it appear that your child runs your life, which in some respects is true. Ways in which they do this will be discussed in the section on Child Power. But what *you* do, say, think, and feel are the principal factors governing the relationship. This applies most intensely in the period of childhood, but do not believe for a moment that it has little bearing on the adolescent or young adult. Just notice how your young adult child watches your facial expression and picks up on some subtle feeling you have about him or someone else, feelings you aren't even aware of. Observe how interested he is when you drop your voice in discussing some point about him with another person. It simply isn't true that adolescents or young adults don't care what you think and say. For the most part, their "low key" responses are not what they seem.

A Method for Parenting

As the concept of parent power is grasped, your sense of guilt (if you have it) may diminish and you may feel that you have some influence in the direction that your relations with your offspring will take. And you do. You may be able to follow a simple method which can relieve your tension and change the course of your parenting. This method has gradually evolved in my work with parents. It seems applicable to most parent-child stress situations. When used as a *preventive* with an anticipated problem, or with an existing problem, no matter how insignificant or profound, it usually bears fruit in improved communication and reduced tension.

One of the most interesting discoveries I made was that practically every group member, regardless of cultural or economic background, shared certain basic parental attitudes. These cut across all racial, religious, and ethnic lines. Neither affluence nor cultural traditions influenced those attitudes. Naturally, the content of the discussion material varied according to background. But parental attitudes in one locale closely resembled parental attitudes in an entirely different locale. Running through every group were the common factors I have already mentioned: parental self-doubt; disappointed expectations; a sense of helplessness, especially when lines of communication were absent; and much guilt, shame, anger, and tension.

Three-Step Method for Problem Solving

Three steps in the method for problem solving are: *identification* of the problem or issue; *planning* or seeking alternative courses of action; and *acting* upon or testing each alternative until one is found that clarifies issues and reduces tension.

The first step, *identification,* refers to the specific factors in the situation. In order to identify, you must place your finger squarely on the problem in order to find out *what* is going on. What causes this impasse between you and your child each time a particular issue arises?

In asking yourself what happens when an argument starts almost every evening at the dinner table, you may discover that you are interrupting your teen-ager halfway through his statement because you "know" what he is going to say. Maybe you do know, but you don't realize that he resents your omniscience because it's officious and it makes him feel stupid. He may also resent your rudeness.

In asking yourself why your baby screams whenever you put his snow suit on him, you might reveal your irritability at having to go out in the cold with him so he can get some "fresh air"—and you dislike going out into the cold.

Sometimes, when it is impossible to identify a problem by yourself, you may have to talk with your spouse, your friend, your neighbor. But I urge an initial attempt by yourself. The mind is a wonderful instrument, and is frequently unpredictable. It may just come to your rescue if you give it half a chance.

Once identification has taken place, you are ready for the second step. That is the *planning* phase: thinking of what to do about the situation. In planning, the *hows* are investigated. How can you approach this issue with your child in a new way? What *alternative procedures* are open to you? How can you test these alternatives? How can you keep from becoming irrevocably discouraged by your failure to communicate with your child?

During the planning phase thoughts seem to fly right out of your mind as soon as you become aware of them. Perhaps paper and pencil will be useful—and solitude! Alternative solutions should be jotted down as soon as you think of them. Don't censor anything. Ideas can easily be rejected later. Hang loose with them. In that way, within minutes, you may have a group of possibilities right there in front of you, in black and white. You can mull them over and consider their relevance to the situation confronting you. An impossible alternative might even point the way to a possible one. These too may be discussed with someone else. You become closer to that person, whoever it may be. You begin to get a better perspective on the situation, and to feel less overwhelmed by it.

Some people are capable of identifying a problem and finding alternative solutions to it in the course of their ordinary thinking habits. For others, this silent communication with oneself as a new approach to parenthood remains in the realm of fantasy. Most people have to *decide* they want to give deliberate thought to the matter at hand and then try to focus their thoughts on the subject.

Perhaps it sounds absurd to say, in effect, that if you want to think about something, sit down and think about it. But that is exactly what is necessary, especially when you are new at this kind of deliberation. Most people take time only to think of so-called important decisions. They rarely give frequent parent-child bickerings the same consideration. They do not pluck themselves out of the maelstrom of daily living and say to themselves, "Now I am going to give myself fifteen minutes of uninterrupted time to think about this problem." The most that is usually done, and then only when a problem has reached an intolerable stage, is to declare, "We've got to talk about this," and then proceed to bumble through another fruitless encounter.

I am suggesting a more purposeful move. And I am suggesting that you make this move long before the intolerable state has been reached. For at this later point, your *potential for positive parent power* may have fizzled out, and you may require professional help.

Furthermore, I am suggesting that this top-priority attention be given not only at times of moderate or severe stress, but at any time in your relationship with your child, perhaps daily or weekly, or monthly. Such ongoing consultation with yourself, your spouse, or a friend about your child's development can in no way be regarded as an oddity. After all, you do want your child to develop wellness, and you want to enhance your relationship as he matures. And surely, you want to *prevent* the development of serious neurotic attitudes that might affect his adult life.

The third step in this method is that of *action*. Difficult as identification and planning are, step three—action—is even more so. Now, something tangible must be done. Action is accomplished only by *doing*. You can plan and talk about a trip for years—but until you pack and get on the plane, no trip exists. Action takes a great deal of effort for some people who spend inordinate amounts of time in the thinking, planning phase without ever moving on to action, or indeed without ever having clearly established (identified) what it was they were out to accomplish in the first place. In addition, step three is the one that requires the most courage.

A parent may delay acting on a wish to ask his fourteen-year-old boy where the party is being held because he's afraid of the child's contempt. Then the parent is furious when the child is late getting home and he has no idea where to look for him. Is it easier to be angry with our children than to ask them a simple question?

To identify a potential or actual problem, to organize a plan with alternatives, to decide that it is relevant to the issue and discuss it with a spouse is one thing. But to put the plan into action requires a willingness to depart from the tried and true. That takes tremendous courage. It also takes stamina and ability to withstand discouragement, for there is no guarantee that your plan will be effective once it is put into action. Another and yet another plan must be tested if previous ones fail. If your ten-year-old child is afraid to go into a shop alone, you might have to try five or more alternatives before you find one that gives him the opportunity to leave his position of anxiety.

If one alternative doesn't work, there are nine others, twenty-three, or fifty-eight. All you have to do is sit down and think about them. You'll discover your own nine. Then try them out, one by one, until you find a suitable one. Remember, you will have a lifetime relationship with your child. Isn't it worth a little time and effort now?

In using this method, keep several points in mind. One is that it can't be practiced all the time. That's not because it has no continuing pertinence in family life, but because it would be unnatural to use any method all day long. This would create such extra tension that the good accomplished by the use of the method would be undone by the feeling of "I *must always* do this for my child." No. Indulge yourself in your old habits of not thinking and of jumping at your child because you're so much ahead of him. You might as well think of it in that way, because you're going to do it anyway. If your child accuses you of "regressing," admit it and tell him you're trying. But expect him to try too.

More important than any method is your need to relax more, to be less grim in your approach to your children. If any method is taken as a must, it can become rigidifying. The point is to develop *appropriate flexibility,* but please, not flabby permissiveness! You can design your own method of parenting based on this outline, but only if you find it useful for your family.

When you feel you've found *the* way to handle a situation and it has worked, don't be surprised if it fails after a while. What was effective with your children in December may not be so in March. What was great on Tuesday may fall flat on Saturday. What did the trick at dinner may cause hysterics at breakfast. There is *no one way* for anything when you're dealing with children—just as the boughs of a tree never bend the same way when a breeze stirs them.

Countless direct and indirect references to and explanations of these three steps will be made in these pages. So remember: 1) exploring and identifying the issue at hand; 2) thinking through and planning for alternative approaches; and 3) acting upon your plan. The three steps may be thought of in many ways: to know, to plan, to act; to listen, consider, perform; understand, contemplate, test; see, think, do; what, how, now—take your pick.

Double Message

Very often, the identification of troublesome features in a relationship is made even more troublesome because of a complication I call the *double message.* A double message occurs when a person says one thing and implies another. There are different forms of the double message. "Do you really want to go out in the rain?" may mean, "I don't want you to go out in the rain." Even brief messages can be complex. "I'm having Ray over for supper," chirps your daughter. "Oh," you murmur. Meant as an acknowledgment of her announcement, you are really saying, "What—that guy again!"

These are fairly obvious double messages. A more subtle and well-used form is that of the *equivocal no*. It is used with youngsters when they want to go somewhere or do something. This *no* is equivocal because it contains an element of *yes* as well as suggestions of other feelings, often in conflict with each other.

The equivocal *no* is a no which is frequently uttered before the parent has given himself a chance to consider his response. It therefore carries elements of unformed, random thoughts. It is a no which is not straightforward, clear, firm, or direct. It may sound that way and the parent may intend it that way. But even if no one else knows what's going on, your child senses its equivocal nature and is left to deal with it as he sees fit.

In essence, what comes across when the equivocal *no* is uttered is a kind of *yes/no* message. The parent may be aware of his yes/no stance. But more often he is not, and is deeply troubled when his child gives him a hard time over what he believes to be a firm **no**.

To say no equivocally when your youngster wants something is to encourage nagging and coaxing until the child gets satisfaction. While not clearly aware of your yes/no message, the child picks up the equivocation and tries to strengthen the yes side of it because that side suits him. "Can I have the green boots?" meets with, "No, the brown ones will go better with everything and won't show wear so much." Fine. But can you leave it at that? What kind of mommy are you, do you think, to deny your daughter green boots? Is your reason a good one? Not to her. And maybe you don't think it's a good reason either.

The child may sense your feeling that it's not a good reason. She may feel that you're being unfair and as a result, she won't "like" you. Burdened with these crosscurrents, your no comes across as less than firm and final. She picks this up, and, playing upon your fear of rejection (not being liked), asks until you give in, really pleased, finally, that she rescued you from your guilt feeling of being such a "mean" parent. Mind you, all this may be unconscious on either side until the youngsters reach a certain level of wisdom. Then they're onto the little game most of the time, and depending upon their personality and character structure, will make use of it somehow.

Remember, though, that this is usually all played out without parent awareness. It cannot be brought out into the open by you without raising the question mentioned earlier under identification. *What* is going on here anyway? Double messages are insidious and so difficult to identify because they are often flatly denied or very well rationalized. A later section will elaborate on double messages.

Parent Power

Parents know that children need food, shelter, and clothing. Most of them know that children also need warm and affectionate relationships. What too many of them do not know is that qualities of warmth and affection do not thrive in *tension-bound parents*.

I shall try to define the tension-bound parent throughout this book, and show how a *tension-free parent* might eventually evolve from the former. I shall also try to identify the worries and concerns of parents that influence attitudes and behavior toward children.

As an identifying, thinking, planning parent, you can find out how much more you know about rearing your child than you thought you knew. You can find out how to have confidence in your previous experiences. You can come to recognize and appreciate the wisdom you have acquired. You can learn how to apply your common sense to resolve parent-child tensions.

Sometimes parents are good for and to their children; sometimes not. Most times, they are in-between, with occasional excursions to the extremes. But whatever you are, you all exert a powerful impact on your children, for better or worse. You cannot avoid having this impact. Your child cannot escape being influenced by it. Parental impact is the most powerful influence to which human beings are subjected.

Do you know that your power can be used to encourage growth? Do you know that it can be used to retard or destroy? If you do not, then you, along with millions of parents, are probably rearing your children by a hit-or-miss method, perhaps missing more than hitting. Whatever you are doing, remember that you are having a very important impact on your child—the most important of his life. It is this impact that we shall continue to explore.

For Emphasis

The following are several points that I shall underscore repeatedly.

1) Parent tension exists and is prevalent in most homes.

2) Parent tension can be prevented or alleviated to some extent.

3) Parents do not intend to create tension, are often unaware of it, and do not know that it can be resolved.

4) Parents cannot accept their natural limitations and at the same time expect too much of themselves and of their children.

5) Parents have many strengths and resources left unexplored and unused.

6) Parents have it within their power to rear their children as they see fit, but are unaware of that power and do not use it effectively.

7) Children have the power to show their parents how to grow as parents, and how to be welcoming instead of rejecting.

8) There is a way for parents to help themselves without arousing more anger, guilt, conflict, and anxiety.

This book tries to avoid theorizing and preaching. It presents material which I have gathered from twenty years of work with patients and the garden variety of parents and children. Although almost all parents will recognize themselves saying and doing the things described here, no criticism is implied. But parents will be asked to view *the ways in which they wield their parent power.* If dissatisfied, they will be asked to consider what effective alternatives they can use. I am trying to help them to learn to raise this question and to answer it for themselves. No book can answer it for them, for there are probably as many answers as there are sets of parents.

To repeat, this book tries to encourage you to develop confidence in your own method of child rearing so that you are not divided when you approach your children. I hope to provide you with the tools that will help you develop your own method of approaching, coping with, and solving potential or full-blown problems between yourselves and your children. With these tools, you can assume and maintain full responsibility for your own method of child rearing. No one else can tell you how to raise your child. I can only suggest ways you may proceed with your work as a parent. To each his own.

CHAPTER II

Step One—Identifying the Problem

Human exchanges consist of at least two elements: that which is intended, and that which is actually conveyed in words and feelings. Because words do not often match feelings or intentions, and because the people concerned are usually unaware of these discrepancies, reliable communication is chancey. Where satisfying relationships are desired, however, it is very important to figure out what is actually going on. Otherwise, all remains in the realm of fantasy. To identify the actual, then, is to state the facts of the matter and not the fantasy. An example can best explain how an honest attempt at communication can become clouded.

You're Not Listening

Mrs. Abel, the mother of a fifteen-year-old boy, complained that her son never talked with her. She found it increasingly difficult to start a conversation and felt that she and the boy were becoming more and more estranged. She attributed this to the fact that he was fifteen years old and that he was "rebelling," as all good teen-agers are supposed to do. Nevertheless, she took small comfort in that and was unhappy with the situation. When asked to identify the problem, she said: 1) her son was fifteen; 2) he was therefore rebelling; and 3) he never talked with her.

In working with her, I accepted these statements as only a partial explanation, and began to help her with further identification. The following dialogue took place.

"You say he never talks to you?"

"Well, hardly ever."

"When does he speak to you?"

"Oh, he never does."

"Does he talk with you in the morning?"

"He's pretty grumpy in the morning."

"Did he talk with you this week?"

"I don't remember. He just doesn't seem to want to talk with me."

"You haven't talked with him all week, then?"

"Oh, yes, we've talked sometimes."

"When?"

"I don't remember."

"Did you talk yesterday?"

"Well, he comes bursting in after school and he's starved and so full of everything. So I give him something to eat, and he starts to tell me all about school. I'm usually busy then, so I tell him to tell me later."

This revealed that the boy was eager to relate the happenings of the day while he was still very much involved with them. It seemed, however, that his mother had no interest in what he had to say to her at such times.

Asked what followed, Mrs. Abel said, "He eats and goes out, or does something in his room, or gets on the telephone. Then later on, after dinner when I'm finished with the dishes and the kitchen, I ask him to tell me what he wanted to say earlier. 'Aw, forget it,' he says, and no matter how much I try to get him to talk, he just won't."

At this point it was clear that the boy did try to talk to her, and wanted to talk with her, but that the timing seemed to be off. He wanted to talk at three-thirty and she wanted to talk at eight-thirty. She was not interested in what he had to say earlier, and he was not interested in saying anything later.

I asked Mrs. Abel whether she wanted to find out more about the situation. She agreed, and the identification procedure continued. We chose a specific day when the boy had come home and she rejected his "talking." On that day, Mrs. Abel was putting away some groceries as she prepared dinner. I asked her whether she was able to cook, put things away, and listen all at the same time. It appeared that this was possible. When asked if she was doing anything else, she said that she was thinking.

Often this "thinking" that a person does while cooking, cleaning, or doing household chores is fantasizing. It is common with people who are working at tasks which are not intellectually demanding. It is a habit not easily relinquished because of the comfort it provides in the course of daily living.

Because of her own needs, then, Mrs. Abel is unable to accept her son on his terms (when he wants to talk). Thus, identification of the actual facts in this situation were the following: 1) It was not true that the boy never spoke to his mother; 2) for her own reasons, she had no interest in his school activities at that time, and therefore had no interest in him in relation to those activities.

From the boy's point of view, he cannot understand the separation his mother makes between being interested in him (which she professes to be), and not being interested in his concerns. He *is* his concerns at any given moment. He feels: If you reject my concerns, my enthusiasms, my joys, or my sorrows *as I am experiencing them,* then you are rejecting me. This is hurtful, and he withdraws to protect himself from further hurt. It's a love-me-love-my-dog phenomenon. Containing its own rationale, such a problem is not usually open to other rational discourse.

If this woman can appreciate the destructiveness of her poor timing, she can prevent further estrangement from her son. It might also be helpful for her to remember that she is the only mother he has, and that he still needs her concern, attention, and affection.

But this parent cannot suddenly become interested in her son's doings. She may, however, be motivated to try to show interest at another time. If this can be done, two things may occur: 1) The boy may find it pleasurable that his parent listens to him for a change; 2) the parent may find it pleasurable that her boy is talking to her. Such an exchange may lack the parent's deep interest in the content of the conversation. But her effort may help to plant the seeds of a genuine interest in reestablishing communication with her son. That is enough

for a start. In time, it may be possible for both to move closer to the
goal of a mutually satisfying relationship.

It must be emphasized that the son was clearly trying to communicate, spontaneously. But communication is a two-way system. His
antenna was sending out signals, but hers was not receiving them.
Therefore no communicating was possible. Although some signals are
so weak that it is almost impossible for parents to pick them up, these
were loud and strong. But even such unmistakable signals may be
completely overlooked. It is something of a tragedy that such good
intentions on the part of both were misunderstood to the point that
each felt the other was rejecting and intrusive. In the afternoon, the
woman felt that her son was intrusive and he felt that she was rejecting. In the evening, he felt that she was intrusive, and she felt that he
was rejecting.

Limits

Certain women have difficulty with adolescent boys because their
total experience with them is so limited. Unless they have lived or
worked closely with them at some time in their lives, they have no
first-hand information. They have to rely on the husband's interpretation of the son's developing sensitivities. Living with a teen-age son
these days doesn't automatically make one cognizant of the pressures
and stresses he may be experiencing. Whether or not an adult feels
that the adolescent's problems are valid is beside the point. Suffering
is always valid for the sufferer, regardless of the observer's opinion.
If the youngster is to feel welcomed then, his anguish must be recognized (not indulged) as such.

Let us examine most women's experience with teen-age boys. As
daughters themselves, it is unlikely that their fathers gave them any
detailed description of the trials and tribulations of their adolescence.
If they had brothers and were good observers and confidantes, they
are probably the best informed. If not, then they remained relatively
uninformed. Dating boys, and subject to the results of adolescent
inner turmoil, they had no way to understand that turmoil—unless
they were somehow privy to what was going on in the evolution of
the adult male. Their own husbands are not likely to have outlined
the details of their own early years, especially the aspects which made

them feel most anguished. If husbands do this at all, from the perspective of ten, twenty, or more years later, seemingly intolerable past experiences and feelings fall easily into a new place, softened by humor, nostalgia, or even pride.

In terms of understanding some of the basics of male adolescence, most fathers have an advantage over their wives because they were "there" themselves, even though it was another place and almost another era. This would not necessarily hold true for the father who, as an adolescent, lived and accepted only one way and is therefore completely closed to those aspects of his son's teen-age years which seem at such odds with his own.

Not knowing, not understanding, and perhaps not even being interested in her son's "middle years" (don't be shocked, there are a few), yet having to deal daily with the many caprices of adolescence, a woman may display attitudes that are too strong, vague, fearful, timid, equivocal, or inappropriate. These are the attitudes which "turn off" youngsters. Making demands and having expectations that are appropriate for an eight-year-old are not appropriate at fifteen. Teasing, playful, protective, prideful approaches sometimes have to be soft-pedaled in these middle years, with both girls and boys. They suddenly see a playful mommy as a very silly one of whom they may feel ashamed, or for whom they feel contempt. Ashamed of themselves for having those feelings, they try to go along. But they have not yet learned to handle such feelings; and their shame and guilt may twist them into being surly, rude, or withdrawn.

Please! I'm not saying you should turn off your spontaneous reactions to your children. I'm only describing what actually happens in some families and what may be going on in some adolescents' minds. It may never happen in your family. If it does, it's up to you to deal with the information in any way you see fit.

Two other points are important. To the extent that your attitudes toward your children are not put-ons—that is, not deliberately designed to have a certain effect, and are easy and relaxed, in keeping with the circumstances—your children are less likely to be turned off by you. What most adolescents will not accept are attitudes that are insincere or inappropriate to time, place, and age. The second point is that their hypercritical, too-demanding view (yes, demanding, because they expect you to be someone you are not) very often subsides or disappears after a few years, whether you remain friend or foe. As friends, your adult children will accept your shortcomings and hang-ups with good humor and often unexpected compassion. As foes, they merely resign themselves with a sort of sour, shoulder-shrugging acceptance: "Well, what can you expect of them?" But no set of parents has to continue such a relationship with their children. For even if it's not good now, you can always change it in the future. You have plenty of time, and they'll give you chance after chance after chance. You just have to be willing to reach out a little and try to identify the stumbling blocks that stand between you.

From the position of almost total ignorance of a teen-age boy's physiology, psychic stresses, and preoccupations, some women don't have much going for them as they try to cope with the many rapid changes taking place before their eyes. No sooner do they feel comfortable with one change than another has replaced it. These mothers have no way of knowing that every year or two will bring a whole new ball game. Even though such mothers may have earned their merit badges for making it through their offspring's childhood with relatively few traumas and much satisfaction, there is no guarantee that paradise will continue. At nine or ten, things have already been changing, perhaps imperceptibly, while Mommy is still in the happy blush of innocence with her "little boy." But by twelve at most, if she's been unaware, it hits her all at once. Not only are subtle changes continuing to occur, but more obvious ones startle her.

One day, she finds out that a complete stranger is occupying her home. His personality, appearance, habits, and needs are unrecognizable to her. Yet she's still washing his dirty clothes, placing meals before him, chauffeuring him around. She's the same. She knows she hasn't changed. So who is this little stranger who stomps around, whose irritability flares up when you talk to him in the way you always have, whose eyes begin to reach the level of your eyes, who looks at you quizzically, sometimes critically?

It's a tough spot to be in, Mom. But it can be handled without tremendous upheavals if you can recognize that something different is happening. You may not know which changes are taking place yet, but at least recognize that changes are occurring, that they are swirling all about you. That is the first step. The *what* of identification is the existence of many changes in your child. From there, you go on to the specific changes. Your son snatches the phone from you when you announce sweetly, "Honey, there's a little girl on the phone for you," and snarls, "H'lo," because he's embarrassed that the caller heard his mom call him "honey" and refer to her as "little girl," and so forth and so on. It doesn't make much sense, true. He's still a "honey" to you and always will be. And of course the girl *is* a little girl. But how do they actually hear it? Who knows? Maybe they think it's patronizing. Ask them.

In fact, *any* reasonableness on your part may be met with seeming unreasonableness on their part. You don't have to understand or explain it right now. You hope your bewilderment will lead you to initiate a conversation much later, or the next day: "You seemed irritated the other night when I called you to the phone." Or, "I felt you were angry with me the other night," or whatever. "Was there anything I did that bothered you?" If you get nowhere, you can try again another time, or make further observations. Finally you may have to proceed on the basis of your own assumptions. That is, even though you've called your son to the phone for years with "honey" and it was quite all right, now for some reason unknown to you it is no longer acceptable. That's it, like it or not. If you want to deal with it to relieve any distress you may be feeling, then go into your consultation room and start consulting with yourself about ways of approaching your child, yourself, your family attitudes and practices, ways which may have a salutary effect on this troublesome impasse.

I have used examples in this section which refer mostly to boys. However, with appropriate modifications, what I have said applies to girls as well. Also, some fathers find themselves in the same position with their daughters as mothers do with their sons. Their experience, knowledge, and understanding of girls is often so limited that the many despairs, frustrations, and sensitivities to which their daughters are subject leave them utterly baffled.

Changing, Always Changing

After eight, ten, twelve, or more years, the cozy, comfortable, loving good-night kiss after your youngsters are in bed turns them off. If that happens, a common recourse is to push you away. The reasons are various. A kiss may remind them too much of the babyhood which

they are trying to thrust behind them. Or, if they happen to be angry
with you, they may withhold that kiss to express their anger. They
may experience a mild sexual response which could be embarrassing
to them. Whatever it is, they are seldom aware of anything beyond
a vague discomfort and irritability, and they would find it difficult to
explain. Certainly, they would not attempt to do so unless pressed for
an explanation.

If there does seem to be sudden disinterest in that kiss, but you want
to continue with it, try kissing perfunctorily on the forehead, or before
they get into bed. If you decide to omit the kiss, your heartfelt "Good
night, sweetie" may suffice. There are all kinds of ways to handle it.
Try a few and see what happens. If nothing works, it's no tragedy if
you can't continue with that kiss.

But try not to feel hurt. If you want to, ask if they want to continue
it. If they don't, don't feel rejected. You asked and were answered
honestly. Be thankful for that straightforward bit of communication.
There are many other times during the day when you can kiss, pat,
poke, touch, or hug—times that are not quite so critical as that time
of the long-standing, reverent good-night kiss. Although for many,
there is no cut-off age for kissing or other show of affection, it is just
part of some children's development that they don't want to be physically fussed over.

For you, that phase is just over, like diapers, formulas, and watching every step. There are welcome "overs" and there are sad "overs."
It's nobody's fault. No post mortems need be held. Of course you'll
miss it. But have no regrets. It was sweet while it lasted. Pack it away
in your memory kit. If you must have a little girl or boy to kiss good
night, adopt one, or kiss the neighbor's, or wait for your first grand-
child. *Or you can always keep preoccupied with your youngsters' current needs and your very own.*

Clues

How can you know when it's time to use the three-step method I
presented in Chapter I? Well, if you don't know definitely that something is amiss, there are clues. If you notice consistent irritability at
certain times such as weekends, dinnertime, etc., that you can't account for, it may be time to do a little identifying. If you find yourself

regarding your offspring's friends with greater affection than you feel for your own children, and think, "Horrors, don't I like my own children as much?" it's time to do a little identifying. When too many "nothing" conversations turn into absurd yellings back and forth, take heed. When there's repeated lying, disappearing, sulking, spending too much money, incessant loud music, bad tempers, car accidents, the time has come.

Perhaps the best clue is your own level of discontent. All children, and indeed all parents, are difficult to be with at one time or another. I'm not talking about the ordinary irritations and clashes; I mean a chronic sense of discontent, of disappointment, of suffering for which you can find no cause but which seems to be more acute in your relationships with the children. These feelings will indicate to you that all is not well in your family.

More obvious times are the often repeated arguments, serious refusals to cooperate with what seem to you reasonable requests, tears, recriminations, and the like. It is usually not wise to try to resolve anything while tempers are hot and vindications are being sought. It is more prudent to let things cool for a bit.

Get Away

At any point of serious difficulty or difference with your youngster, try to remove yourself from the arena as soon as possible. There is no point in prolonging an exasperating, stormy impasse. In a quiet, solitary place (sometimes the bathroom is the only place) ask yourself: *What is the matter?* It may be that you don't like your son's or daughter's language, hair, friends, study habits. Say to yourself: What is the issue here? What are we arguing about all the time? Am I somehow disappointed? Am I expecting too much? Am I angry each time I see my expectations thwarted? What is it that galls me? What makes me blow up so easily? What makes me unable to have a conversation that does not deteriorate into a stupid, bickering exchange? What was it specifically just now that caused this altercation and distress?

Take a few minutes away from everything. You may be surprised to find that all kinds of thoughts will occur to you. If you feel that you are beginning to get an idea about what is wrong, but you're not sure, test it. See if you can duplicate the circumstances. See if the same thing happens. Sometimes you may have to play around with it awhile. You may have to observe different family members' reactions —to notice if there are feelings of resentment, uncertainty, or guilt with which your children are struggling. You have to know what role your youngsters' friends and companions play in arousing family tensions.

Look carefully into all the possible conditions that may contribute to the outcomes that you find unbearable and which cause you pain and suffering. This process is less complicated when younger children are involved. It becomes more complex, however, as your child matures. But with a little practice, you may find yourself identifying at times without even trying.

That Was Then

A nine-year-old boy, after having been a fairly well-mannered boy all his life, had become sulky and rude to his parents. Their lecturing and scolding seemed of no avail. One day his father yelled at him, "What on earth is the matter with you these days? You used to be such a pleasure to have around." The child wasn't sure that it was a question his father wanted answered. "Do you really want to know?" he asked.

"Yes, I really want to know."

"Well, I don't know for sure. But you make me feel like a baby."

"How?"

"The way you and Mommy order me around."

"How do we do that?"

"When you tell me to do something, like picking up or putting my bicycle away. I don't want you to tell me those things when my friends are here."

The boy suddenly looked surprised. Apparently he himself hadn't known clearly what was bothering him until he actually said it. Many children cannot usually articulate such feelings and do not as a rule. But this child was directly asked and was honest and uninhibited enough to come right out with it. Such a response attests to large depots of shared family experiences which led him to believe that he could trust his father with the truth of his feelings.

These parents were not "ordering" him any differently from the way they had in the past, when he had not objected or cared. But at nine, and before his friends, he felt humiliated. This wasn't intended. The parents were doing what they had always done. They were not being more officious. They hadn't changed. But their child had. His change (a very common one, to say the least) required a change in them before harmony could be restored.

Recognizing that the boy was unhappy because he felt they were treating him "like a baby" was identifying the problem. He was not out to annoy or frustrate them. He was merely growing. His irritation with them was the result of their lagging behind him. It so happened that this father had asked and had been told what the matter was. But very often parents will say, "Why didn't you tell us?" to which the classic answer is often, "Why didn't you ask?" which may be a kind of cover-up for the child's not knowing how troubled he was or why. Can you fight that one?

And More Questions

When identifying, carry on a dialogue with yourself. Ask questions like these: What was my voice like when I said what I did and my child responded so rudely, or in what seemed an inappropriate manner? Was I patronizing or condescending, or sarcastically critical? What was my facial expression like? Did I look forbidding, disgusted, condemning? Was I really asking a question, or was I issuing a directive?

If I want to issue a directive, do I feel I have the right to do so? Can I do it? Am I afraid to do it? If so, why? If I am afraid, do I have the courage to try to overcome that fear? Or do I think it inappropriate to issue a directive at all? How would my spouse feel if I gave an order in that tone? My friend, employer, employee? Is it because I don't want to come across as a drill sergeant that I avoid making any demands? But then when I do, is that exactly how I do come across? Can't I stand myself for appearing that way because then my family won't love me? But who's to be the commanding officer around here if not I? Somebody has to call the shots sometime. Am I making unreasonable demands?

I know that children don't know how to run a home or a family.

I can't expect them to do that. I can't expect them to make decisions they're not equipped to make or that I don't want them to make. I don't want to have them decide that we should go camping on our vacation, when we parents want to rent a little cottage at the seashore. And if I don't want them to tell me that, I don't have to ask them. I can just tell them what we are planning to do. That's our prerogative as parents.

So what's the big deal? They have another sixty or seventy years to do just as they please. I don't have to feel bad if we parents make the decisions for now. But why couldn't I say to them, "If you had a choice, what would you like to do?" And when they say camping, couldn't I say, without churning inside, "That's a nice idea. Maybe we could do it next year. Because that takes a lot of effort and we would like to relax at the beach this year." Presto. Decision made without tears, fights, hysterics, mean mommies and daddies, and rotten kids.

If you're willing to submit yourself to that kind of scrutiny (and of course all those questions may not be necessary or relevant for you), you'll find an easy entry into step two of the three-step method, the phase of planning and thinking through *how* you can solve what is troubling you. Your answers to some of those questions will provide you with a list of many alternatives of action.

Starters

Make up your own six questions as "starters." They should be pertinent to your particular situation. For example: Am I angry about clothing scattered on the floor? Am I angry with nonchalant, passive attitudes? Am I disappointed in their disinterest in work, in appearance, etc.? Am I angry because she is so much like my mother-in-law whom I don't like very much? Do I despise his disinterest because it reminds me so much of myself and what I despise in myself? Does his self-destructiveness reveal my view of myself as parent, as spouse, as person?

Am I frustrated with my own life? If so, can I take it out on anyone else but my child? Must he be the repository for my bitterness and disappointment? And is that because I don't have the awareness or perhaps the courage to place the responsibility upon myself or complain to anyone else in a more searching way? If any of this is true, can I look for relief? Do I depend too much on my children and my spouse for life's satisfactions? Is there any way I can enlarge my own life? Do I have any interests of my own with which I can relax, which are not inevitably bound up with my family? Is there too much togetherness in my family, to the exclusion of not enough *to-oneness* with myself? Do I really need some of this to-oneness? Can I talk with my spouse about this? Has she ever thought about these things? Does she have a need like this? How often have we talked about things that have only to do with ourselves? Or are we always concerned or worried by children, budgets, and other materialities of life?

Do we have inner, spiritual needs that we never think about or talk about? When I go to my house of worship, what do I think about there? How to make another dollar, or save one? Do I just fantasize about pleasant things? Do I ever spend the time to think about real and practical ways to improve my communication with my spouse, with my children, indeed with all the people who are significant in my life? What do I think of myself—am I a dodo that I can't think of these things?

Any child can. Any adult can. Certainly any parent can who wants to improve the quality of his parenting and of his entire existence.

Unemployed

One woman stumbled upon a significant but unexpected finding when she noticed that she was becoming more and more cranky with her three teen-agers, who weren't involved with any of the serious problems she was aware of in other families. She found that she was being snappy and sarcastic, even with their friends. One day, one of them asked her if she felt ill. She said no, but the question puzzled her. Then when she saw her face in the mirror, it was pale and strained.

She was not a particularly attractive woman, but her children had always said that Mommy had a "happy face." It certainly didn't look happy now. It looked angry. Surprised, she thought, "What am I angry about?"—and then she felt tearful.

Talking with her husband later that evening, she related what had happened. "Well, were you angry, or were you just tired?" he asked.

"But why should I cry?" she asked, ignoring his question.

"What were you crying about?"

"I don't know." He had the good sense to keep quiet for a moment. I say "good sense" because when a person admits he doesn't know something, he will often start seeking to know. Sure enough, after a few seconds, she said, "I felt sad."

"I thought you said you felt angry."

"No, I said I looked angry when I saw myself. But I felt sad when I cried."

"What have you to feel sad about—your lost youth?" he chided. Distracted by her search, she did not take offense at this.

"I feel I've lost something, but I'm not so sure it's my youth." She smiled. "Not that I'm happy about that either."

Several days later, the same thing happened. A basement room had been arranged for her teen-agers to entertain themselves and their friends. Several youngsters trouped down there, carrying trays laden with chips, juice, cookies, cake, and paper cups. As soon as they disappeared down the stairs, she felt like crying again. She went into the bedroom and looked at herself. She saw the pale face again. This time it looked sad and tired, rather than angry. "What under the sun is the matter with me?" She sat on the bed and repeated, "What is the matter?" She reviewed her many concerns. There were no overwhelming worries, no financial crises, no major illnesses, no calamities. "But I've lost my children!" she suddenly exclaimed—and the tears flowed.

Of course she had—and of course she hadn't. She had lost her babies, her little darlings who were always underfoot, needing her for this and that, telling her about the goings on in school, scrambling about to get her to fix something, take them somewhere. Yes, that was gone forever. And here she was still wanting to hear them bubbling around her, asking her questions, making her feel needed and important. They had moved on. She had been left behind. A sudden flare of anger shot through her. "I shouldn't have fixed the basement for them. Then they'd have to stay here with me." She smiled sadly. "What a fool I am!"

Eventually she realized that she felt bereft of her occupation as mother and was indeed angry with her children who, she felt, had "fired" her. She was also resentful and envious. For while she was being left fallow, they were having a great time with companions, music, noise, and the exuberance of youth. Her irritability and disagreeable manner toward them were outcomes of a complicated set of forces that were motivating her behavior. Preoccupied with her sense of loss and her anxiety over being "unemployed," she was not relishing the richness of fleeting moments of companionship with her offspring—her "children" who were on their way to becoming her peers.

Stick With It

Don't expect to accomplish such a thoroughgoing identification as that without a lot of practice. But you can see how one phase of identification leads to another. What is required is to *stay with it.* Many family situations are as complex as the one just described, and many are not. But all can be clarified to some extent if you are willing to take a little time. You can also see that the task of finding alternatives of action becomes possible only after such identification has been made.

This first step of identification establishes the *what* of the issue. The questions here, and many others, can help you to find out what is causing stress between you and your children. But please remember that while identification is necessary to any shift in attitude, it is only one part in a constellation of three moves. Having made this first move, you can go on to planning your alternatives. For that, you'll find some guidelines in the next chapter, which covers step two of the method for parenting.

CHAPTER III

Step Two—Planning

S TEP TWO OF THE METHOD for parenting involves thinking through and making plans deliberately designed to relieve parent-child stress and to resolve the problems we talked about in step one. We can now use the information gathered in step one of identification to find suitable alternatives of action which should help bring about some change in communication and other difficulties common to most families. Where step one exposes the *what* of the problem, step two investigates the *hows*.

Time and Place

This *planning phase* requires time and thoughtful attentiveness to the matter at hand. It may require consultation with a spouse, and sometimes with other persons. When I say time, I do not mean hours or days. I mean fifteen minutes, five minutes, or an hour if necessary, rarely more than that. The length of time is not the significant feature of the planning phase, however. It is the quality of the time given to it that is important. Preferably, that time should be taken in a quiet, solitary place where you can be free of other commitments and distractions.

Do you know that very few parents ever go into a room alone merely for the purpose of contemplating a problem or making a plan? You will find, however, that when you do this, you are able to focus on a single point and can often arrive at conclusions which might be impossible to reach when your mind is cluttered with the usual distractions of family life. You can now make sound decisions based on thoughtful conclusions.

I cannot overemphasize the importance of taking some quiet time for the planning of step two. Naturally, the place and time of day depend upon your routine, occupation, activities, age, and number of children, etc. If older children are in school all day, you have a wider choice than if they are very young. In that case, the only time might be in the evening after they are in bed. If you work in an office, you might be able to take a few quiet minutes to think and plan. If you live in a crowded household, you have to be more resourceful in finding your time and place. Some parents have told me that a locked bathroom is their only refuge.

Planning does not come naturally; it has to be practiced repeatedly at first. That is why it requires an uninterrupted segment of time. Later on, it comes more easily. At some point, it may become possible to plan an alternative at the moment of conflict between you and your youngster. Just a few seconds of contemplation may allow you to offer a thoughtful alternative. If you can do this, you will not have to open up the issue another time. As you work on planning, you will build up confidence in your ability to come up with something useful. Also, you will be able to trust yourself with alternatives which arise on the spur of the moment. But don't expect to be able to do that right away. Anger and distress will not permit it without sufficient practice.

Any idea you come upon might be considered as an alternative, a possibility. Write it down immediately. Keep paper and pencil ready. Don't let your thoughts frighten you. They can be discarded then and there if not suitable or feasible. Keep your sense of humor about them. If you place a censor upon your thoughts initially, you will interfere with the free-flowing logic you must depend on if you are to work on the matter at hand. A censor will lead you into other pastures which might be more interesting to contemplate, but which may be irrelevant.

Two Is Better Than One

Sometimes both parents are involved in identifying and planning. If they are agreed on the issue at hand, the work may go more quickly and not seem such a chore. A fourteen-year-old girl told her parents that she had gone to a party where the parents of the hostess were not at home. They did not immediately tell their daughter of their disapproval, for fear of hurting her feelings. But they talked together and realized that they did not want her to go to unchaperoned parties.

They felt "square, old-fashioned and untrusting" about their attitude. They also felt that their previous attitude of openness with their daughter was in jeopardy. What they did not realize at first was that they were not being open with her by not voicing their disapproval. While parents are certainly entitled to decide not to be open on all occasions, their thinking nevertheless was at fault, for openness goes both ways. One cannot be open only when one is approving. Disapproval may also be open and aboveboard. It is this very openness which permits discussion on the reasons, attitudes, and circumstances surrounding the disapproval. To approve of your fourteen-year-old daughter's wishes is easy and pleasurable. To disapprove and still maintain open communication and harmony takes a little more doing.

In discussing this matter quietly between themselves, the parents were able to discover why they did not want their child in such a situation. (This was the first step—identification.) Some of their reasons seemed tenable; some did not. Among the tenable reasons was their own anxiety and discomfort.

They then had to decide how to proceed. (This was the second step —planning.) Would they forbid her to go to such parties? Would they forbid her to go to all parties until she was older? Would they permit her to have parties only at home? Would they speak openly about their feelings to her? Should they follow one of their plans without giving her their reasons?

They decided to be frank, offer their reasons, tell her how uncomfortable they felt when she was not chaperoned, and hope that she would cooperate with them. If she would not accept their position and cooperate in some way, they were prepared to forbid her to go to any party unless they were sure that parents were present.

Even though this is a common and troublesome situation in many families, the concerns of these parents may seem insignificant to you. But please try not to be "turned off" by the mundaneness of this example. I offer it only to show how effective this method can be when used conscientiously.

Bedtime Horrors

Another common problem for parents is children's bedtime and its accompanying irritations. Many parents are plagued with the child who takes one, two, or more hours to settle down each night. Such a child is usually quite young, but may even be six or eight.

The first thing to do with this problem is to identify 1) whether or not one or both parents want to "get the child out of the way" at bedtime after a long day for everyone, and 2) whether or not the parent's irritability mounts when this activity is prolonged. Parents who have this problem often exclaim, "But I've tried everything!"

Everything usually refers to a set of activities which are gone through in regular consecutive order, and include games, drinks, stories, etc. No serious evaluation of the situation or effort to change attitudes has been made. Each night the problem is approached with optimistic defeatism. Caught in this bind and hating it, parents do not believe that the situation can be any different. They resolve that they will not "give in" this night, but they take no occasion during the day to consider possible alternatives.

Two problems often undermine the efforts of parents who have difficulty getting children to obey reasonable demands. One is the giving of *double messages*. That was discussed in Chapter I and will be referred to frequently. A double message is a message which is not clear to the child and which conveys unwittingly the parent's uncertainty regarding his own position on a particular issue.

The second problem derives from the parents' need to behave in a permissive manner, whether or not permissiveness is indicated or appropriate. These two often overlap, for if one is going through the motions of permissiveness and yet not feeling permissive, then obviously the child is being given two messages: 1) You can do as you please in this circumstance; and 2) you must do as I say. Put another way, the child hears: 1) It is your bedtime; and 2) it is not your bedtime. Which message is he to follow? If he wants to continue playing and running around, he follows the part of the message that says: It is not your bedtime, you can do as you please.

If that's what you really want, there's no problem and you'll be bored by reading this. If it's not what you really want, however, you have to try to state that clearly to yourself. That would be identifying the problem. Then you'd have to sit down and decide what you want to do about it and how you are going to do what you want to do. That is the planning stage.

Permissiveness

True permissiveness with offspring of all ages can only be a condition of inner responsiveness to the child's need or demand. Either the child's behavior or wish is "all right" with the parent or it is not. If it is not, then any show of permissiveness is a pretense, albeit an unconscious one. When the parent is applying the principle of permissiveness without feeling permissive, it becomes a pseudo-permissiveness. A permissive state is an inner state, an attitude, expressed by the presence or absence of certain words and deeds. One cannot be permissive without feeling so. Permissiveness is not for everyone, nor for all times or occasions, because it may not be appropriate; nor can everyone have a permissive attitude.

Parents owe it to themselves to discover their true feelings and notions of child rearing so that they can avoid gaps between what they truly believe and how they act. The greater the discrepancy, the greater will be their sense of uncertainty, frustration, and failure.

Alternatives for Bedtime

Having to go through certain procedures every night at bedtime, parents indeed feel that they have been through everything. When that situation was discussed in a group setting, parents came up with some of the following suggestions: No stimulation before bedtime, including roughhousing, playing games, stories, TV, etc.; a warm bath with minimal playing in the water, followed immediately by bed and lights out (with night light if necessary); a warm bottle of milk in the crib; a glass of water with ice on the night table to anticipate the complaint that the water was too warm; talking it over with spouse, relatives, neighbors, pediatrician; seeing a professional counselor to find out: 1) if both parents are working together on the problem, or are subtly undermining each other's efforts; and 2) if they are feeling guilty for not being permissive enough. Various parental stratagems may or may not be useful. More important is the parent's opening awareness of the wide variety of available alternatives. This awareness brings to the parent's attention that not everything has been tried. In any case, the decisions will be those that are most suitable for a particular family.

Change

Too often, parents resign themselves to a pattern of behavior in the child which causes distress to the entire family. They hoodwink themselves into believing that they are merely assuming a permissive attitude. But resignation is not permissiveness even though it may seem so on occasion. In the case of resignation, no relief can be achieved, for change can be brought about only with consistent effort to establish a different pattern for the child. It is unlikely that deliberately pointed effort, carefully considered in the context of the problem, would meet with failure in most cases. Failure is usually due to "too little too late," and not to an intrinsic failure factor.

Planning refers to finding alternatives to old attitudes or ways of doing things. No one is out to hurt anyone when changes must be made. This does not mean that some members of the family may not be threatened and made anxious at the idea of change. But we have to remember that this is only an unfortunate by-product of change and one that is relieved when it becomes clear that the change will be useful.

Change is necessary for growth. Compared with adults, most children change easily; they cannot avoid it. Adults do not change easily, and often try hard not to. So there is a basic clash between the child's need to change in order to grow, and the adults' wish to remain safe and secure where they are.

That creates a profound difference in the stance of the adult and the child. The undamaged child has little or no apprehension about change. It is as natural to him as breathing. One day, four-year-old Clemmie climbs a little tree in the park. Another day, she climbs a larger one. What should she do, climb the same little tree throughout her tree-climbing years? Watching her little girl, Mommy's heart starts to beat rapidly. She is afraid Clemmie will fall, so she tries to confine her to the little tree. Clemmie demands change, so she cries and fusses. Mommy takes her home.

Mommy decides that she is unwilling to feel afraid when Clemmie is in the park. What are her alternatives? She can argue the point each time, which is what most parents do. She can let Daddy take his daughter to the park on the weekend and let him handle the tree-climbing. She can reflect upon what the other mothers of four-year-olds do. She can stand beneath the tree when the child climbs, so that if a fall occurs it will be broken. She can keep her daughter out of the park until she feels that Clemmie is ready for the larger tree. A few minutes must be taken to think this out.

A decision is then made about which alternative is best. She finds that she cannot move against her feeling of fear. She knows from her previous experience that she must respect that feeling, for she would become more anxious if she did not. But neither can she infect her child with her low tolerance level for anxiety. A compromise must be reached. She has to relieve her fear for her child's safety, and yet provide her child with the opportunity for limited freedom in which her curiosity can continue to expand.

In making a decision, this parent is learning to trust her growing child to make constructive changes. She is also learning to trust herself to tolerate fear and overcome timidity, which are also constructive changes. She doesn't really want to keep her daughter down with the three-year-olds. But she doesn't want her heart in her mouth, either. Where is the line to be drawn? She must consult with herself, her husband, or some other person to plan her next move.

Having done so, she decides to go to another area of the park where the trees are too high to climb. Then she has to plan for different playmates and a shift in her daily routine. But it all works out and there is no fussing when Clemmie finds herself in a new play area.

Such a procedure can be applied whenever necessary. How much anxiety you are willing or able to put up with is always a question. To what extent are you willing to deprive your child of the chance to grow? It works both ways here too. A mother who must see to her own anxiety problem must impede her child's growth in some way, unless she can find a suitable alternative to relieve her tension and at the same time let the child grow unhampered. It's a delicate balance to be weighed, so that neither parent nor child suffers needlessly.

While Clemmie's mother seems to be procrastinating about meeting the challenge of the larger tree, she is making deliberate efforts to deal with the problem. Perhaps, in the long run, she will be ready for the larger tree sooner. In the meantime, she maintains her sense of security and is a more contented Mommy. She has found and chosen her alternative.

Alternatives to "Punishment"

It is almost impossible to predict what alternatives will pop up when one is open to ideas. Mrs. Dain told a parent group that her thirteen-year-old son was taking things that did not belong to him. She had threatened that his father would beat him every day if he did not stop. One parent responded by saying that Mrs. Dain was obviously aware of a problem and was trying to help her child. This approach precluded any defensiveness on Mrs. Dain's part.

The question was raised as to the possibility of handling the matter in another way. Mrs. Dain suggested that perhaps the boy was "jealous" because his elder, chronically ill sister went to a clinic every week where she had two of her own "special" doctors. This mother was deeply concerned and spent a great deal of time with the girl. She was often irritated by her son's lack of cooperation when she was tired from "all the work I have to do for your sister."

During the discussion, Mrs. Dain realized that the child had not had much opportunity to be "special." That thought led to another. "Of course! He's special now, since I have to give him attention because he's been taking things." If he could not get attention one way, he was going to get it another way. She decided to show him some "specialness" by going shopping with him for trousers he needed. After that, they had a hamburger together. It occurred to her that she had not been alone with him, away from the family, for a very long time. Some time later, she planned to get tickets for a ball game and to persuade her husband to take him, leaving a younger brother at home.

Her boy's stealing had provided Mrs. Dain with the opportunity to slow her rushing drive through dutiful motherhood and consider alternatives of action. Beatings had seemed like a tried and true solution. But she admitted that her threat hadn't worked anyway. As a caring mother, she was open to the idea that there might be another way of dealing with the problem. So when she paused to think, she came upon valid insights.

In this characterization of the *parent-bound* woman, I am referring to one acceptable view that Mrs. Dain may have of herself. This is the self-image that we appeal to, even though we assume that it is inter-mingled for her with other, less acceptable views. There was no doubt that Mrs. Dain was convinced of her good intentions. Our interven-tion did not concern itself with the validity of that point. It had to do with *creating openings*. These openings could effect improved com-munication between mother and son, and bring about a greater sense of well-being.

Alternatives to Consistency

Everybody talks about consistency in parenting—but it is rarely found in most families. The alternative to being generally consistent as a parent, which is almost an impossibility, is being consistent within yourself during a parent-child encounter. Your child should have the feeling that your position on any single point is consistent within itself.

This is what I mean when I speak of the alternative of *unequivocal response*. The unequivocal parent remains consistent with his posi-tion, whatever it happens to be at the moment. If he wants to change his position, he is free to do so, of course. But he must inform his child of the change, give reasons if he cares to, and then be one with his new position.

Another way of talking about consistency is to bring in the double message. This double message is at the center of inconsistency. So all I'm saying is that you can try to identify your position on any one issue and then plan to be *one way at one time*. It is not a change in your position that confuses youngsters. It's only confusing when the child feels that you yourself don't believe in your own position at a given moment. The only way certain parents are consistent with their children is by consistently giving out double messages. That consist-ency is not due to the desire to be consistent, but to unconscious motives which leave the parents without a choice regarding the quality of communication they maintain with their children.

When you recognize that you are being inconsistent in your position, you tend to deprecate yourself. You feel guilty for not being consistent. You may respond to guilt in destructive ways. Too often, the wish for consistency turns a wishy-washy, double-messaged, pseudo-permissiveness into a foolish and inappropriate rigidity. Those are two extreme alternatives, neither of them useful or satisfying.

Do You Really Want to Listen?

As another alternative of action, a parent could plan to approach a teen-ager by saying, in effect, "I've been thinking about how we always get into a snit when we talk about appearance (or drugs, sex, or other subject). The other day I was thinking about that and I realized that I was unhappy about it—that there seems to always be some tension about it when we're together. I thought of a few things I could do or say to you. But somehow I couldn't decide what. Then I decided to just tell you all the things I had thought of and see what your reaction was, and maybe see if you could help me to arrive at a better way for us to live together."

Your seventeen-year-old might at least be intrigued by such an approach. He (or she) might also be drawn to your new attitude, your direct, help-seeking approach. Were you to plan such an approach, you would have to be prepared to reach no conclusion, receive no commitment or promise, whatever was broached. You would have to plan to keep to what you started, only sharing your wish to improve the quality of communication. If you kept your "cool," it is unlikely that he would blow up as usual during such discussions. He would believe you when you said you wanted a reaction. A reaction! How about that! When was the last time you asked for that—and meant it?

Lots of mothers and fathers ask their children for reactions and opinions, then prevent them from saying anything. Or if they do, they don't listen. And if they listen, they do so only to direct their own arguments more forcefully. Sometimes they seem to listen, but are really thinking about their own next move, designed to clobber the "reaction" and make their point irresistible. This is a common game between older children and their parents. Some fathers are skilled at this, especially professional people who are experienced at influencing others. This is not wanting to know someone's reaction; it's just fooling yourself into thinking that you can make someone believe you want to do something you don't intend to do.

So if you plan to say to your youngster, "I want to get your reaction to this thought of mine," you'd better mean it. He'll listen to you the first time and believe that you really want an honest reaction. And you'd better be prepared to keep your mouth shut and *wait* for a reaction. If it is forthcoming, it might not come out immediately, all nice and shiny. He may have to stumble and bumble around because he doesn't have a reaction all polished up waiting for you to ask for it.

On the other hand, he may be able to come out directly and hit you with a truth that can be quite unsettling. You asked and you got. So be ready. If you don't think you can stand the heat, don't ask for it. You may be better prepared later on. But if you ask and don't mean what you say, and don't wait for a reaction, he'll see immediately that you're up to your old tricks and lose trust (once again) and go into a sulk.

It's hard for parents to believe that their children want them to talk with, listen to, share. Your children are sometimes angry with you because of the many disappointments when you said, "Let's talk," and *you* did all the talking; when you said, "Tell me what you think," and *you* did all the telling; when you said, "What's troubling you?" and then delivered a lecture. Perhaps it sounds as if I am saying that parents just talk too much. But it's more than that. You talk so much because you're tense for any of a hundred reasons. Maybe you feel you have to inform, set straight, control, guide, win at all costs. If you're not a talker, maybe when you do talk it's usually some form of overt or covert put-down, so subtle that you don't even know it yourself and you insist that you're not putting anyone down. In a sense, any put-down, whether or not you are aware of it, is a way of talking too much.

So here again I'm talking about *double messages.* You say, "I want you to talk," and you mean *you're* going to talk. You say, "I want your opinion," and then you hammer your own across. These double messages are everywhere. They surround us. They pervade every aspect of your family life, at all ages, on all subjects, in all seasons. Verily, the double message could be called the message of all occasions, by all parents, for all children. *Now is the time for all good parents to come to the destruction of their double messages.*

Step two, then, the planning phase, is that one focusing on other possibilities. These other possibilities are referred to as alternatives. Any idea you have may be considered an alternative course, although not necessarily applicable to all families. This planning phase is the thinking through. Remember—the identification process exposes the *whats*. The planning process helps you to find the *hows*.

CHAPTER IV

Step Three — Action

ACTION CONSISTS OF DOING something specific, something explicit, something concrete. It is the *doing phase* of the parenting method. Besides an obvious act, doing may consist of verbalizing one or more alternatives discovered through the planning in step two. The effort necessary to utter even a few words, however, may often be great. If those words are required as a possible prerequisite to change, however, the effort must be made. Without it, all remains in the realm of fantasy. By remaining silent, the parent practices a kind of self-deception, with the continuous, daily sop, "I'm going to say that tomorrow."

Effort as Action

Don't expect guarantees, though, that such action will bring about the desired result. On the other hand, remember that without some new action, it is nearly certain that nothing new can happen. At times the action may be a non-action, such as deliberately not doing or saying something that you ordinarily would under certain circumstances. That may sound contradictory. But you know how difficult it is to keep yourself from following an old pattern when it is habitual, like criticizing or nagging. It is difficult even when you know that those actions may conflict with your goal. A deliberate effort is required to keep quiet under such circumstances. I consider that effort action also. In other words, action is any *follow-up* to the planning stage of step two.

Failure Is Par Too

In action there are always risks. The most inhibiting is the risk of failure. If you identify and plan and do not act, you cannot be faulted for failing. But as soon as you perform an act or say a word, then you or others can judge you.

A teen-age girl had been given a traffic ticket for speeding and endangering the lives of a car full of teen-agers. Her parents decided to place limits on her by saying that she could have no more than two of her friends in the car at one time. When she had a minor accident, however, they were angry and condemning of each other because each felt that the other should not have encouraged the imposition of limits, since the daughter's rebelling against these limits may have been responsible for the accident. And unconscious, vengeful forces could indeed have been at play in the girl. But it is also possible that she simply ignored the limits; after all, she did have four other people in the car when the accident happened.

Instead of condemning, this couple needed to reevaluate their action and either reenforce it or find other suitable alternatives. Their mutual condemnation removed the focus from the need to prevent another such occurrence. They had permitted themselves to be shamed by their failure, and their daughter would suffer because of that.

Infinite Varieties

Action takes many forms. A couple were traveling with five young children. After the novelty wore off, the children began squabbling over games and toys intended to keep them happy and occupied during the trip. The parents tried reasoning, adjudication, rewards, and threats. Finally, exasperated, the mother, Mrs. End, screamed,

"If you keep on fighting over those toys, I'll throw them all away!"

The children were shocked, but only momentarily, for the eldest remarked reasonably, "Mommy, you know you wouldn't do that." "Just try me!" she snapped grimly. Daddy was wise enough to keep out of it.

Later, the children started squabbling again. Mrs. End waited until they reached a rest area, then asked Mr. End to stop the car. She got out deliberately, amid a flurry of questions.

"What did we stop here for?" "What are we going to do here?" Telling her husband to keep the engine running, she turned to the children. "You," she said, "aren't going to do anything." With that, she opened a rear door, removed two toys that had been the subject of argument, walked to a trash container and dropped the toys into it. She brushed her hands with an attitude of finality, and before they could even register their astonishment, she got back into the car and Mr. End drove off.

Silence reigned so long that the younger children fell asleep. Mr. and Mrs. End felt pleased at their successful move, and were in a fine mood when they stopped for the night. The children were rested and in good spirits and everyone was on good behavior the rest of the evening. Furthermore, although there were many whispered conferences about whose turn it was to play with which toy or game, there was no more bickering over the toys.

That action may seem extreme to some people. They may complain of wastefulness, of meanness, etc. But that action was the one Mrs. End chose. It worked for her and she was satisfied. And that's the point. No one has to do what she did. Each family can find its own particular action suitable to the circumstance and compatible with family attitudes.

Mrs. End recognized that she was not angry in devising her plan as a possible solution to an irritating situation. In fact, she felt somewhat amused at her expedient and was relieved that her exasperation had forced her to take a stand. By her unequivocal attitude, careful planning, and definitive action, Mrs. End had succeeded in cutting through her habit of double messages and had given a single one for a change. She had said, in effect: "This will not be tolerated any longer —period!" It apparently served as a relief for her children as well. Now they knew exactly what she meant, what she wanted, and they knew the consequences of their behavior. As is so often true with little ones, certain simple, uncomplicated, and straightforward actions often speak louder than words.

Little Children, Little Problems

Clear and definitive action with young children helps to establish limits and avoids the confusion of double messages. I am not recommending the throwing away of toys on a regular basis. I am underscoring, however, the principle of the unequivocal limit as it relates to particular circumstances.

Coping with stressful situations in this way helps parents to accept their responsibility to exercise authority effectively. Parents must find their own metier. They will learn that limit-setting is a relief to both parent and child. They develop greater confidence in themselves as they "practice" appropriate applications of their authority. Or, to put it another way, as they practice the art of parenthood they grow to respect their ability to be effective parents. Their children grow to respect that ability also. Children expect parents to exercise authority. They are not automatically opposed to it, as some people think. As long as it is kind, fair, reasonable and relevant, they can accept it.

Parents are often worried that their children won't like them if they exercise their parental prerogatives. In some instances, therefore, they try to behave like their children's peers, which they definitely are not. They may resent this posturing, even though no one is making them do it. They disregard their children's contempt for their lack of dignity.

This is especially true of teen-agers who are "turned off" by their parents' attempts to behave as "one of the kids." When a parent is naturally and spontaneously a kind of playmate, he is usually accepted as such by the child. Most children love such parents dearly, because they can be great fun. But when certain mannerisms are put on in order to win favor, children can sense an intrinsic artificiality and may be embarrassed or disgusted by it. They want their parents to be themselves, not actors or actresses. They tend to love the staid, more reserved parent just as well, even though they will not prefer him as a playmate.

If parents learn direct ways of behaving when their children are young, they are better equipped to deal with more complicated exchanges in the teen years. Children are relatively easy to live with in the early years. But one cannot be an indifferent parent who neglects his development as a parent in those years and then expect to cope with some of the complex events that take place as children grow toward adulthood. Learning to cope effectively early is the best preparation for coping later. Prevention of small stresses and problems teaches one how to handle and/or prevent later stresses and problems.

Except for obvious handicaps and serious matters of physical health in early childhood, it is well to remember: "Little children, little problems—big children, big problems." First learn to deal with the little ones. Then the later, larger ones won't seem so overwhelming.

Nothing Good

Mr. Fare complained that his son "never does anything good." I thought he meant that perhaps his youngster was a delinquent or that he was a kind of misanthrope for whom goodness was only to be ridiculed. But I had misunderstood him. What this father meant was that the boy never did anything *well,* according to the father's standards and expectations.

Whenever Mr. Fare asked his son to do a chore, his pattern included one or all of the following: 1) Giving detailed instructions on how to do the job, even if the boy had done it before; 2) cautioning the boy about all the mistakes he could make and those he had made earlier; 3) implying that the boy couldn't do the job the way he expected it to be done; 4) indicating that he knew the boy probably didn't want to do the job at all; 5) expressing anger that the boy was uncooperative; and 6) declaring that he didn't like the boy's attitude about doing household chores.

You can see why the boy had no interest in being cooperative or even in being around his father. But more than that, the boy's confidence was shaken each time, so that he approached the task feeling tense, awkward, and self-defeating. Because he was only a small boy, he could not do the chores as well as his father, who was experienced. Yet when the boy revealed his ineptitude, the father blamed him, expressing disappointment that his son's performance was poor. This was the basis for the remark, "My son never does anything good."

It never occurred to him that most eleven- , thirteen- , fifteen- , or seventeen-year-old boys are unable to do even simple tasks with the same know-how as an adult. Even a simple job like sweeping out a room or mowing grass with a power mower can be difficult. Some youngsters may be very adroit, but others don't realize that there's a little more to such jobs than meets the eye. They may not realize, for example, that sweeping motions must cover every square inch of the surface of a floor, and indeed must be repeated two or more times if all dust and particles are to be swept up. Most youngsters feel that if a broom is moved quickly over the surface of a floor with some attempt to cover most of it, the floor will be swept clean.

When a teen-ager indignantly whines, "But I did sweep it!" you can believe him. Maybe it doesn't look swept, but he did sweep it. Depending upon one's goals, one can either let it be, or one can say, "I see that you did sweep it. But it was very dirty and I think it needs some more attention. Will you go over it again?" Even though the youngster cannot bring himself to sweep it again (for that would be acknowledging his ineptitude), he has learned that a floor must be swept differently from the way he did it. But he may very well surprise you if you have not indicated that he is a "slob" or "lazy," by offering to sweep it again. Parents often forget that their children might wish to please them. Very young children enjoy pleasing their parents, and they still do as teen-agers—believe it or not! But if they are unkindly criticized, they will lose their incentive to please.

As for cutting grass, youngsters find it difficult to mow in straight lines, or to overlap each row so that no grass is left uncut between the rows. They do not know how to avoid rough spots which can damage the machine. Each task has its own special requirements such as these.

It Takes Time

A mature, experienced man is a kind of expert at these chores, even though they are essentially simple and require no training or special aptitude. But clearly, experience does contribute to a fine-looking job and to the maintenance of a well-functioning machine.

Few youngsters can have the incentive that their parents have to produce clean floors and well-cut lawns. They might care a little. But they just cannot care as much as you do. They don't do the job poorly just to irritate you. However, once a rebellious pattern is set up, then a not-caring, frustrating stance becomes a non-discriminatory, inappropriate, total attitude of defiance against your authority. I am not addressing myself, however, to that condition. I want to describe the ordinary, garden variety of parental expectations which drives both parent and child up the wall without conscious or unconscious intention on the part of either.

Most parents are not aware that they can get a child of any age to do anything they desire if they can conduct themselves without critical teasing or sarcasm, but with courtesy (only a please or thank you), pleasant firmness (no double messages), and friendly authority. It works in places of employment or educational institutions. It can work in the home with your own family.

A teen-age boy or girl working at one of these jobs has no awareness of what to look for, and cannot be on the alert, as an adult can, for all pitfalls. It would be too tension-producing to be constantly worried about what might go wrong. What I am saying is that when some of your tasks are assigned to youngsters, you have to be prepared for mistakes. It's part of the package.

If you make it possible for your child to learn from you, as time goes on his performance will improve. But I suggest that the child may never do the kind of job you really want. So be it. Either complain all your life, or be glad that *willing assistance* is being given. I can assure you that it will not remain willing assistance very long if you offer only critical and grudging acknowledgment.

Mr. Fare found that working with his son always ended in some sort of unpleasantness. He was sorry that he could not have "more fun" working with the boy. He remembered the fun he had had with his own father when they hung pictures, repaired doors, painted, played cards and other games. He even got angry with his son when they played cards, because the boy didn't play the way Mr. Fare wanted him to. Remember, he did nothing "good."

New Ways

Mr. Fare also remembered that his father had been a man of few words, a man who never gave lengthy instructions. He had merely indicated briefly how they would proceed. There was a great deal of watching when a new job was done. The younger one had learned by watching and doing. His father's comment would usually be a satisfied, "Well, we got *that* done," which the son took to mean that he had done an acceptable job. Who knows how good his part of the job was? He assumed it was all right because no one ever said that it was not.

Yet here he was carrying on with his own son as if the boy should be able to do a job that required experience. Fortunately, Mr. Fare felt ashamed of himself when he came upon that realization (identification). He could not talk with his wife or even with the boy about his critical approach. But he decided that he wanted to effect some change in his attitude and expectations of the boy. He was able to go through the planning phase without consulting anyone. He arrived at several alternatives. He could 1) stop asking the boy to do anything; 2) commend the boy no matter how poor the job; 3) ask what job was preferable rather than assigning one; 4) encourage the boy to keep busy at other activities away from the father; or 5) have the boy visit relatives or friends on weekends and vacations.

This father even went so far as to consider sending the youngster to live with relatives and go to school in another community, but he quickly discarded that idea, knowing that his wife would probably suggest that he himself live with a relative before she'd let the boy go. Once he had identified his problem, he thought about it frequently. But the time amounted only to a few minutes whenever the subject crossed his mind. Once he had made the initial deliberate effort to sit down and think about it, he found that it kept returning to him.

Finally, he settled on doing as his father had done: keeping silent. He would use neither long-winded instructions nor criticism nor praise. He knew the last would be insincere, and he didn't want to risk that. He also knew that the others would be difficult. What does one say if one is to keep quiet? It's sometimes hard to know that it's done by saying nothing. One woman once said she accomplished this by putting small adhesive strips across her mouth. Her child thought they were playing a game!

Anxiety Rears Its Head

A curious thing happened with Mr. Fare. Having made his decision and feeling somewhat proud of it, he was reluctant to act upon his decision. He kept putting it off. He found himself becoming edgy and irritated with the boy for no reason. So much seemed to be going on within him, yet he had not made a single move. He did not realize that by not asking the boy to help, he was doing something different. Even though Mr. Fare seemed more generally irritated, there had been none of the usual explosions over jobs "poorly done."

However, he felt that he was merely avoiding a confrontation. One weekend, he invited the boy to go with him to buy a new plane. When they returned they began to work on a repair. The father admitted that he had to concentrate the entire time to keep his "mouth shut." He succeeded, and found that his irritability gradually subsided. His action had resolved his doubt about succeeding.

But that was not the happy ending. This man had to keep working on his decision to avoid being critical and did not always succeed. There were other explosions, but less frequent, and not so bitter. On occasion, Mr. Fare was able to mutter an apology for being so critical and acknowledge that the boy was at least trying to do his best.

How Much Is Lost?

Sometimes the attitudes that damage are not obvious, and as we have noted, they are certainly not intentional. Both parent and child may be totally unaware of them. Nevertheless, the damage done may be greater than most parents realize, especially if those attitudes contribute to a consistent style of relating. You can just imagine how disheartening and discouraging it would be for a youngster to be subjected to an attitude which consistently stated the following: You are really so incompetent . . . I can't depend on you for anything . . . you are always spoiling everything . . . you can't seem to learn what I tell you . . . you must be pretty stupid . . . I certainly wouldn't expect you to do anything if there were anyone else around to help me. . . . You can also imagine how a child's self-confidence could be lost or preserved only at a very low level under those circumstances. Such attitudes, explicit or implicit, are self-defeating for both parents and children.

You can believe that your child is not being inept deliberately. He is only doing what he can do, what comes naturally to him at this stage of his development. But he begins to evaluate himself as you evaluate him. If you feel, think, or tell him repeatedly that he is inept, he begins to accept it.

That is how children derive their sense of worth. To the extent that parental attitudes reinforce certain views of youngsters, children will develop these views themselves—as persons who are acceptable to themselves, their families, and the world at large—or as persons who are not.

Something of the feelings a child has during the early years will probably be retained all his life, regardless of any degree of success or failure that he may know. I'm not suggesting that you go to the extreme of celebrating everything the child does. Simple, quiet, appropriate acknowledgments are adequate. Save your praise for special occasions. Think of acknowledgment as a simple statement of fact. "I see you did that," or, "Thank you." (Magic word!) That's an acknowledgment. Leave the put-downs under the rug or in the garage. They contribute nothing to the development or well-being of your child.

It is often disappointing for parents to find that their children are ordinary boys and girls, not the superchildren they have dreamed of in their fantasies. Unfortunately, your disappointment is also a blow to your little one who is probably doing all he can to get you to acknowledge and accept him as he is.

True acceptance is one of the greatest gifts you can offer your child and yourself. It won't be on every occasion, nor is that even necessary. But the child should have the experience of your full acceptance once in a while, anyway. Your disappointment does both of you a disservice. Try to look only for an ordinary little boy or girl. Then the potential of humanness that your child carries within him will never cease to surprise and delight you.

You Win Some

There are times of parental distress when there is nothing to be done no matter how much identifying, planning, or acting you have done. At these times, one can only be patient and wait for the child to overcome or outgrow a particular phase. You may not approve of certain of your youngster's permanent characteristics which surface more completely in later years. Nevertheless, these have to be met with acceptance and respect if you are to maintain an ongoing, mutually satisfying relationship.

At times, parents are disappointed with their children's personality, intellect, appearance, way of relating to their peers, or approach to work and play, and they feel uncomfortable and guilty because of this disappointment. While they say that they are grateful because their children are physically sound, doing adequately in school, and so on, their disappointment nags at them. They become tense, for fear that their joylessness will become apparent. They may regard their children as somehow impoverished, not realizing that an essentially intact but less-than-extraordinary child probably holds more possibility for richness of experience and relating than they do. Potentials, however, must be realized. They may lie dormant many years, waiting to be tapped. But they need to be approached with friendly, affirming patience, not with a tight-lipped, parental "strength and fortitude" attitude.

A child may not have certain highly prized assets as set forth by a society. But he's like an untilled plot of ground. Your affirmation of your child as he is, your care, interest and efforts will serve to enrich that little personality, to bring a shine to those searching eyes. Your new view of your child can help you to experience a kind of rebirth. It's a good feeling and one worth working toward.

The Time Is Now

The action phase is the phase of doing. Information gleaned and alternatives discovered become aspects of a definite course of action, for better or worse. This is where solid, deliberate and pointed efforts must be made. Action might be called the *when* phase of step three. After the *what* of phase one and the *how* of phase two have been considered, the when is *now*.

It is not satisfying for you to only think, worry, or complain about your children. It will be worth your while to go beyond that and do something in the interest of change. Don't be discouraged if your action fails to bring you an expected outcome even after many tries. Remember, if at first you don't succeed, try, try again—and I mean again and again and again. That's all you can do, because when things don't get better, they usually get worse.

So if you are aware that a parent is the primary agent for preventing dissatisfying and unfulfilling growth patterns in children, you cannot afford to let bouts of discouragement stop you. You must be ever-ready to return to the task of prevention. It is truly a great responsibility for us, but an exciting challenge too. It is for us to accomplish if we only will. It takes willingness, stamina, courage, and the knowledge that you and your children can love each other as long as you both shall live. And after that, your grandchildren will reap the continuing fruit of your labors. Maybe you don't care that far in the future. But care a little now.

Part Two

CHAPTER V

Parent Power I

P ARENT POWER EXISTS, FOR BETTER or for worse. It exists whether you know it or not. It exists whether you like it or not. In these pages, you have been presented repeatedly with evidence of your parent power. That power may produce either constructive or destructive outcomes. At any given moment of parenting, you may or may not be aware of your power. You may use it intentionally or unintentionally.

Parent power is transmitted through parental influences, parental impact, fathering, mothering—or smothering—as the case may be. Most people are aware that parents have always had diverse influences upon children. But the specifics of that influence often remain vague. They cannot therefore be grappled with, or studied and held up for scrutiny when that is indicated in order to understand the causes of tension.

Even though much has been written on the subject of parents and children, I do not believe that most parents are aware of the specific, detailed, nitty-gritty, everyday ways in which they exert their power. They do not recognize the minuteness of the processes by means of which their influence creates impact on offspring. They do not know where the wellspring of their power originates, how it flows from those origins, how it is conveyed to their children, how youngsters experience, interpret and respond to its many forms, and what outcomes, great and small, their power may produce.

Why Power?

When we consider influencing anyone, we generally think in terms of trying to effect some change in one who already has a certain substantiality, in terms of experience and opinion. We exert as much pressure in our argument as we feel can appropriately be brought to bear. We are often conscious of what we are about and pursue our goal in deliberate fashion. We think in terms of effecting a change in an individual's way of thinking, feeling, or living. We think of approaching someone who can rebut or defend, someone who may be impervious to influence, someone who can also influence us.

Parent power is nothing new. The term is only an idiom of our time. But there's more than that, for the very helplessness and total dependency of any newborn child make your influence assume the magnitude of omnipotence. That child cannot, for some time to come, effectively defend himself against any harmful elements of the parental environment. If there are any, he makes efforts to repel and reject. Some of these efforts have an important impact (more on that will be said in the chapter on Child Power). But he is really no match for you. The impact of your influence on your child's early life is so great that I believe the use of the term "parent power" is entirely justified.

Parent power has a quality of omnipresence. It is inclusive, pervasive, and comprehensive. The concept of influence is more particular, more circumspect. Power "flobbers" all over. Its impact is felt in every area of your child's experience. It seems to exude from every parental pore into every filial pore, like the air, smog, humidity. One says, "I can feel the humidity in my bones." You can believe that your children can feel your exudations in their bones too, whether or not you mean them to.

For the most part, our children are in no position to resist the influence we exert. They are in no position to sort out the noxious from the benign. They cannot look at us and say, "Look, Ma (or Pa), what you're doing right now isn't very good for me." True, babies cry, scream, are restless, develop gastrointestinal and respiratory disturbances. Older children also have their ways of informing us that all is not well. But how do we know what it all means? Is there too much air in the tummy? Or are they saying, "Get off my back. Let me have a little room to grow this morning without having to deal with your hangups."

If we could interpret their reactions correctly, would we become so conscious-stricken and guilty that we would become all the more tense and be on their backs all the more? That is always a possibility. So before it happens, I'm trying to tell you what might happen to cause distress, so that you can do something to *prevent* it. It might be happening right now, this very day, and you can use your power to do something about it before it becomes so troublesome that you're up the wall. I want you to understand the problem and know that you don't have to stay up that wall too long.

Guilt, Helplessness, and Hope

I don't want to arouse your anxiety, however, by bringing certain things to your attention. But I feel I must inform you of some of the pernicious features which may underlie the tensions in your family. I feel I must arouse at least your curiosity, your interest, so that you will develop an incentive to seek out the roots of your despair. I want to say, "Please don't be anxious. Please don't waste time with your guilt. You are in such crowded company that you would be astonished to know how many mothers and fathers have done all the 'terrible' things you think you have done with your children." But I know you'll feel guilty anyway, no matter what I say. However, maybe that guilt can be alleviated. One way your guilt can be relieved is by your appreciation of the existence of the enormous power you hold and by learning how to use it to your benefit.

You see, one of the reasons guilt remains is that we feel helpless to change the conditions that brought it about. If that sense of helplessness can be diminished at all, then you can move to do something to change those conditions. As they change, you lose your reason for feeling guilty—until the next time! But every little bit helps.

In Chapters II, III, and IV, I have tried to supply you with some means to reduce your feeling of helplessness. (Many good approaches have already been described in the literature.) My implication is, of course, that you are not as helpless as you think. *That is what parent power is all about.* But if you *believe* that you are helpless, then that belief must be dealt with as if it were a fact. I can call it a fantasy. But my calling it that will not change your belief. I have to proceed as if your belief is a fact.

Steps one, two, and three of the method for parenting recognize your entrapment in that belief and are designed to pry you away from it. Sooner or later, if you are to help yourself and your family, you must pry yourself loose from that belief. Clinging to it will keep you in exactly the same position of helplessness that you deplore, and with which you struggle ineffectively.

As you learn to place your finger upon one very small bone of contention at a time between yourself and your child (identification), you may feel more hopeful. As you move toward planning alternatives, you may begin to experience stirrings of influence. Once you have acted upon one of your plans and it has been successful, you will begin to recognize and acknowledge the existence of your power.

As you move in that direction, you will also begin to recognize that your power was being exerted all along, but in ways over which you had no conscious control. When it served your child well, that was fine. When it did not, you felt guilty without understanding that your power was being wielded, but not in a helpful way.

In a sense, once you decrease your alienation from your "power source"—that is, close the gap between your awareness of your power and the power itself—it should become more and more available and accessible to you. Instead of being free-floating, unharnessed, unintentional, running hither and yon, creating havoc or benefit at random, your power can be tapped and applied consciously, judiciously, in the interest of fruitful development for both you and your children.

Power Source

Everything you are or have ever been contributes to the quality of your power source. And everything includes just that—everything. The economic, ethnic, social, and psychological milieu into which you were born is part of your power source. Of importance is the quality of your welcome as a newborn into your immediate family; your early experiences as child, sibling, peer; your experiences as pre-adolescent, adolescent, student, adult; the quality and quantity of your relationships with others; the successes and failures you sustained in any period or area of your life. Included also are the state of your physical health, past illnesses and handicaps, your vitality, appearance, creativity, personality, character strengths and limitations, disappointments, frustrations, neuroses. Everything.

For clarity, it might be well to speak of *negative power* and *positive power*. Negative power could be regarded as power the exercise of which results in unforeseen, unintentionally harmful, hurtful or otherwise deleterious effects. Positive power will have helpful, beneficial, or otherwise salutary effects. Negative power may be regarded as any parental impact which has detrimental effects on your children, and positive power as that impact which results in generally acceptable growth-producing effects.

Don't think for a moment that negative power is more powerful than positive power. It may seem that way because it is often associated with pain or distress. But positive parental power exerts a tremendous influence also, sometimes completely unknown, yet influencing the development of many of our strengths.

Money in the Bank

I like to think of positive power as *money in the bank*. Not only is it there to be drawn upon in time of need, but it is constantly accruing interest at an unusual rate—maybe 50 or 100 percent! At such a rate, you can see that it might never run out. But this resource has another unusual characteristic. As it is drawn upon to meet the exigencies of daily living, it is immediately replenished by the very experience that drew upon it in the first place. Clearly, it has a magic quality which causes it to grow and grow.

Perhaps you think I am being fanciful. And perhaps I am. But I have witnessed this process over and over in those persons who draw upon their strengths (money in the bank) repeatedly; who engage wholeheartedly in life; who give freely of themselves yet seem always to have an endless supply of whatever it is they are giving—be it knowledge, comfort, creativity, or good mental health.

Teachers who give and give to their students without thought of extra recompense continue to experience joy in their work. They don't run out of ideas, nor does their fund of information dry up. Businessmen and politicians who work hard and wholeheartedly in the interest of the public often enjoy the fruits of their labors. Volunteers are frequently known for their endless resources of enthusiasm, industry, and optimism. Workers in the arts do not deplete themselves by producing and producing: As they age, unless they suffer ill health, they seem to find more and more to draw upon.

Where does all this energy, this vitality, this interest come from? It comes from your bank, that bank into which you and your parents, by means of their positive power, began to make deposits from your earliest days. I'm not referring to the trips, the vacations, the schools your parents provided for you, nor even the food, clothing, and shelter. While all of these *may* serve as deposits into this special bank, I refer more specifically to a quality of experience found so often in even the most fleeting moments: How your parent's hand felt when you crossed the street or when you had your hair combed; the uncomplaining way your mother washed your teddy bear or that rag of a security blanket; the arrangement of the dandelions you brought in; your parent's companionable silence on a bus ride, taking a walk, fishing, working or playing; the patient way your father ran after a ball and threw it back to you again and again so that you could not miss it; the way he made room in the car trunk for your favorite toy; how he produced chewing gum and chocolate on a long drive; how your mother held you on her lap when you hurt yourself so you could cry and not feel silly; the expression on their faces when you said something that had to do with nothing at all, but which was *you*. Little things, big things, thousands and thousands of things, years and years of them, an endless procession of experiences.

Now you are drawing upon your bank to make deposits in *your* child's bank. You didn't know you were doing that, but you are. That's part of your power. Whatever riches of humanness that you possess within yourself (and there are ever so many, some of them perhaps long unused) are now, by means of positive power, being poured into your children. And so they produce, link by link, a slim but endless, shining, golden chain of experience with which your child may thrive and grow.

You have seen examples of the use of negative power throughout this book, and there will be many more in the following pages. So I shall not belabor the point here with more illustrations. No doubt you will have little difficulty recognizing them. Let me only repeat: Don't despair over them. If you can recognize your own negative power, you are in the best position to change its character. Without that recognition, there is little you can do, for you may not even know that tension exists until it has become a serious problem beyond your power to solve.

Other Resources

It would be an oversimplification if I were to leave you with the impression that parental influences were the only sources for the development of your personality and character structure. In concert with all that parental influence provided, both positive and negative, you have made your own contributions to your development. From the time that you began to relate to your peers and a world wider than that of your family, other influences went into the creation of your individuality, with all its strengths and shortcomings.

Using all available resources, you became the artist, and you wove the fabric of your being. You continue to weave it each day, as new stimuli, new experiences impinge upon your consciousness. Whether or not you are aware of it, you decide upon the colors, the threads, the design, the tone, the mood, for your daily life. With few restrictions, you can create it in any way that you choose. If colors are drab, threads thin, the overall design can compensate and can express your aliveness. You can take help wherever you can get it. But the fabric you weave is of your very own making. To recognize that is to recognize the truth of your power to effect change—perhaps not in last year's pattern, nor even in yesterday's, but in today's and tomorrow's, and the next day's. This opportunity is always open to you, if you will give yourself that freedom. No one else, no other authority can provide you with it.

CHAPTER VI

Parent Power II

ARENT POWER REFERS to the total impact a parent may have on a child's development. *Parent output and input* refer to an infinite number of actual *message units,* verbal and nonverbal, overt and covert, intentional and unintentional, direct and indirect, conscious and unconscious, which originate in the parent and which permeate the familial atmosphere.

Input and output have to do with the *content* of parent power. A little further on I'll describe *parent "vibes,"* a refined aspect of output and input. Vibes serve as the wrappings for output and input, as their means of transmission. In a loose sense, input and output refer to the *what,* vibes to the *how,* and parent power to the whole thing.

Output

Parent output refers to verbal and nonverbal feelings, thoughts and deeds that stem from parenthood, but which are *not directly intended* for your child's edification, consideration, or use at the time of output, or ever in some cases (especially parental tension, which is also output). Parent output includes manifestations of parental attitudes, values, needs, fears, conflicts, desires, dreams, wishes. Most parents are not conscious of the extent of their output. Even though this output is not directly intended for child consumption, it is nevertheless clearly related to your child, for it would have no existence whatever without a child in the home. There are both positive and negative outputs, and either can come from an affectionate, optimistic, flexible nature, or from a tense, pessimistic, rigid one, according to personality, state of mind, and circumstances.

In the position of parent-person, you say, think, or do things which are directly related to your being a parent. These things differ from the things you would say, think, express, or do as, for example, a housekeeper-person, a breadwinner-person, or a lover-person.

A friend has called to ask you to attend a boating class with him. The thought crosses your mind: If I learn about boats, then I can take my son out in a boat sometime. "Yes," you reply, "I'll arrange to come every Wednesday night." That is a simple parent output. What you might have said as a nonparent-person, we cannot tell.

A neighbor wants you and your spouse to come over for refreshments on a Saturday afternoon. You'd like to go, but that neighbor is not exactly welcoming to your children. "No," you decide, "I don't think I can get away." That's parent output.

These are obvious forms of output. There are countless other verbal and nonverbal forms. Tension is a very common nonverbal output. But it certainly may have a verbal component. The lovingness of a loving parent is output. Flexible sensitivity is output. Listening, accepting, welcoming are outputs. A parent-person's facial expression, posture, and voice that are related to a child's presence are outputs. Outputs can be decisions about schools, vacations, furniture, friends, automobiles, location of homes. So-called child-centered homes are loaded with parental outputs. The more child-centered the home, the greater the number and variety of outputs.

At times, the atmosphere in a home can become so laden with outputs that a visitor may be inundated by them. Depending upon his personality or interest in your family, he will be able either to tolerate that atmosphere, or be repelled by it. If you have ever wondered why certain of your friends have somehow just drifted away, ask yourself if you were perhaps subjecting them to too rich a mixture of parental output. You can be both a friend-person and a parent-person at the same time. Your friends don't mind a little of the other as long as they can relate to you primarily as a friend-person.

It is also possible to be a parent-person and a spouse-person simultaneously. In that instance, what you say or do can be interpreted as the output of a parent-person as well as the expression of a spouse-person. For example: "I do think, dear, that we ought to go to the seashore this year on our vacation. It will be relaxing and fun for all of us. The children can learn how to swim, and you can paint, sail, and lie in the sun. It will be nice if you take the children with you when you do something, but they will have plenty to do if you prefer doing it alone." The parental output here is clear-cut. The statement expresses interest in the children as well as the kind of vacation the spouse might enjoy.

Input

The principal difference between input and output is that *input is intended to directly influence a child* in some way. Inputs are the thoughts and feelings you try to *put into* the child. Input is meant for the child's benefit, guidance, edification, information, development, and use. However, even though input is *directly related* to the child and intended for his or her use, the parent may very well be totally unaware that he or she is attempting an input. In other words, the intention to influence may be a conscious or unconscious one. Under some conditions, where it is unconscious, the parent may deny it if so confronted. Where it is conscious, the parent will use whatever means to accomplish his or her purpose. That purpose is to influence with useful information, tools, attitudes—all that encourages and enhances growth as you conceive of it for your child.

"What a generous child you are," you exclaim, "to share your toys with your little brother." The conscious intention here is to 1) inculcate an attitude of generosity; 2) impress the fact that generosity is a worthwhile characteristic; 3) indicate that generosity is pleasing to Mommy and Daddy; and 4) keep it going so that you don't have to deal with anticipated future squabbles over toys.

I do not want to give you the impression that parental inputs and outputs are being put down—or up, for that matter. They are simply being labeled and described, for they exist whether we admit it or not, and by any name you please. A parental input is any verbal or nonverbal feeling, thought, or deed that you express, consciously or unconsciously, in order to exert a direct influence on your child. While parental output is not directly intended for the child's use, parental input is strictly intended for the specific use and benefit of your child.

Off Course

That parental input does not always contribute to healthy growth often comes as a surprise to well-meaning parents. Much input, seen subjectively as caring, loving, and guiding, can be viewed objectively as evidence of hyprocrisy, overprotectiveness, or as a device to encourage dependency. The teaching of caution may be viewed as invoking anxiety, and parental expressions of doubt may be recognized as compulsive suspiciousness.

The child playing at the edge of the water at the beach, whose overcautious parent holds hands too tightly and repeatedly refers to "that big wave," senses parental tension and may come to feel anxious, instead of merely cautious, about the water. The mother who speaks and behaves as if every street crossing is an encounter with hostile forces out to destroy her and her child will inspire unrealistic fear and lack of confidence in her child. Such negative inputs (and outputs) are intended to teach only reasonable caution. But they convey a *message of extremes,* and often strike wide of their intended mark.

Rather than merely demonstrating in a relaxed manner ways in which waves and traffic can be dealt with, a message of extremes implicitly states that *all new experiences, and selected old ones, have to be guarded against, for they are untrustworthy and may cause untold damage.* This is clearly not an aspect of all new experiences, but a belief of anxiety-prone parents who cannot cope, anxiety-free, with certain experiences themselves.

Such parental input is surely not intended to do more than convey an appropriate or reasonable amount of fear, if any, so that caution is exercised. But what is a reasonable amount of caution? Does caution have to be taught by instilling fear? What is it that instills fear in addition to caution? Is it a simple message of caution, or is it the obvious signs of anxiety in the too-tight handclasp, the slightly con-

stricted voice, the repetition of words, the fearful (uptight) counte-
nance? All these implicitly say, "That is a terrible monster out there,
and you must always be cautious or it will get you!"

A child does need clear, thoughtful, unequivocal reminders when
in a position of danger. But these reminders need not be so repetitious.
Beyond that, an alert parent is needed where continuous awareness
is required to ensure safety. Neither your anxiety nor the child's will
accomplish that. When he's older, you will not have to be so alert. But
if anxiety is aroused in the child, the best he can do is to avoid the
danger altogether. This may be fine for some parents. But you must
know that if it becomes a pattern, he will be deprived of a spirit of
adventure, enthusiasm, optimism, and joy in anticipation of new experiences. Once such a pattern is established in early life, it often dogs
a person for years.

Output⟶Input

Sometimes parent output becomes parent input. This may occur
when you suddenly realize that something you are saying or doing
might make a dandy little input. So your intention shifts and you try
to put it into the child, for you believe that it will be useful there. And
it very well may help the youngster to grow in a way that gives both
parent and child a sense of well-being. Such an outcome results from
many a parental input. However, in some instances, the outcome of
well-being may occur only for the parent; that is, you may feel good
about the result of your input, but the child may not. On the other
hand, he may reject the parent input and feel neither good nor bad
about it. If you have certain expectations based upon your inputs, you
may be disappointed when these are unheeded.

Disappointment then becomes a parental output which can be felt
by the child, even though you may not intend it. Where disappointment is used as an input—that is, the parent deliberately tries to
influence the child with it—two motives may be found: 1) Disappointment is being used as a spur to urge the child in the direction the
parent wishes him to go; 2) the parent unconsciously wants the child
to feel guilty, so that the child will rectify his behavior in some way
to please the parent.

Parent Tension

There is no way a parent-person can avoid putting out or putting in. When the components of these processes are expressed easily, spontaneously, and appropriately, the child may be easily, spontaneously and appropriately influenced. And so he learns how to live with comfort and relevance in the world.

However, qualities of absoluteness, must-ness, and should-ness in parents—regardless of the child's circumstances, necessities, or wishes—arouse parental tension. Feeling its impact from the parent, the child is puzzled and confused, or is made anxious. He reacts in one or more of the many ways children may react when they feel that their connection to the most important people in their lives is fraught with tension.

Children's sense of well-being (especially very young children) is incompatible with parent tension. Even the happy, healthy child feels uncomfortable in the presence of a tense adult. If the adult is not important to the child, that tension does not matter very much. But where the teacher, or the babysitter, or the parent exude such tension (vibes), the child can be made to feel quite uncomfortable.

If there is no counterbalance for such tension, the child may be damaged by not achieving his potential. Where tension flows from parents continuously in the form of various outputs and inputs, the child is indeed in a quandary, for he cannot just walk away and ignore them. Because survival depends upon these people, the child is obliged to discover ways of dealing with tension-producing factors in the environment. Surely a formidable burden for a child!

Politics of Parenting

Much goes on between parent and child that mandates the child's preoccupation with security. But how can you expose and understand the politics of parenting? What are the actual exchanges? How do you engage with your children? What motivates them to listen or not listen, to respond or not respond? An understanding of the actual hows and whats of parent-child encounters can lead to an appreciation of the tremendous power the parent wields, through output and input, in everything the child feels, is and does. As you grow to appreciate your position of power, you are better able to redefine your position, and perhaps relinquish a position of fear, timidity, immaturity—feelings which have caused the child to be fearful and uncertain as well.

The "battle" persists because of the existence of two fearful, uncertain adversaries who have had to resort to a sort of covert violence in an all too common, hurtful parent-child relationship. Where the parent understands and accepts the power he holds, he can no longer be drawn into the position of adversary, for he can no longer view an offspring as an adversary. Indeed, there is no contest, for the child is not even an equal—rather, a young, tender, innocent, uninformed being who needs gentle parental guidance. With that he can grow into a person who can feel secure because of his continuously evolving sense of autonomy. All the institutions, monies, professionals, and studies cannot accomplish that. Only a parent, as a primary preventive agent, can help the child grow with a sense of selfhood and to a deep conviction of self-worth. All other means act only as secondary measures.

As parents, you may identify with many of the vignettes presented throughout. Perhaps you will come to a greater awareness of your own constructive or destructive involvements with your children. Through these vignettes, the parent is repeatedly confronted with his or her part in the relationship, and is repeatedly exposed to the possibility of alternatives.

Parent Vibes

Parent inputs and outputs are comprehensive concepts and therefore complex ones. They include everything that comes from a parent in the context of parent-child relations. One component of that "everything" is the feeling component which was loosely grouped in Chapter V with nonverbal elements of relating. But this feeling component can be further defined by separating it from certain other nonverbal communications such as facial and body expressions, tone and quality of voice, flushed or pale cheeks, respiratory rate, etc. Even grooming and general appearance can be included among nonverbal elements.

A nonverbal feeling component includes whatever conveys the subtle, intangible, emotional overtones of anything that can be seen, felt, or heard. I refer to those overtones as *parent vibes,* to use another of our "now" idioms. Parent vibes are the intangible, often unrecognized "radiations" which seem to emanate from parents and which convey one aspect of a message or a complete message in itself.

Total unawareness of those vibes is possible and often the rule with some parents. Nevertheless, these vibes may totally influence the outcome of any human encounter. Parent vibes are often the conveyers, or carriers, for covert, unrecognized messages. They are operant in the *double messages* I described in Chapter I and to which I have frequently referred. Parent vibes often make it possible for youngsters to know what you want and mean, even though you yourself may not know what you mean, so you say something else (double message). But your parent vibes may be spelling out the message loud and clear.

Reading Vibes

It takes a straight (unconfused) child to "read" these messages. Babies are best at it, because they are the least contaminated by anything that can impair their perception of those "radiations." When Mommy or Daddy is tense, baby senses it. Your parent vibes convey the message of tension to baby.

But if young children are barraged with double message after double message, they become confused and lose to some extent the capacity to read the vibes aright. Verbal and other nonverbal aspects of output-input demand and capture their attention, and they lose the sharpness and sureness of their earlier perceptions.

A tense parent (*conveying* message number 1 that says "No") but also smiling, cajoling (*giving* message number 2 that says "Yes") is difficult to read. The child may feel vaguely that if he follows the smile accompanying message 2, he'll collide with message 1. If he senses the contradiction of 1 and 2, then he clearly goes counter to message 2. In either case, he is afraid he cannot achieve the desired outcome. Wanting to go along with or please the parent, he is caught in his own conflict. He cannot be straight with himself and choose the one message he prefers, or none, and risk the consequences. In this case, he is too busy trying to please an unpleasable parent.

Put another way, the child may respond to parental conflict by creating a conflict of his own—a sorry outcome indeed. Yet often it cannot be avoided, for parent tension is conveyed by vibes even if overt verbal and nonverbal clues are controlled.

How It Happens

The youngster comes out feeling that he is wrong if he responds to the overt message, and wrong if he responds to the covert message of tension. Such a feeling of being wrong no matter where you turn can result in feeling uneasy, guilty, "bad." The parent asks, "How did my boy develop such a bad feeling about himself? He's had nothing but love and consideration." Yes, he's had love and consideration. But there's been much more than that. He's had the benefit (!) of your tension, sometimes completely unknown to you, yet being continually conveyed through your parental vibes. You never intended him to know of that tension or to be burdened with the conflict from which that tension began. You didn't even know yourself that it existed. So how could you have prevented your child from being influenced by it?

Nevertheless, that is the course parental vibes may take; that is the harvest they may reap. A youngster cannot know that your tension has to do with you and not him. Children's natural egocentricity leads them to believe that parental tension, as expressed through irritation, impatience, pessimism, anger, hostility, cruelty, etc., is directly related to them and points to their shortcomings—in a word, their "badness." That is how your teen-ager developed such feelings about himself. In a way, you had nothing to do with it; yet you had much to do with it!

I referred earlier to emanations from parental pores to offspring pores. These are of course the vibes I'm describing here. Nowadays, for the reasons I've outlined, many young people are trying to get away from their parents because they often feel tense and helpless in the face of parental vibes. Young adults accomplish this by moving out and going to work, or by going to college and avoiding parents at vacation time.

Younger children, not ready to leave with their parents' blessings, may follow a more destructive path and effect this separation by "running away." (Running away is a complex business, and I'm mentioning only one factor.) But the persistence of certain parental vibes in some homes is antithetical to children's developmental needs and can sometimes elicit such tensions and anxiety that youngsters cannot tolerate it. Instead of approaching parents and saying, in effect, "I feel awful about something. I'm not sure what it is. But can you help me?" they run away. They hope to find help which cannot come from other youngsters they know who are just as impoverished, despairing, and needy as themselves. The use of drugs and excesses in sex are only some of the means they use, believing that these will compensate for an inexorable sense of hollowness.

Pollution

If you have ever been aboard a large ship for a long period, you are familiar with the feeling of the steady throb of engines and the vibrations they cause. You may have had the feeling of wanting to shout: Will you stop a minute! There is a quality of intrusiveness in those vibrations. After a while, however, you grow accustomed to them and can live with them. But there is always a sense of intrusiveness. We might call it a form of *sensory pollution*. It's there, surrounding us at all sides, and jarring us continuously. It is a total intrusion, and not unlike the air pollution to which every city dweller is subjected.

It is unkind perhaps to imply that parental vibes are a kind of pollutant. I'll qualify this by saying that parental vibes may be regarded as pollutants only when the messages they carry have an adverse effect upon the youngster.

In this decade, vibes have a different quality. Many things that you do now have been done many times before. Why haven't they been injurious to youngsters in the past? you may ask. Perhaps they weren't harmful because the past was another world, another time—because there has never been so much of so many things or so many people before. Priorities have changed. That's the way it is. And what difference does it make, anyway? Here we are now, in this decade, with the world as it is. It isn't anyone's fault—or it's everyone's fault. Take your pick. Feel guilty if you want to. But that will be a waste of time if you are interested in helping your child, and it will add to the harmfulness of whatever is already bothering you and your child. Many parents know that something has gone wrong. Yet many haven't a clue as to why it has happened. Worse yet, it will keep happening. And some parents are not going to be able to inform themselves as to the true nature of their relationship to themselves and ultimately to their children, spouses, and everyone else in the world.

Kinds of Vibes

All people generate, emit, and receive vibes. As I have noted, vibes occur independently of our consciousness of either emitting or receiving them. As an aspect of parental power, vibes are just there, like it or not. There are vibes that make us happy; vibes that make us sad. There are vibes which intrude, demand, jar, excite, stimulate, anger, frustrate, intimidate, or burden; those which comfort, pacify, calm, strengthen, reassure or please; those which leave one indifferent, cold, distant, puzzled, isolated, or despairing.

The quality of vibes depends upon the kind of person a parent is. Even making a fair share of parental "mistakes," a sincerely reaching-out parent, whatever his personality or philosophy of parenting, probably emits more vibes of a comforting nature than of a disquieting nature. Vibes of an unremittingly demanding parent excite anger, resentment, and rebellion in offspring. A distant, indifferent, unresponsive parent emits vibes that generally "turn off" a youngster. Each parent who is interested in his child's welfare is obliged, therefore, to investigate his own vibes, discover their nature and the uses to which they are put, and attempt to effect changes which may improve the quality of his relations with the child.

Not All Bad

Dealing with change leads to a new view of yourself and your parent vibes. Remember that a new approach could result by following the three steps of the procedure described in Chapters II, III, and IV. If you are wondering about the primary source of your conflict and tension, consider that human attitudes, behavior, and stresses evolve from cultural and familial patterns over which we have little control and which are repeated to some extent in each succeeding generation. You came by your inner conflicts as honestly and unintentionally as your children have come by theirs. Surely you can forgive yourself; for you, your parents, and the society in which you were reared "knew not what they did."

But take heart! For if there are parent vibes which injure and damage, there are surely vibes that heal and promote well-being. These are the vibes I referred to in the section "Money in the Bank." These vibes are part of the hundreds and thousands of little pieces of living that provide your child with the strengths and wisdom of his years. Your task then is to emphasize positive vibes, those which encourage growth—and to better understand negative vibes, those which undermine, which "put down," and which corrode the edges of your child's potential and self-worth.

Evaluation

Sometimes parental outputs and inputs are great. Sometimes they are not so great. And sometimes they are quite poor. Most parents fall in the range of not so great with occasional flashes of great as well as poor. Great or poor, parents are generally unable to evaluate themselves. One problem is the parent who does poorly but thinks he is great. It follows that he wonders why he is having a hard time with the child. It doesn't matter whether or not a parent who produces a positive output knows it. What does matter is that outputs and inputs are growth-promoting.

Another problem is, however, that when you discover that your outputs and inputs haven't been great, you tend to become so disheartened, so discouraged, and so guilt-ridden that you make yourself even more tense. Or you rush out to read everything you can find. In this state, you interpret what you read in absolutes. It's either this extreme or that extreme. It is often difficult to grasp, in terms of a continuum, the innuendos that authors make. While they may talk about one response, they also imply a wide range of responses for any one circumstance. This breadth of view may be missed by the parent seeking to quickly reestablish a feeling of comfort. Reading is not much use to the person who is at the low end of the range of parental effectiveness. If serious problems already exist, such a person needs other help, possibly from a trained person.

Impact, Impact

It should be no surprise to you that children adapt to parental outputs and inputs without awareness on their part. As they grow, almost everything they do is patterned, more or less, after the methods, attitudes, and values that you espouse. This includes the way they eat, handle toys, dress, move, talk, play games, etc., as well as the way they think and feel. Of course, there are exceptions. But you must remember that your constant barrage of inputs and outputs has repeated impact.

Parents are sometimes amazed, not so much at the similarities of taste and habit between their children and themselves, but at the exaggeration of such characteristics in their children. This exaggeration has also been noted in regard to ideas, where so-called radical youths come from homes where liberal views have been discussed and weighed. However, a young lifetime of listening to forward-looking, theoretical constructs does not confer instant competency when one attempts to apply those constructs in the context of one's own life.

Parents seem to underestimate the possibility of their offspring's misinterpreting their open but considered and questioning attitudes toward experimentation. With what they take for implicit parental approval, therefore, some youngsters transform any new idea into an *instant experiment* without careful appraisal or with little regard for consequences.

An understanding, for example, of political experimentation, in any area of institutional or private living, requires study and experience. While bright youngsters can grasp complex concepts easily enough, it is not likely that they can fully appreciate the subtleties, historical significances, socioeconomic factors, global implications, and human needs that cannot be ignored in any thoughtful contemplation of a new or revolutionary idea.

Under the guise of espousing freedom in any of its many forms, some parents merely afford themselves an opportunity to give vent to their unconscious frustrations, hostilities, fantasies, and other inner conflicts. By means of parental output and input, children may receive many distorted messages which they cannot interpret accurately. Not only may such messages mar perceptiveness and judgment, but they may also becloud and jade a youth's permanent outlook.

What a child is by the time he reaches adolescence is largely, but by no means completely, the result of what parents have put into that child in terms of output and input, from the day of birth. The adolescent has also been influenced by teachers, peers, and the mass media. The influence of the these latter factors is not inconsiderable. They are not, however, the decisive factors in the molding of personality and in the way each youngster views himself and the world. To be sure, they are significant factors, but they are only additives to the basic parental outputs and inputs which make the principal impact upon offspring. Parents are the primary agent responsible for the health of their children.

Background

It might be useful at this point to offer a brief summary of the theory of human development which best helps me to understand human behavior and motivation.*

Reflecting the stresses and tensions of the entire society in which the family is rooted, adult members of each family pass their own conflicts and anxieties on to their children. Conflicts in the culture augment personal, inner conflicts, leaving parents incapable, in some instances and to some extent, of feeling genuine affection and concern for their children. Where parental conflicts are irresolvable and tension persists, children cannot achieve the sense of security and self-confidence necessary for coping with life. Instead of attending to their spontaneous, joyful growth, they are required to develop tension-relieving means of relating, whereby they may feel safe in a world they view as potentially threatening, rather than open and welcoming.

I cannot fault any generation, for your own problems with security and self-confidence started in babyhood with your parents, they with theirs, the latter with theirs, and your child's with you. There's no point berating you or your parents. As I have repeatedly stated, I am interested only in bringing to your attention certain conditions, beliefs, facts, and fantasies, so that if you are so inclined you may have some frame of reference for beginning your own investigation.

---

*Dr. Karen Horney's theory of neurosis and human growth, as described in her works. See epilogue.

Understanding an individual's insecurities requires an exploration of beginnings. There, one will find an environmental matrix of conflict, anxiety, and tension. Such environmental factors do not permit the experiencing of comfort and welcome that babies require for optimal growth.

A degree of rejection, experienced principally through parental tension, is well tolerated by most babies. But where tension is too great, the baby reacts with fear, expressed through physiological distress. To the extent that circumstances continue to produce the need to reject tension, the child will produce a reactive tension of its own. Should that tension remain unbroken, the baby will generate anxiety in response to parental stimuli which are not intended as such, but which the baby experiences as threatening to its well-being.

Later on, anxiety-provoking stimuli may be more obvious. How many of you have seen a mother striking her child repeatedly, hard, while holding a skinny little arm so that the child cannot escape? I suppose an occasional beating is of no great danger to a child as long as there are evidences of parental love. That child is capable of learning that the parent has a vile temper that has to be tolerated. But where such behavior is not mitigated by clear evidence of sincere welcome and acceptance, then it could easily confirm an earlier feeling that danger exists everywhere and that it must be guarded against at all cost.

It is impossible to say exactly how little children feel threatened, for they cannot tell us these things. They can only express physiological discomfort, which may fluctuate markedly from mild to severe distress. Where disease is ruled out and the child continues to show great distress, one can only postulate that tense parents emit vibes that cause discomfort in their babies. I believe that most, but not all, functional feeding, skin, and gastrointestinal disturbances in infants are probably outcomes of a baby's stress reaction to the discomfort in response to parental conflict, anxiety, and tension.

Busy with such concerns at the outset, a baby is distracted from total involvement in its own growth. If anxiety-provoking conditions persist, the child of two or three is already hampered in its psychic development. Anxiety developed early in life, in response to threatening stimuli, requires a child to evolve survival means against it, for anxiety is not compatible with comfort. The child feels that the only way to achieve some measure of comfort is by constantly elaborating and refining survival techniques as the need arises. Although the child remains unaware of this effort, much energy, vitality, and intelligence necessarily go into the work. Thus the neurotic character evolves.

Having developed attack measures or other means useful for ensuring safety, this child could respond with hostile aggression to a peer's friendly or affectionate approach. The parent is puzzled.

"Honey, why are you throwing sand at the little boy? He wants to play with you." Although some degree of withdrawal is common for many children, another child may respond with extreme withdrawal to a peer's approach, even though companionship is desired and needed. "Honey, come over here," says Mommy. "Don't hide behind the shrub. That little girl wants to play with you. She won't hurt you." The child's inability to respond positively to friendly overtures points to rootedness, even at an early age, in a compulsive form of behavior. In this case, compulsiveness is measured by an inability to alter attitudes and practices which clearly serve to create and maintain unwanted distance from others.

Remember that I am describing only one aspect of neurotic growth. But most often, neurosis is formed in bits and pieces scattered throughout the course of one's early growth and is mingled with healthy elements for which parents have also laid the groundwork and to the development of which they have contributed significantly. If parents become aware of any problems early, and are willing to make the necessary efforts to reassure their youngsters and help them to feel more secure, it is likely that some of the damage may be undone.

While compulsive patterns do not always interfere with a child's general development, there is no doubt that the quality of that development, or at least of the child's sense of satisfaction, will be interfered with in some way. Such a child may have difficulty learning and enjoying. Childish spontaneity is interfered with. Guardedness is the order of the day. A bright child is often ashamed of his performance and cannot know that that performance rests upon a base of anxiety and not upon stupidity. Any tension that child experiences will produce continuous distractions in efforts to grow. Such a youngster can only conclude that he is somehow deficient, inept, incompetent, inadequate, and therefore undeserving. Families may unwittingly feed into such beliefs with teasing, light remarks about shortcomings, thus confirming the youngster's feelings of inferiority.

To some extent, these inferiority feelings and other attitudes cause responses of exasperation, impatience, anger, unkindness to our quick, thoughtless barbs. The stronger the children are, the more the negative parental responses roll off their backs. But to the extent that they are damaged, even the smallest barb is sometimes experienced as a slashing wound; tolerances are at low ebbs and seemingly innocuous hurts are often responded to with total rejection.

The children cannot be faulted, nor can the parents. Everyone does what he does in good faith, with the best of intentions, or in ignorance. Most children cannot be expected to know about the things I have just described, nor to understand them, nor to care very much about them. Even if they did care, there isn't very much they could do about them. But for parents, even a fragment of insight can serve as a point of departure from old ways, embedded in ignorance, to new possibilities; for parents have greater wisdom and greater capacity to understand, to care, and to do something about their caring.

CHAPTER VII

Parent Power III

YOU MUST BE WILLING to pause and take a look at yourself and your family. That takes effort. You have to see what is wrong and what might be done to improve conditions. That takes effort. And you must have the courage to act upon your findings and deliberations. That takes effort.

I know I've said all that before. But that's the key, the secret if you will, the magic that will help you to change tension-producing attitudes and habits into less charged, disturbing, and troublesome family relations. I cannot promise you anything but possible relief from that tension if you will try, and keep trying, to do something different.

In this section I want to discuss some troublesome areas of parental concern, including fear of school and attitudes of the divorced mother. This material will further illustrate facets of parent power in particular circumstances.

Like Mother, Like Daughter

The child of a very conscientious mother who loved her child "before she was conceived" was riding her tricycle in a park where concrete steps were adjacent to the bicycle path. Looking away from her conversation with another woman, she saw her daughter riding toward the steps, her legs pedaling furiously. The woman flew after the child and "saved" her just as she was about to tumble down the steps. There was no way of knowing whether the child would have fallen—but that was the mother's story. She was convinced that her daughter was about to topple down those steps.

At any rate, this mother reported that she "calmly" removed the child from the zone of danger, but had to go home because her fear reactions had made her feel faint. She then reported that she remained highly anxious for weeks thereafter, and that her anxiety interfered with her general well-being. She could not relax, sleep, or eat well, and actually lost several pounds. Can you imagine the quality of her outputs and inputs during that period of time? How shrouded in anxiety every communication must have been!

Several questions come to mind. Was the child really in such danger as the mother imagined? She had bicycled in the same place many, many times, as had other children. Would the child really have plummeted down the steps, or would she have stopped, as other children always did? If it was so dangerous there, why did she allow her daughter to play there?

The child had been "saved" without a scratch. So after an initial, uncontrollable fear reaction, what was the anxiety all about? Obviously, the child was not continuously at the edge of a precipice. Why all the fear? Was this extraordinarily devoted mother shocked at her own incompetency as a mother? Was it so staggering that such a thing could even remotely happen to *her* child? If there were no real danger, why had she imagined it? Was she making too much of a rather pleasant, nondemanding afternoon activity? Was she trying to justify her "sitting around all day with nothing to do but watch the baby"? Was she resentful that her devotion and conscientiousness had reduced her to a mere baby watcher, so that she had to add some excitement and danger to the task in order to make it seem more worthy of her talents?

During the period of this mother's anxiety, the child began to show evidence of fearfulness when she went to the play area. Later, she avoided playing with children outside. Not until her mother's anxiety subsided did she return to playing with her peers.

School Phobia: Parent's or Child's?

School phobias cover a wide range, from mild to very severe. They may occur from nursery school through high school and college. They may be disguised by physical illness, learning or behavior disorders. I shall confine myself here to the mild forms occurring in children during their first days at school.

Such children may or may not have an older sibling already attending. They may look forward to attending school. But their preparations for the opening day of school are often attended to with more grimness than joyous anticipation. Whatever the early signs, these are the children who fuss when the time finally comes and who cry and balk when they get there. Sometimes they can stay and sometimes they cannot. Parents usually feel that these children need time to become "adjusted" and are willing to stay with them or take them home, with the promise that they'll return tomorrow. Unless this is resolved in two or three days, the parent may find that the child is afflicted with a form of "school phobia."

At this point too many parents try to rationalize the problem. "He's too young for school." "She's too sensitive for all that confusion." "The teacher isn't very patient." "The classroom looks depressing." All this serves to avoid looking at the problem. The fact is that the child is frightened. That fact must be identified before any progress can be made.

Then one has to rule out or cope with all the things that might be frightening. When those are either eliminated or dealt with, one has to look to attitudes within the family. This child has seemed to be looking forward to school. Yet when the time comes, he becomes tense. Has an older sibling been intimidating the child because of jealousy that the position as the only "school child" in the family will be eliminated? Has Daddy announced that now all manner of things will be learned and many games will be played with all the other kids? Is that a little too much for a kindergartener? Or is it Mommy whose voice grows a little quavery when she speaks of her "baby" going to school? Is she infecting her child with her sense of loss? Is she infecting her child with her anxiety at being left alone without her "baby"?

So the question of whose fear, the child's or the parent's, must be raised. Sometimes it's Father who tends to be timid about entering into new situations. Sometimes it's Mother's equivocations about school. On the one hand, parents seem to say, "Rah, rah, you're going to school next month." But something about their faces and voices seem to belie that joy. Again, little children are confused by the double message: 1) Daddy says school is good; 2) Daddy seems tense when he talks of school so there must be something scary about it. In this way the child picks up the vibes of anxiety that either parent may be emitting. If the fear is purely the child's, a little detective work may uncover the cause. But if it is a deep-seated fear, it may resist your efforts to uncover it.

Reasons for Mother's anxiety may have to do with feelings of impending uselessness or emptiness when a child is away from home. She is in conflict because she wants the child to leave, yet she doesn't want to lose her main reason for existing. Unaware that anything is troubling her, Mother has made no moves to fill an impending void, nor is she able to prevent her child from receiving the message of her equivocation.

Whether or not Mother understands her motives is of little importance at the beginning of the school year—unless that knowledge would immediately relieve her anxiety, which is unlikely. All she has to know is that her child is frightened and that she and her husband can do something about it. These facts must be established first. Then appropriate alternatives must be found.

The goal now is to get the child into school as quickly as possible and not to treat the parent. One thing that works well is to remove the anxious parent from the scene of action when the child has to get ready for school. If it's Daddy's anxiety about a new situation, he should be up and out of the house before the child awakens. If it's Mommy's anxiety, she should keep out of the way. Daddy can take over for a few days. That's all it may take. His child's getting a comfortable start in school is worth a few late-to-work mornings.

Other alternatives could include a friend, neighbor, babysitter, older child, etc., to take the youngster to school. Arrange for a car pool with other children's parents. Before school opens, moves should be made to familiarize your child with the school building, school-room, and teacher, if possible.

All children may be a little tense about their first day in school. But 95 percent of them make it and will come home the first day telling you how wonderful it was. You know your own youngster. If you think he'll be one of those who may not make it the first day, try to prevent any difficulty by making the path as smooth and as familiar as possible. If you feel your apprehension growing, plan ahead with your own alternatives, so that the child does not have to share your anguish.

I have placed the greater responsibility in this situation on the mother, because she is the person who is usually closest at hand and therefore open to greater involvement. But let it be noted that the father may be just as involved in his child's fear of school as the mother; his parent power may be as influential as the mother's. But the first consideration is to identify the source of the vibes that contribute to the child's apprehension. The other parent can then use parent power to help the child through a trying time.

Children of Divorce

For the most part, and even in these "open and enlightened times," divorce is a miserable business. There are three general phases of this misery: 1) pre-divorce; 2) divorce; 3) and post-divorce. Statistically, the first is worse than the second, and the third may be the worst of the three. The following section will describe some of the factors which can harm or help the children of divorce.

Edge of Divorce

The *pre-divorce phase* starts when incompatibility, unfaithfulness, or other causes become evident. The "injured" party may suffer most deeply here, although the so-called "guilty one" does not get off scot-free by any means. This is the period of suspicious watchfulness, of waiting, ostensibly to see if the problem will be resolved and to determine if the marriage is still viable.

There may be tremendous anguish during this phase, and many persons consult with therapists at this point. Any marriage can be saved in a pre-divorce stage if *both* partners want that very much, for it is often only ignorance or stupidity which brought it to this stage. Sometimes this phase may serve as an "eye-opener" in a situation where neither partner desired or actively brought it to pass, but they suddenly found themselves in the phase.

Where one of the partners wants to save the marriage, it might succeed if 1) that partner uses all his or her resourcefulness and strength to preserve the marriage; 2) the other partner is indifferent but willing to "go along"; or 3) the marriage is pseudo-maintained out of passivity, convenience, or fear. When one partner resists and covertly or overtly undermines efforts of the other, the marriage has a poor chance of survival.

Parents often try during the pre-divorce period to keep children ignorant of the problem. They feel that should the divorce not take place, the children can be spared any possible trauma. If it does take place, there's always plenty of time to inform them. In view of an ofttimes very prolonged pre-divorce phase, one may conclude that there is hardly any constructive purpose served in subjecting children to such a long period of anxious uncertainty.

There are many arguments for and against telling children of an impending divorce. In the pre-divorce stage, however, the possibility of reconciliation is always present. If children are informed then, and the divorce does not take place, they may be left with a residual anxiety which may flare up whenever the parents go into a "divorce mood."

The argument for telling in order to explain the high tension in the home may not be valid, for that tension will be present regardless. One has to ask whether the added knowledge of an impending divorce contributes beneficially to an already damaging situation. In the final analysis, however, each parent, knowing the strengths of the child, will make the decision based on his or her own principles of communication and philosophy. There is no rule.

Surprisingly enough, the pre-divorce phase can run from six months to many years. A reasonable average is perhaps two or three years. While that seems like a long time, there are two common reasons for it. One is that time goes by; the partners wait for a holiday to come and go—for the end of the school year, summer, or whatever else "for the children's sake"—and a couple of years slip by.

The other reason is that most people find it difficult to make sudden major changes in their lives. They become anxious about making the wrong decision, or changing their status, or any of the other usual considerations. So they have to grow with their anxieties gradually and get used to the idea, even though they may accept the change in principle.

The occurrence of that anxiety explains the hesitancy of the wife or husband who promises an extramarital partner a divorce so that they can marry. This hesitancy is also prolonged because of the children. Most parents are loath to leave young children and want to "wait until they are a little older."

In terms of straight information, it might be useful to the spouse who does not want a divorce to know that even when the partner asks for one, there may be a great deal of time available in which one can work to restore affectionate confidence. That is not done by bitter recriminations, angry depressions, hysterical threats, but by careful self-evaluation, hopefully leading to insight and growth. Then, whether or not a divorce takes place, the "abandoned party" turns out to be way ahead in the end, in terms of self-development.

I know I'm calmly suggesting that you do one of the hardest things in the world—"a careful self-evaluation." But remember, I said "straight information." All I'm hoping is that you might learn something you didn't know before, that things can be done to help you. But you have to know that there is something to do before you can do it. If you already knew this, well and good.

For the extramarital partner (lover) who has been promised divorce and a new marriage, this information may also be of some use. If there are young children, status and prestige at stake, or financial pressures, the divorce may be many years away. If the lover wants to wait five or more years, well and good. But he or she should know of that possibility and plan accordingly.

I want to make clear that there may be no intentional duplicity present in making plans for divorce. When the lovers are together and promise divorce and marriage, they may very well be wholeheartedly sincere about it. That is why they are so credible to each other. They mean it *while* they are saying it. Although a lover may lie intentionally, I'm referring only to the man or woman who is sincere at the time.

On the other hand, when the lover is with his or her marital partner, he is also sincere in feeling that he cannot make the break, cannot wrench himself away. So promises may also be made to the spouse, and these are as real and sincere as those made to the lover.

It seems to depend then upon where the partners are situated and with whom. The situations described may indicate a namby-pamby person to the reader, but such is very often the case when such circumstances exist. Then, it would seem that the abandoned spouses are in a stronger position than the lovers, if they want to preserve the marriage and are willing to make necessary efforts. A wise spouse who wants to maintain a marriage can know how to do it if he chooses. And a wise lover can know how to stop wasting time after a fair number of sincere but empty promises, and seek elsewhere for affection, companionship, solace and security.

Divorce

Divorce is usually sought because one of the partners can no longer accept the other. He or she wants the spouse to be a different sort of person, which is hardly possible. To use an absurd but graphic example, if I cannot accept you because you have blue eyes, that must mean I want you to have eyes of another color. Obviously that can't be. If I cannot accept that impossibility, however, and I insist upon your having blue eyes, then I can never be content with you. If I feel forced to remain with you, I shall be constantly disappointed and angry with you and make us both unhappy.

A marriage containing years of insistence on an impossibility may follow. Couples fluctuate from hopeful insistence to disappointment to hopelessness to anger and back to insistence again. It's one of the vicious cycles of life, often making its participants as vicious as the cycle they are caught in. Having said that, let me add that the secret of all good relationships is each person's accepting the other as he is. This applies in marriage, between child and parent, and anyone else.

This second phase, divorce, can be better or worse than the first phase, depending upon the needs and wishes of the partners. Many spouses admit to great relief when the decision is finally made and the process is set into motion. Others, wanting reconciliation but feeling that the decision to divorce is irrevocable, feel hopeless and may become severely depressed. That is a most trying time for both parent and child. Whatever they have been told, children feel the sharp lines of tension in the home at such times and react to them as to any other negative parental vibes.

This phase can last from one to two years—one year to get around to filing after the decision has been made, and one year until the final decree. It can be done sooner, but many find that they cannot rush through for the reasons I mentioned. If parents could just let that period run its course, let the time pass, and live their lives as fully as possible, it would be a relatively tranquil time compared with the pre-divorce phase.

There is no law stating that the time of divorce must be a deeply traumatic one. With the decision made, the element of uncertainty is removed, and children can feel more settled. During such a troubled time, they take every cue from the attitudes of both parents, not only the one with whom they happen to be living. Too often, however, this phase becomes a time for recriminations, squabbles, intrusions, and hysterics over child custody, none of which is conducive to steady, stable, comfortable development in children. If parents never cooperated before in rearing their children, this is the one time to start trying.

Post-Divorce

The quality of the post-divorce period for children again depends mainly upon the quality of the parent's attitudes, personality, activities, friendships, financial condition, etc.—that is, the parent they are living with. It is truly the time of greatest loneliness and anxiety: lonely, for one is actually alone now, having been with someone (for better or worse) for many years; and anxious, because the acute anger and suffering of the pre-divorce period and the involvements of the divorce period are over. This is it. It's all over. There's nothing left to get excited about. One feels abused, abandoned, empty.

Because a child usually remains with his mother, she will be the focus of interest. Her children's moods, attitudes, and feelings of well-being will parallel her own. These feelings are almost completely dependent upon the mother's, and not upon the number of hours or times the father visits with his children.

Besides providing fairly and without dispute for them, the most important thing the father can do for his children now is to avoid letting them feel that he is rejecting them. That is done with attitude, not with presents, trips, or removing children from the mother. Such acts may unwittingly serve to undermine the important goal of the mother, for she wants as much evenness as possible in the children's home life. Deliberate undermining, which may be overt or covert, attempts to discredit or ridicule attitudes and belittle plans made for the children.

While Father is not required to say what a great woman Mother is, he needs to know that a disparaging attitude will hurt his children far more than it will hurt his divorced wife. He needs to remember also that whatever the future holds for any one of them, she will always be the mother of his children. If, through his efforts, he succeeds in eliciting from his children any ugliness of feeling toward her, he should know that their subsequent guilt will be his responsibility.

This situation cannot be a one-way street. What applies to Father applies to Mother as well. Whatever love any of us have for our own parents should not be tampered with. There's little enough love around as it is.

If Mother feels her abandonment and loneliness very keenly and conveys her feelings, through parent power, to her children, they will suffer along with her. The major task such women have is to try to break away from outputs stemming from suffering. It can be a herculean task, and they can use all possible help from friends and relatives. If women can believe that leaving their suffering is the best thing they can offer their children, better than all the physical care, outings or vacations, they may be encouraged to make all necessary efforts to change the quality of their outputs and inputs.

Divorced women feel guilt or shame before their children for depriving them of a father. They must remind themselves again and again that they intended no such unhappiness, and that it is a waste of psychic energy to dwell on the subject. Neither shame nor guilt has a place in the family of divorce, nor has self-pity. Too many other problems must be dealt with.

Divorced mothers must not brainwash themselves into believing that the child's well-being depends on having two parents. That will be transmitted to children through outputs and inputs, and they too will feel deprived, impoverished, and ashamed without a father. I'm not saying that they will not have some of these feelings anyway. I'm only saying that mothers can add to them.

All children need *at least one healthy person* to rear them. Two or ten are fine. But only one is really necessary. If you can be that one, you don't have to worry about your children's being deprived. They are seriously deprived only if you feel deprived and transfer that feeling of deprivation to them by means of negative outputs and inputs.

So to the divorced parent, man or woman, I say: Take heart! You can go it alone *if you want to*. Here are your alternatives: End the rotten, miserable business; get down to the beautiful business of your own development and your children's growth; move your children and yourself toward an optimistic future and joyousness. It's all out there waiting for you. Do it! Now!

CHAPTER VIII

Child Power

N OW LET'S TAKE A LOOK at *child power.* Remember that when I use the word "child" I mean offspring of any age, unless I clearly specify a particular age.

At birth, an infant's temperament and physical status influence the parent's responses to him. Healthy, vigorous, demanding infants with a loud cry may please parents or intimidate them. Quiet, compliant infants may please them or worry them. Fussy, whining infants fatigue and irritate them. The allergic or colicky infant drives them up the wall. The response depends on which feelings are aroused in the particular parents. Already, within the first few days of association, you can see the impact an infant may have upon parents. That's power.

The lives of at least two people may be radically changed by the arrival of a baby. Two young people without a care in the world about where, when, and how they once occupied themselves during their leisure time are suddenly thrust into a disorganized routine of living, about which they have little or no knowledge and which is not particularly conducive to their well-being. I didn't say that the baby was not conducive to their well-being, but that often the new routine is not.

Anxieties about this little stranger's comfort become the order of the day. There is often great joy also, for there is nothing so exciting, so adorable, so rewarding as a gurgling, contented baby. But should there be any problems of feeding, sleeping, etc., the anguish is just as great as the joy. That's power.

The pleased, happy baby is no problem after the first few days, when parents have made the necessary adjustments. The pleased, happy parent is no problem for baby. But how does baby fare with a worried, fatigued, or irritated parent? Even the healthy baby may respond to such a parent with restlessness, sleepnessness, or gastrointestinal distress. That may further disquiet the parents who begin to wonder what they are doing "wrong." "Babies are not supposed to be this way," they think. "I must be a poor parent." They do not know it, but Baby is already exerting a powerful influence on the family.

Words *Will* Hurt

A parent's sense of insecurity makes him or her doubt his competence. To doubt one's competence is realistic and is not the issue here, for the inexperienced parent cannot become experienced or competent overnight. Nor, for that matter, can the experienced parent remain competent at all times. Unfortunately, however, this truth is not accepted. The parent is busy denigrating himself, rather than setting about to investigate the quality of his parenting and taking steps to improve it.

For the most part, people hurt themselves. Children or others seem to do the hurting because they say things that merely coincide with the same hurtful feelings one has about oneself. That can happen whether or not one is aware of his own feeling.

If someone tells you, "Oh, what a monster you are with your green hair," you are surprised, shocked, or amused. You may feel that the person who said it is kidding, drunk, or crazy. It is not likely that you would feel upset, for you are fairly certain that you are not a monster with green hair. Thus the remark could not "hurt" you. If you were entertaining guests in your home, though, and one of them said that, you might be embarrassed for a different reason. You might feel that you made a mistake in inviting such a person, and that now your other guests are thinking that you are a fool. Your own feeling causes you to inflict the hurt upon yourself. But the hurt has no relation to "green hair."

Limits

Very young children exert an awesome power over their parents. Just watch any parent with a little one in the park, on the street, or in the supermarket. That supermarket! Almost any toddler can make a fearsome shrew out of almost any parent there. By checkout time, both child and parent are tired, patience has worn thin, and tempers are tattered. Many mothers become embarrassed, ashamed of their inability to control their toddler's flailing arms clutching at anything within reach, or their quickly moving feet, carrying them beyond sight and sound.

It seems not to occur to parents that an ordinary marketing tour is too much for most little children. They often become tired and cranky long before Mommy is ready to leave; and she often does not take necessary measures to relieve them, for example, by doing the rest of her marketing another day. Inconvenient? Of course.

A mother and her young child were at the checkout in a supermarket. The child's hand strayed to the goodies temptingly displayed. Knowing from previous experience that these were not to be touched, the child looked inquiringly at Mother. Mother didn't say a word but just looked down, very evenly. They stared at each other for maybe ten seconds, and then the child looked away. Little fingers caressed the chewing gum. Again the child looked up. Again Mother returned a long look. There was no frowning, no smiling—just looking. A third time the child looked up and after a few seconds, smiled at Mother. Mother smiled back, and kept looking. The child then grabbed Mother and gave her knees a big hug. Mother fondled the child and then asked her if she wanted to sit on the window seat while she checked out. The child seemed to have forgotten about the chewing gum and was content to sit down.

I don't have to describe what usually happens when mothers start to discipline their children about keeping their hands off things. This was an extraordinarily eloquent piece of discipline. Everything was crystal clear to the child, and there had been no harsh words, ugly feelings, or spanking. Children respond to such quiet discipline; however, if they have already been spoiled by harsh disciplinary measures, it is difficult for both parent and child to shift to a new method. Many tries are necessary before success is achieved. And it is achieved only when the parent can be very clear-headed as to the nature of the message. If the parent described above had smiled too early, the child might have taken the smile for a signal to grab the object. Angry or disapproving behavior could have unsettled the child. Subsequent behavior might then have been erratic and therefore contradictory to well-being, which always depends upon Mommy's kind regard and not upon her anger.

Child Politics

Children of any age who fuss about being left with babysitters control a good part of their parents' social life. They also control the quality of their parents' enjoyment, because once out of the home, such parents often, but not always, remain tense about their young-sters' "suffering" at home. That suffering is usually in the parents' minds, and does not relate to what is actually going on at home. Such parents keep busy with phone calls and other needless concerns throughout a supposedly enjoyable outing. They don't know how to take time off. It is well to know, however, that parents themselves have brought about this kind of child power.

Such child power is apparent also among teen-agers. Who needs to be told how parents squirm and suffer under the unintentional cruelty inflicted upon them by youngsters who know all the ploys of getting their parents "off their backs." They know how to nag mercilessly to impose their demands. They have been known to withhold love in reprisal for some real or imagined hurt.

All along the line, children have developed their own *politics* of dealing with their parents. Each family has its own brand. These develop initially as defensive maneuvers against unwitting parental onslaughts. Where the nature of parent power is positive, the child has no need to develop *counter power* to deal with it. But when parent power is wielded indiscriminately and injudiciously, offspring have no choice but to develop a little extra power of their own in order to maintain a semblance of autonomy. That their power becomes indis-criminate and compulsive at times adds yet another layer of difficulty to the parent-child complex.

At first, most children try to be reasonable with parents and point out simple truths. If parents remain unresponsive, children develop other ways, sometimes devious, and often become fairly clever with maneuvers that make parents feel guilt and submissiveness. Teen-agers, especially, see through the tissue-thin rationalizations that many parents use. Not only do they see through those rationalizations, but they develop contempt for their parents as well.

In order to respect and love you, a teen-ager does not need to admire your intelligence or capability for success as measured by external standards. But he does need to feel your true concern, and to know that you can be depended upon for straight responses to comments and queries, including "I don't know."

I Know What You Need

Children have the capacity to be the pivotal factor in the well-being of their parents. That does not apply to all parents, but only to those whose well-being depends on their interpretation of the well-being of their children. If that sounds confusing, it's because it probably is. But perhaps it can be explained better by breaking it down into the following steps:

1) The parent, or parents, decide what the youngster needs to feel content. It may be a particular activity, a particular friend, a particular outing.

2) The child goes bicycling, or watches TV, or buys a magazine, or plays a game, and is content.

3) The parent, overlooking the contentment of step two, is waiting for one of the outcomes of step one, feeling that unless that is achieved, the child cannot feel "good."

4) The parent suggests, fusses, or is silent but remains "uptight," waiting for the child to show the *expected* signs of well-being.

5) As those signs do not appear (other signs are being grossly misread), the parent becomes all the more tense. His own well-being is thus being interfered with and he cannot be comfortable until something in step one comes to pass, or the child goes to school or to bed. Then the parent can relax. But the process begins again the next day.

Such goings-on occur most prominently on weekends, holidays, and during vacation time when children are not occupied with school or work. I do not overlook the need for parents to plan suitable activities for younger children, especially for city dwellers who cannot easily run out into the street without concern for safety. I'm only pointing to the distress of the parent who is so dependent upon what an offspring does or does not do. That restricts the parents a great deal and prevents them from exploring each day for their own satisfaction.

Such parents suffer because of a particular belief they hold, a belief based largely on fiction. Many, many parents have a fictional image of what a "good" parent should be. That image may be saintlike or some form of superparent. Since few parents are candidates for sainthood or ultrasuperiority of any kind, that image is a fiction. However, the parent doesn't realize this, and so he retains that image continuously, although it is less distinct at some times than at others.

The view has partly to do with a long list of services, cheerfully and relentlessly delivered. But more important, it includes continuously flowing love from parent to child, regardless of annoyances the child causes. Any honest parent knows what a fiction that is. But some parents cannot stand thinking of themselves as not loving, even for a minute. When they are angry with their children, they often have to go through the charade of assuring a child of their love. Children don't ordinarily expect you to throw them out of paradise forever when you get angry. They don't doubt your love that quickly. They know that right now you are angry—period. Unless you show continuous evidences of dislike, rejection, deprecation, you don't have to reassure children of your love every time you get angry. If you really dislike and reject, they will probably sense it, no matter what else you say or do. As I have indicated, children sense how you feel about them by your outputs and inputs. Even though they may not be clear about it, nor able to express it, they pick up your vibes and their meanings.

Child Output and Input

Similarly, children have their outputs and inputs. They don't care as much about their effect on you, however, and are much more truthful with their feelings than most parents are. Some children simply don't like their parents. But they acknowledge their dependency upon them. They know they need them for all kinds of support, and for the many goodies which flow from parent to child. But they often may not like them because the parents are not likable, or because they are too tense, too intrusive, too overpowering, too demanding, rejecting, indifferent, or unkind. That doesn't mean that the child does not stand ready to like his parent if the parent becomes more likable. Children are usually ready to change their view of the parent if given the opportunity. While parents are not as flexible as children, they need to know that months and years of time are available in which to effect a shift, so that each one, parent and child, becomes more likable to the other.

Parents cannot tolerate being in the position of the unliked parent; they feel all the pangs of poor parenting. A most troublesome aspect of the adolescent years is that, at one point or another, so many adolescents make it quite clear that they no longer adore their parents in the way they did as little children, and in fact may find them crude, rude, or inconsiderate. Whether or not a parent deserves such an evaluation is not the point here. Parents cannot accept that view in any case, and such feelings give rise to strong responses. Here again, we see the power of the child to upset the entire equilibrium of the parent by a perhaps too hasty, thoughtless and unkind evaluation expressed mostly through child output. Nevertheless, the parent falls into the trap. He strikes back, either defensively or offensively. Neither is called for, but this happens in some families.

At first parents are shocked, then terribly hurt, disappointed and disillusioned. "I've given this child the best years of my life and this is the thanks I get!" They become angry and may strike back at the child in a hurtful, vindictive way. They may be cowed by such accusations, feel deep guilt, and become depressed. They may try to become more submissive so that they will be better liked, but this ploy succeeds only in incurring either the contempt or guilt of the child.

Dealing directly with the dislike by trying to overcome it with a frontal attack is not often successful. Nor can such adolescent vibes be taken altogether seriously by the parent. Although almost every adolescent goes through such a phase, sometimes little need be done except wait until it's over. But where there might be some justification for the feeling, the parent should try to understand how he or she is being unlikable, how too demanding, too intrusive, too overpowering.

Such an investigation does not require the existence of guilt feelings nor breast beatings nor despondency.

Difficult? Yes. "Now why doesn't my sixteen-year-old seem to like me?" That's a tough question; but raising it opens up a broad channel for you, and the task at hand becomes less formidable. To the extent that your youngsters are clear-headed and not utterly cynical about parents, they are the ones to help you understand how your vibes have come across to them. That is part of their power. Now the question is—can you accept that?

It is fear of that dislike—"not being loved by my child"—even very early, that leads so many parents into a form of behavior popularly known as parent permissiveness. I shall discuss that at some length in another section. But I want to say here that what passes for permissiveness is usually not permissiveness at all. It is a kind of hodgepodge, pseudopermissiveness, designed (often unconsciously) to fool both parent and child into believing that, under the banner of "ensuring my child's love," the parent is agreeable to, approving of, and enjoying many sometimes irritating, obnoxious, unacceptable, disgusting, inconsiderate behaviorisms. This approach often leads to the so-called "child-centered" home, which is not a true reflection of existing parental feelings.

The Child-Centered Home

A child-centered home binds parent to child and child to parent. Of course, a home may be naturally child-centered from 7 to 8:30 A.M., or 3 to 5 P.M., or 7 to 9 P.M. if children are young and attending elementary school. If they are teen-agers, it's child-centered perhaps from 5 to 8 P.M. where their concerns are discussed after school, where they are listened to attentively (not *ad nauseam)* at the dinner table. But it would seem that a happy home should be Daddy-centered at certain times of the day or week, Mommy-centered at other times, and centered on individual children in the context of special family events. In other words, the focus of attention may be turned to whoever seems to require it at any given time.

If a home is determinedly and inexorably child-centered, other members of the family will be deprived, for there is only so much time and energy available in any one day or week. Parents, like any human beings, go from one extreme to the other. They are horrified by the old saying, "Children should be seen and not heard," so they have swung over to having children's noises prominent all day—at play, at meals, with guests, at bedtime. It's a wonder children aren't completely exhausted with all the talking and noise they are encouraged to make all day long. No rule says a child must be allowed to make as much noise as he can, or that a child cannot be told to be quiet on certain occasions. What is important is that the requirement be imposed fairly and reasonably and that the child have plenty of opportunity to express himself.

Such decisions can be made by the parent. But the child is often given the task of making decisions he cannot make and does not want to make. No child should be put in that position. There are so many decisions that are within a child's scope. He need not make them all.

The Demanding One

You've all seen how youngsters rule their parents in the most minute ways. Sullen children are carefully observed by anxious parents for signs of contentment. When they see those signs, they are delighted. Rude children are often spoken to in the most gently questioning tone by submissive parents when a good, clear, firm tone is required to deliver a particular message. Some parents spend a great deal of time preparing certain foods, arranging activities to please their children, and then stand around like the people in the TV commercial, waiting for "El Exegente" to decide their fate.

Many children are demanding only because they have been encouraged to develop that way. I daresay there are parents who feel that such characteristics show strength and a quality of leadership. And if you are willing that every activity of yours be interfered with, every meal disorganized, every conversation interrupted, even every night's sleep disturbed, that is your business. All I can say is that if you are unhappy with such a state of affairs, it need not be. But you're the one who will have to change it. The youngster cannot because that is the only way he knows of being and relating. He will follow your lead, but you will have to initiate the changes. It won't be easy. It might take years. But it can be done. You'll notice little changes as you work at it, and they will be gratifying. And from a long-range point of view, when you consider that you'll probably have something to do with your offspring for the rest of your life, the effort might become worthwhile. What's more, you'll be doing your child an important service.

The Teacher

Elsewhere, I said that your child can teach you how to be an effective parent if you permit it and if you can watch, trust, and listen to him. When little children seem negative, they are not trying to bother you. Your thinking that only interferes with a recognition of the message your child is trying to give you. If you trust your children to know their feelings, then you can learn from them.

A two-year-old boy kept throwing his new synthetic blanket on the floor during the night, and his mother would find him covered with his pillow. She scolded him and finally pinned the blanket and pillow in place. The next morning, the blanket, along with the crib sheet and padding, had been pulled off and were on the floor. Mother was furious and screamed at the child. "What is the matter with you? Why do you do that to your new blanket? You *are* going to use that blanket."

Years later, she learned that the child was uncomfortable with synthetic fabrics. When his woolen baby blanket was replaced by a synthetic blanket, he felt uncomfortable and did the only thing he could to help himself. He removed it. Had his mother not been involved in what *she* regarded as a power struggle, she might have heard his eloquent plea.

A little girl screamed whenever her mother put on her snowsuit and boots. By the time they were ready to go out she would be perspiring and Mother had to dry her. One day, before they reached the screaming stage, Mother asked, "What is the matter? What are you fussing about?" The child replied, "Your hands are too hard." Now you might not know what that meant, but this mother knew immediately. She was always rushing, and when she put the suit on her daughter, she would push, pull, and shove with quick, strong movements to get arms and legs where they belonged. Her movements were not gentle or playful. They were hard. They expressed her impatience, her resentment at having to give so much time to dressing and undressing. The child felt anger through her mother's output. That frightened her and made her uncomfortable. She said Mommy's hands were hard. It was the whole Mommy who was hard. Fortunately, this woman was capable of listening to her little girl and learned a great deal from just that one small sentence. Outings were more pleasant afterward, when Mother was able to quiet down, be more leisurely, realize that there was no great rush, and let her child do most of her own dressing.

There is no dearth of instruction, advice, and information from older children and teen-agers. They are all quite eloquent, but parents may not be listening. To listen doesn't mean to swallow every word, or to fall flat on your face with gratitude for the information. To listen means to hear, to attend to, to comprehend a message *once in a while*. That only takes a few minutes here and there. You don't have to devote a whole day to it—you couldn't do it consistently anyway. Only now and then. Parents sometimes think they listen, but they are only going through the motions. What you hear has to be reflected upon and responded to. As I say, the whole process may take only a few minutes.

When teen-agers say something outlandish, they are not completely unaware of it, and they don't expect you to swallow it whole. But the parent who does is caught in the bind of having to reject it, point out its absurdity, and may wind up ridiculing and belittling in the process. If the statement is taken with a grain of salt, none of that is necessary. The parent can then attend to the message and deal adequately with it.

Your Rights

Your efforts to be a successful parent are supposedly for the child's benefit. If so, and you are in a quandary as to how to proceed, try going to the source. I expect that your child knows what he needs from you in terms of attention, interest, and affection. But each child has a particular way of expressing his needs, and children in a family may differ markedly. So if you find out first what your child needs, you may save time and eliminate considerable worry. If you overlook obvious signals from your child, and make up his or her needs in your own mind, you run the risk of overlooking reasonable and necessary needs which will remain unmet, and of setting up an antagonistic style of relating that will spread to many other areas.

Don't get the impression that every squeal, pout, and demand must be courteously and consistently attended to. No parent has the time or sincere interest for that, nor would it be conducive to rearing healthy, self-reliant, affectionate children. I refer to needs that only the individual concerned can know about. You must exercise judgment, however, in deciding what's reasonable for you to attend to and what's not. If your boy fusses continually over some food and it's not vital to his nutrition, omit it. He's telling you he doesn't like it. Maybe he's allergic to it. If your little girl doesn't like a relative who thinks she's adorable, listen to her. Maybe her great-uncle has bad breath.

So many of the little things that don't really matter shouldn't be allowed to determine the quality of your overall personal relationship with your child. It's not worth it. Eliminate whatever points of stress can safely be set aside and focus on those essential to growth and self-discipline in your child. You'll find that there really aren't so many of these latter when you count them up. Too many concerns over your children are like chaff. You want to gather only the wheat. Let the chaff blow away. You don't need it and neither does your child.

Part Three

CHAPTER IX

Parenthood Is Not
a Natural State

I T IS AN INTERESTING FACT that the word "parent" has no common verb form. The words "mothering" and "fathering" have become common in recent years. But these forms are still used as nouns. There is no other way to say "to be a parent." No one can say, and be grammatically correct, "I parented my children pretty well, I think."

One can say, "I raised my child or I raised my cabbages." One may even say, "I reared my children or I reared my horses," depending upon the depth of feeling one has for the horses. Of course, one cannot say, "I parented my cabbages or I parented my horses," because it's obviously impossible to be a parent to any but a human child.

Parenting

But why make an issue of it? Only because parenting is probably the most important job in the entire world. That is a broad statement, but that's the way I feel about it. Anyone is free to disagree.

Parenting is certainly widespread on our planet. It is safe to say that more people are parents than anything else. It appears that most educational institutions have not felt it necessary to belabor the issue of parenthood in any large way. It is interesting to note that some 1,600 hours of instruction in mathematics are given from grades one through twelve (not including homework time), yet in many schools not one hour is given to the analysis of satisfying human relationships. Of course it is important for all children to know how to count, add, etc. Yet a majority of the public probably uses only fifth- or sixth-grade-level math. How long would it take a child to learn that much math if he started later?

Some believe that learning mathematics teaches a youngster to think, but I doubt it. It has been my experience that many children, as well as adults, have some kind of hangup regarding math. Next to failure in reading, failure in math is what makes children *feel* most deficient and incapable of grasping abstract ideas. This extends to other areas with some children, leaving them with the feeling that they cannot learn easily.

But this is not a treatise on mathematics, and I am all for including it in the curriculum. But I am in favor also of a revision in the timing and in the content.

I suppose it has been assumed that since so many people were likely to become parents, they would manage somehow to bumble their way through parenthood. This is, unfortunately, exactly what has happened. People have bumbled through as their parents did, and as their parents' parents did.

The strongest argument in favor of the bumbling policy in parenthood has been the use of the good old maternal, or parental if you will, instinct. However, I believe with others that this instinct is not as ubiquitous or as sacrosanct as it has been made out to be through the years. I do not doubt that many human mothers would indeed fight, lie, cheat, steal, kill, or die to protect their young. Parents may have to do all these things in certain parts of the world, even today. But in many other parts of the world, parents are not forced to these extremes.

Furthermore, if we equate this instinct with that of the animals and say if animals can rear their young without learning how, why cannot human beings do the same? I don't know, but it's obvious that too many cannot. It is probably safe to say that human beings could rear their young to the point that animals do, given similar conditions.

However, the human condition is much more complex than the animal condition. In the latter, the animal parent must make a home and forage for food. A human parent can do this fairly well if he is employed. If not, then it may be even more difficult for him than for the animal. Then, the animal parent must teach the young how to find food and shelter for themselves and to protect themselves from enemies. The human doesn't know who the enemy is, if indeed there is one; so this part of the task becomes confusing.

If a mother's instinct told her how to rear her young, and also ensured that she would naturally love her child, then she (as well as the father, who, one presumes, has a fatherly instinct) would also instinctively know how to let the child grow in such a way as to permit it to develop the essential independence from her *at a proper pace*. In this way, she would not produce one of the many troubled children we find today.

One can probably say that by the time a child is twelve or fourteen, or even earlier, he has been taught the essentials of survival. If humans lived in a natural state as do animals, there would not be much else to do about it. For by that time, the children would be ready to procreate and they would be off, with their own caves, foragings, and young. And so it would go, with the so-called parental instinct having stood them in good stead.

But there is hardly anything natural about the way human beings conduct their lives. Even the simple basics of food, shelter, and clothing have become monumental complexities. The poor little old maternal instinct was never designed to provide a child with the wisdom, strength, stamina, and integrity to withstand the barrage of all that contemporary society has mustered.

Add to this the complexities of education and the even more fantastic ones of interpersonal, intergroup, and international relationships, and one becomes almost buried in interweavings and entanglements. And lest we forget, we must include also the intrapsychic complications one develops for himself. It takes more than instinct to grapple with all of these developments in our lives.

The basics that instinct can give one's young are simply not adequate to deal with living in our society today. What about the parents who did an adequate job? Where did they learn? They did not have to go to school to become educated in how to be a good mother or father. Nor does one necessarily have to go to school to be a good historian or mathematician. If a child has someone in the home who is adept in these subjects, then he may learn there. But if no one at home knows anything about them, nothing can be learned unless one goes out to learn. And so those fortunate people who have had kind, self-respecting parents were learning from their very early days how to be patient, self-respecting parents also.

I've mentioned respect as a basic ingredient in family living. Where does love come in? The fact is that one cannot love when one does not respect. Parent-child feelings may become very complex and confused. What passes for love is often a lot of other feelings within the range of human responses. But I believe that love can grow upon respect in almost any relationship, if given half a chance.

These are some of the reasons why I say that parenthood is not a natural state. Although they become biological parents at the moment of their offspring's birth, people do not suddenly become parents in a comprehensive sense. As I have stated earlier, people are not educated as parents. There are few effective programs that prepare one for parenthood.

Very recently, the Department of Health, Education and Welfare has begun to sponsor programs for parent education. But it will be some time before the concept of *prevention through parent education* becomes a concept compatible with reality, and a feature in all educational facilities. For the most part, parenthood is suddenly thrust upon you and you may naïvely believe that you are prepared for it by virtue of having experienced pregnancy. "Hah!"

Well-meaning, smiling relatives may say nothing about the trials and tribulations of parenthood. They have either forgotten or they don't want to worry you. In either case, they are to be forgiven, but not depended upon. Relatives either give too much advice or too little. If they give too much, you are loath to ask them anything. If too little, you are also loath to ask, because you think you should know it all. Again, hah!

Every Parent Does His Best

One day, many years ago, I was interviewing a couple whose adolescent son was very sick. He had been admitted to a psychiatric hospital where I worked. It soon became clear that their own attitudes, values, and needs had played a large part in the evolution of the boy's illness.

With tears in her eyes, the mother said, "I don't know how this happened, Doctor. We always did our best!"

"Yes, indeed," I thought, "you probably did. But your best was apparently not very good." And because I believed her, I felt very sad, for I suddenly realized that every parent, everywhere, probably does his or her best under the given conditions. But the given conditions are often just not good enough for a child to thrive upon.

Every parent wants to be a "good" one. But what is a good parent? There are so many ways of defining a good parent. But I think that the basic ingredients of good parenthood are two: *respect* for one's fellow being, adult or child; and patience, which one will have if a capacity to respect another human being exists.

I've said that most parents have the best of intentions toward their children. No parent is a poor parent deliberately. How, then, do such intentions misfire? I have raised the following questions repeatedly here. Can one explore the nature of good intentions and discover precisely how they may damage? Can parents be helped to understand that their ignorance is curable if they have the desire to be cured? Can they learn in specific ways to avoid destructive outcomes with their good intentions? Raising such questions and struggling with them are ways of making parents' best a lot better.

Help Yourself

In a practical sense, parenting can be learned only step by small step. I have suggested that you ask questions of anybody who will answer them. But do some comparison shopping. Get several responses to the same question and then choose the one with which you feel most comfortable. Reading is useful. But here again, don't swallow everything you read. See if it suits you. Go to discussion groups and lectures. Every little bit may help, especially getting out for the afternoon or evening. That kind of relaxing may make parents less tense the next day than anything they may hear at a meeting.

The trouble is, couples expect to be full-blown parents from the first day. They quickly become dissatisfied when they find themselves bumbling around, as anyone must who takes on the most important and difficult job in the world without a day's training! How else could it be?

Of course, you can't run out that first week and ask all the questions and read all the books. But since you're with your baby much of the time anyway, you can learn a great deal from the child. He will be delighted to let you know when he is uncomfortable, hungry, sleepy, or playful. You should try to have someone around in the beginning to reassure you that you will neither break, drown, nor starve the baby. Once you have the basics of handling, your best teacher is your own child.

Your baby will communicate by some very direct and simple means. If you are paying any attention, you will pick up those communications and act upon them. Baby care can be a relatively benign time for many parents, except for those with problems they had long before Baby arrived.

Childhood Is Natural

Contrary to the unnatural state of parenthood, childhood is a natural state. Children do not have to learn how to be children. They just are, without trying. It's all they have to be, while parenthood is imposed on top of everything else you are by the time you achieve that status.

Because a child automatically needs a parent (and let's not forget that!), he is perhaps the person who can best guide you about being a parent. He doesn't say, "Look, Dad, this is the way to do it," but the messages are there if you will look for them. The process of teaching and learning is a reversible one, however, with the child or the parent in the role of teacher, depending upon the exigencies of each encounter. The child either learns or teaches as the need arises, because he is just doing what comes naturally. But, as I have indicated, you are not as flexible. You have to learn every step of the way. This requires a deliberate approach with which no child, fortunately, has to be burdened.

Babies Change

However, once you have learned how to be parent to an infant—
lo and behold, he is no longer an infant. He is a playful, wakeful
baby who wants much more of your time. And once you learn how
to be a parent to a nine-month-old baby—presto chango!—he is a
toddler.

At that point, very little of your previous expertise is of much use,
for the toddler is a completely different person. A world of crib,
carriage, playpen, bathinette, and other such limited areas suddenly
changes into the entire house, the sidewalk, street, and unlimited
horizons. Once a child is mobile under his own power, it's another ball
game.

When Baby is running about, things become more hectic. Baby
wants more only because his horizons have expanded so. The parent
does not know just how far Baby can go. When there is a discrepancy
between what Baby thinks he can do and what Mother thinks Baby
can do, trouble starts. Baby tries to convey information to Mother,
but she cannot understand it. Either she is not listening, not looking,
not patient enough, or just incapable—though that is rarely the case.
It doesn't take more than average intelligence to be a fairly successful
parent. But it takes a tremendous amount of listening and adjusting.

New Children—New Parents

In essence, then, you become a new parent with every new phase
your child goes through—the wonderful ones, the terrible twos, the
terrific threes, the friendly fours, the fearful fives, and so on and on.
Each year brings you a new kind of child. But who can be a new
parent each year? Who *wants* to be a new parent each year! Maybe
you *will* want to if you know it is necessary, and if you are watching
for the signals you are given as your child changes.

Stop, Look, and Listen

Don't think that I am saying that you should "go along with" your
child every time he moves a muscle or opens his mouth. I only urge
you to observe your child. Get to know him well. Read signals. Then
you'll be in the best position to decide what you want to do. Your

child cannot dictate your role, but he can make you aware of his needs if you will get to know your child.

Growing Up

Sometimes you are happy with your child at the age of five or six. He's cooperative, friendly, cheerful. He goes to school, eats what you prepare, plays, and sleeps. You could go on forever like this. This is just what you expected parenthood to be. You think you know what it's all about now, and for all the years to come. Forget it.

When that child hits eight or nine, you are informed unequivocally that he wants more autonomy. You won't know when to let him be, and where to interfere. You may not read the new signals, and then you'll wonder why he suddenly becomes angry, rebellious, and won't cooperate as before.

You do not want to leave those lovely sixes and sevens because it was so pleasant and such fun. You knew your ground there. So you fight it—this new demand for autonomy. Your child fights you. You cannot win because he's only growing; that cannot stop. But if you fight hard enough, you can crush the child to some extent. He then might seem to you more like sixes and sevens again. But it will not be a natural state. The child will suffer in some way. It's true that children are strong and resilient, but they are not stronger than their parents.

A Light Hand

If you can remember that your child is growing, and that he (or she) somehow feels that growing, you may be more sympathetic to erratic changes. He knows he's bigger, stronger, wiser, more informed. He may not be able to tell you this, but there's no doubt about it. He's ready for more experiences, more risks. He's not afraid of the things he wants to do. But you are. This is a big moment. Are you going to let your child grow without having to deal with and perhaps be infected by your anxiety? Are you going to let the child move into each new month, watching carefully and restricting only those demands you have thoughtfully considered and decided that he is not ready for? You will be permitted to interfere to some extent without resentment. In fact, you will be permitted to interfere quite a lot.

Children can be surprisingly reasonable. They have no natural instinct to fight you, but will if you provide the grounds.

You cannot, however, have it all your own way. You cannot restrict the child only to those experiences about which you have no anxiety because these might possibly be too few for optimal growth. You will have to pluck up your courage and let him be. These years are perhaps the most exciting for the parents who are not frightened by the boldness of their children, who rush to meet each day with joyous anticipation. In these years, you can see your child's adult personality begin to unfold, the manner of confrontation he will make to a wider world. Most children need help from their parents in these years. While children seem brash, impatient, all-knowing, they too have fears and trepidations. But if you are caught up in a struggle to keep them from growing, you will not notice the areas in which help is needed, and you will fail them.

This is a tight rope to walk. It is not wise to push a child beyond a comfortable level. (Many parents do this with gifted children.) Yet it is not helpful to overprotect and keep children from doing things they feel ready for.

Parents need to trust their children's judgment more, for they often seem to know the limits of their abilities better than their parents do. They will not, therefore, usually push themselves beyond these limits. When your children want to do something new, ask how the decision has been reached. You'll find out some interesting things about your children.

The Adolescent

But even if you "make it" past your child's ninth or tenth birthday, you enter a whole new world in eleven to thirteen. You are a new parent to a new child. By now, however, you have hopefully established some basic principles by which your family life is governed. As long as you, as parents, respect these principles, the children will usually do so also, regardless of age. A common example is young adults' attitudes about holidays. If you have kept them all along in a certain way, and they have been enjoyable, your adult children may very well look forward to family traditions—even though they may grumble a little.

In general, if the road has not been too rough up to adolescence, it should not be too difficult through it. But there is no guarantee that this will be so. Here again, the situation is the same. The struggle between parent and adolescent is essentially one of not observing signals. This is referred to as a communication gap, and in a sense it is. For if adolescents are disappointed with their parents' obtuseness, they quickly stop communicating in all respects. Parents feel hurt and abandoned, often following suit and making no attempt to let their children know, in a civilized manner, their thoughts and feelings on various issues. They may only express disappointment and anger when they are sufficiently aroused, and that is the extent of their communication.

By the time your child is in the second decade, the parent-child situation may have well reached the "impossible years." It is then that the adolescent may make a valuable contribution. Motivation may be attributed to a wish to alleviate tension between child and parent.

The adolescent now has available many years of experience with parents and a rapidly developing ability to contemplate, consider, weigh, to observe relationships other that those in his own family. This young person, with the wisdom of his years (however few they may be), might make a contribution toward the reduction of tension in the family by making repeated efforts at being understood and at understanding his parents' concerns. This might be done inoffensively, by questioning, by listening, by offering information.

Again, it's a two-way street. Adolescents complain that parents don't listen, and parents complain that adolescents don't listen. If both complaints are valid, can the adolescent be the one to take the first step? He is usually the more flexible, the less tired, the less discouraged. Perhaps he can initiate where the parent cannot.

If children are entitled to their parents' regard and concern, are not parents entitled to their children's? Or are neither entitled to anything? What is important is that people living together, young or old, can make a contribution to a satisfying relationship. The responsibility for this is neither the parents' nor the children's, but a shared one in which both parent and adolescent may have the satisfaction of seeing a degrading family condition become one of some dignity and mutual respect.

No Easy Job

I've tried to hurry through the entire developmental years in this section, touching only briefly on specific points. But the main point is, I hope, clear by now. Parenting doesn't come easy. It doesn't come free. It has to be worked out and given time, interest, energy, compassion for self and for the child. It requires watchfulness, attentiveness, willingness, and loads of flexibility—not mushiness. Even with all this, mistakes will abound. It can be no other way. But successes will also abound, and for these, your child will be grateful. He won't tell you that now. You may have to wait ten or twenty years to hear it. But believe that he'll forget most of your "garden variety" goofs and wish that you could too, for guilt feeds on feelings of failure. Let them blow away and start each week anew.

Quality Parenting

In case you are thinking that this parent business is too much for you, you must understand that you cannot be expected to be busy parenting twenty-four hours a day and seven days a week. Less is fine too, as long as it's *quality parenting*. The quality is the important thing, rather than the quantity. The rest of the time, do some growing yourself. The growing parent is the happy parent. And the happy parent usually rears the happy child.

Read everything you can; play, study, work, socialize, love your spouse and accept all those limitations that you know by heart. These won't blow away, you can be sure of that. To do these things takes purposefulness and interest in yourself. Arrange your time so that the children are not "all"—because if they are, you'll find, paradoxically, that they won't be nearly enough for you.

And finally, let me pass on to you some advice a wise man gives to fathers. "The very best thing you can do for your children is to love their mother."

CHAPTER X

They Never Say Anything Nice

Y OUR FIFTEEN-YEAR-OLD DAUGHTER is wearing a new dress, or a new hair-do, or boots, or coat. "How do I look?" she asks, pleased with herself. Now stop! What do you suppose she wants to hear? Remember, she's not showing you her faded old jeans or tangled hair. She is not likely to say, with obvious pleasure, "How do I look?" when she has those on. It's already indelibly inscribed in her brain how you think she looks in those. If you never said it again (which you will—about 3,422 times more), she would know it to her dying day. In sixty or maybe seventy years, when you are gone but not forgotten, your seventy-five- or eighty-five-year-old daughter will remember how you felt about her faded jeans. So don't be worried that she doesn't remember it now.

When your fifteen-year-old daughter asks, "How do I look?" all she wants is one sincere word. That word may not be too much of a problem for most parents. But the sincere part—there's the rub. Okay, so you can say lovely, or great, or darling, fine, good. But can you mean it? And if you don't mean it, should you fake it? And if you fake it, aren't you being a liar? And if you're a liar, won't your dear, sensitive, perceptive child know it? And if she knows it, won't she think you're a hypocrite? And if you're a hypocrite, won't she lose respect for you? And if she loses respect for you, won't she have contempt for you? And if contempt, why not dislike? And if dislike, why not hatred? Shall I go on?

Give a Little

Let's slow up and go back. First of all: Here's your fifteen-year-old whom you are supposed to love. (More about that later.) The chances are pretty good that her face, at least, is clean. So, as far as she is concerned, she has made an effort to please you as well as herself. But she wants a little confirmation from you. Can you give her that little confirmation so that she can bounce out and go wherever she is going with a good feeling? Is this too much to give a fifteen-year-old today? Maybe later that evening, if an older boy is trying to make her believe that he will love her forever if she "goes all the way," she might be better able to make a choice that will be in keeping with her own well-being. She will not be driven to feel that she'd better get a little "love" whenever she can. The girl who leaves home with a good feeling doesn't need to look for it with this boy, or in any situation that will compromise her in any way.

About Meaning It

Secondly, how can you be sincere? I suppose if you don't like your daughter, you will find it difficult to say anything nice. But if you love her a little, or have ever loved her, bank on that love. Here she is, open to you, vulnerable to whatever you say or do. Know that you are not just a helpless parent at that moment. Know that you are powerful. You can, with one word, with one facial expression, with one inflection of your voice, change her mood from good to bad, or from bad to good, if she happens to be anxious about how she looks. If that isn't power, I don't know what is. You have it in you, that instant, to be a "fairy godparent." Is that bad?

Can you remember some time when she was a little girl, and you did indeed think that she was adorable? Can you feel compassion for her tender fifteen years (yes, she's still tender even though she may seem to you tough and unfeeling sometimes) and for her dependence upon you? If she didn't need you, she wouldn't be asking. If not compassion, can you feel pity for her? Can you just feel how nice it must be to be fifteen and about to have a little adventure? Can you feel that maybe she cares just a teensy-weensy bit about you, even though it has seemed for months that she can't stand you? Find something, any scrap that can make you feel something good toward her. While you're thinking of all this (and naturally you are) she won't wonder. She'll think you're looking at her to decide how she looks. This shouldn't take more than ten or fifteen seconds. Honest! Try it once if you don't believe me. She'll probably wait.

Kindness

Kindness is many things. It is doing or saying something that usually makes the other person feel glad that you did or said it. It doesn't depend upon how you yourself may feel about something, although if you feel good about something, it might be easier to be kind. But you can be kind, too, if you don't feel good about something. So, whether you feel good or bad about how your fifteen-year-old looks, can you be kind to her and say, "You look just fine, honey," without making her feel that you're lying in your teeth, even if you don't approve of how she looks? After all, you have only a few seconds to make your impact, and then she'll be gone. If you don't like her appearance and you say it, she's not likely to go and change. She'll either be angry with you for your poor taste, or just shrug it off, telling herself, "There's no use talking to them. They never have anything nice to say anyway." And off she goes with her feelings. Either way, it's a loss to you in terms of parental input. The opportunity for something positive between you has been lost. Well, try again sometime, and good luck.

When you're kind, even when you're disapproving, are you being a liar and all those other things I've mentioned? I don't think so. You might have to ask yourself, "What's at stake?" So you don't like her hair that way. But you're kind and say, "It looks O.K." What have you lost? And then ask what you have gained. If it's one good feeling from your daughter, is it worth it? After all, if she really looks horrible in that hair-do, you'll have 298 other opportunities to tell her, won't you? Just look for the propitious moment. I'll guarantee that it will come if you look for it. And then, you don't *have* to say, "Your hair looks horrible that way." You might say, "I think I'd like your hair better such and such a way," or, "With your long, oval face, a soft wave at the temple might make your eyes look larger," or some such thing. You might say, "A little necklace would make your neck look graceful," not, "That cowl neck line makes your neck look like a chicken's," and so on.

You are familiar with the niceties of communication. You use them all the time with friends, with in-laws, colleagues, and often with your spouse. Why not with children? Can't they also be hurt when told they are sloppy, or skinny, or lazy, or stupid? Who can forget that a little kindness will go farther than a great deal of unkindness? For if bald candor hurts and alienates our young, then surely it is an unkindness.

They Don't Listen

This is such a constant cry on the part of youngsters. It is more likely to be heard from teen-agers than from younger children because it takes many years for a child to discover that Mommy and Daddy aren't really listening. Young adult children just give up. They don't even bother to accuse anymore. They just try to go their way and hope that you will let them, once in a while, without hysterics.

"But I hear everything you say," says Dad. "Maybe you hear the words I speak, but you don't listen to *me* and sometimes you don't even hear." What do they mean by this? Your thirteen-year-old son says, "Ma, can I have a dollar?" "Where are you going?" says Ma, having made lightning-like strides ahead in this possible conversation. His question is ignored, even though she would argue about that. "If I know where he's going, I'll know what he needs the dollar for." But, Ma, he's not as smart as you are. All he knows is that you haven't answered him. Of course, whatever a parent says, even more important than words, is the feeling tone, or vibes. Were she to ask sharply, "What do you need it for," he would reject that too.

Affection

It may surprise you to learn that your petulant, snappish, rebellious, and oh-so-independent teen-ager needs your support in so many ways. Teen-agers need affirmation for attitudes and values, confirmation of tastes and opinions, acceptance of their very being, and affection. Yes, affection, even though they seem to bite the hand that is held out to them. They cannot accept the affection you expressed when they were little; they can only reject that. They can get their fondling elsewhere now and don't need it from you. But they desperately need affectionate feelings as expressed by your outputs and inputs. You can't fool them, either. They know when the feeling is real.

When you don't have these feelings, they will return if you try some of the techniques I have just suggested. And don't forget the three-step method—that will help too. You'll find that a concern together with efforts to come closer to your child will be expressed through your outputs and inputs over a period of time. As time passes, your child will respond to them with a little less petulance, and you will respond to that with less irritability. You may eventually reach a détente where you have sufficiently overcome your angry feelings and where friendlier ones take over. At that point you will feel a return of affectionate feelings.

Certain words will spring to your lips. If you know they are not a trigger for snappishness in your child, you'll let them out and they will be accompanied by other outputs of affection. Your child will pick up these vibes, and little by little, you can swing a cool, trucelike relationship around to one with small kindlings of warmth. Seize every opportunity to do so, for heaven knows there will be plenty of times when you will feel only disgusted and dispirited.

It's Over, but Can't We Be Friends?

Tension is so often kept on a high pitch because parents are striving to maintain a parent-child relationship that is finished, that is past history. When a teen-ager rejects you as the authority, it's impossible to ram that authority down his throat. Yet you feel that you still have a duty to perform in advising and guiding. But if the Daddy/Honey stage is over, recognize it and find a new one.

Adults are not as a rule interested in friendships with teen-agers. But there are many different kinds of friendship, and you might consider a friendship with your teen-age child. That doesn't mean that you have to cook or fish, golf, or go to a bar together. Consider what some of the elements of any friendship are. List them for yourself if necessary and see if they are applicable to your teen-ager. You might establish a list called, "Rules of Friendship," and then see if they can possibly be adapted to family use. You might be in for a pleasant surprise.

Planning is so important at this stage because your opportunities for action become fewer and fewer. Always be quick to discard a plan, however, when you see hackles rising, because it's useless from there on. Even though it seems like an excellent plan, your youngster may not appreciate its excellence. Your disapproval of his rejection can only intensify the tension.

Unkind Disapproval

There are many forms of disapproval, forms which have varying effects on youngsters. But unkind disapproval is deadly in any form.

There is a difference between the response of younger children to unkind disapproval and the response of teen-agers. Younger children are often intimidated by it, and they try to restore themselves in your eyes by trying to please. But they don't like that kind of disapproval any more than their elder siblings. However, their dislike goes underground and they are easier to live with. But teen-agers are not so easily intimidated. They are candid and rudely so. If they keep it up long enough, you may throw them out of your heart. Even though they have a large part in bringing this about, they cannot tolerate the loss and they go downhill. This is what makes youngsters so resistant to improvement in family relations. Without extreme efforts tinged with genuine kindness, such estrangement goes from bad to worse.

Such children cannot and will not listen to admonishments. But they will listen like pussy cats if you can tell them, softly and seriously, without accusations, how *you* feel, how the estrangement hurts *you*, what *you* would like to see take place. Without blame, hysterics, or demands for promises, there is a chance for lessening of the estrangement. Remember, they need and want your love. It's up to *you* to find an acceptable way to give it to them.

Why?

Parents are often truly puzzled at their children's rejection of them. They are unaware of the liberties they have taken. They may be very self-indulgent in ways they wouldn't dare to practice with other people. They are often rude, impatient, inconsiderate, officious and unfriendly. Some parents behave toward their children as if battle lines are always drawn. There is no fun, no humor, no play. As soon as children are no longer intimidated by parents, is it any wonder that they reject and show their displeasure openly?

A woman in a shop with her little boy of five was scolding him in a low, vicious tone. He did not respond as she wished, so she whiplashed him with her fingers. If this attitude and behavior are common practice with her, how can he like her? How will he behave toward his siblings when they displease him, and with his peers in later life? Will he imitate his mother?

A woman standing in line with two children, one in her arms, spanked the little one on the legs for squirming and complaining. When she stopped, the older sibling immediately started slapping the child's legs. For that, he got slapped. True, an overtired, pale, thin Mommy. But was one minute given, I wonder, to planning the chores for the afternoon so that she would not be dragging irritable children on her weary rounds? It's hard to believe that some little plan could not have effected a tremendous improvement.

Planning can be used for any situation and for any age. No doubt, such occurrences have taken place often and will continue to do so. This young woman needs to spend a little time with herself and evaluate the annoying, impatient feelings that are becoming the rule between her and her children. Such feelings may very well lead to their saying, in about ten years, "Who—Mommy? Oh, she's so cranky all the time. That's why she never says anything nice."

CHAPTER XI

What Kind of Parent Are You?

T HERE ARE ALL KINDS of parents, and one kind can be as good or as bad as another. Theoretically, one kind is supposed to be better than another. If you substantiate that theory and know that you are that better kind, then give this book to someone who isn't so lucky. But if you're like the majority of parents, then your kind probably isn't the best. So what can you do about it? First, find out what kind you *are*.

Types

I'll name three general categories of parents: the authoritarian type, the permissive type, and the in-between. Each category contains a full range of subtypes. For example, the rigidly inflexible authoritarian; the moderately inflexible authoritarian; the mildly inflexible authoritarian; the occasionally inflexible authoritarian; the occasionally flexible authoritarian; the frequently flexible authoritarian.

Now we move to the in-between category where, if the parent is only occasionally authoritarian, he is something else on other occasions. At the other extreme is the excessively permissive parent; the moderately permissive parent; the mildly permissive parent; the occasionally permissive parent. You can see how I arrive at the in-between, who may be a little of this and a little of that, depending on what is appropriate to the occasion.

Keeping in mind age factors, family, and individual needs, the in-between parent may be extremely permissive if the situation warrants it. He may be permissive in some respects and authoritarian where that approach is indicated and relevant. This, of course, explodes the whole theory of consistency which is discussed elsewhere.

It's a terrible drag trying to be one kind of parent with your head, while your feelings, attitudes and upbringing make you more comfortable as another kind. If you happen to deplore the way your parents reared you, you may want to get as far from that as possible. Yet you find yourself using the same outputs and inputs as they. That's only natural. Your awareness of it is the first step in dealing with it, for you have already identified the problem. You're on your way to solving it if you want to. If it really bothers you, you'll make the efforts I've spoken of in order to effect that change.

That does not mean, however, that you have to go to another extreme and be just the "opposite" of your own parents. That might not be realistic, for you may not be comfortable with such an extreme. But you should be able to find your own level, that is, a position compatible with everything you are and believe. It might resemble what your parents did with you in terms of procedures, expectations, and demands. But don't be concerned about that, for your position will nevertheless differ markedly if the accompanying inputs and outputs are your very own and influenced by your own attitudes and feelings.

The important thing is not so much what kind of parent you are. The important thing is to *know what kind* you are.

Which Kind?

The tremendous advantage of knowing what kind of parent you are is that you can go ahead and be it without all kinds of unnecessary, extraneous, guilt-producing factors entering into your job as parent. First of all, you don't have to keep wondering. Then you don't have to try to be someone that you're not. To the extent that you are not confused about this, your child will not be confused.

When you try to be permissive, and find that you can do it only with gritted teeth, you have to know that you're not succeeding, and that both of you will suffer. The child will suffer because you seem permissive but you're really not, and he has to deal with that duplicitous double message. You suffer because your so-called desirable permissiveness isn't coming off and you're angry, which you "shouldn't be," and so you feel that you're a poor parent. Your knowing when you are feeling permissive and when you're feeling authoritarian will give the child a firmer feeling about you, and about himself in relation to you. He doesn't care much which kind you are, but be only one kind at any one moment, so that he knows how he stands on that occasion.

This runs into the matter of consistency. When I say that it's useful to know what kind of parent you are, it doesn't mean that you will always be the same kind. Consistency is fine if you can have it and under certain conditions. Otherwise, it is neither relevant nor consistent with reality. Furthermore, many parents find it impossible to be what they regard as consistent no matter what they do. So there isn't much point in worrying about it and feeling guilty. You probably wouldn't make it anyway, no matter how hard you tried; so don't hold your breath.

Nature of the Message

The kind of messages you send out to your children when you respond to them will depend upon the kind of parent you are and what you expect of yourself. A young woman was walking along the street with her four-year-old boy tagging along a few steps behind her. She turned and saw that he had picked up a colorful candy wrapper. She came toward him with arm outstretched and, with an expression of utter disgust, snarled, "Where did you get that!"

That was no question, you can be sure. Her manner and tone left no doubt that he was a "bad" boy who had picked up a dirty (disgusting, reeking with terrible, fatal germs) piece of garbage in the street, a thing that would do him untold harm. You can see the *Mommy trap* here. Ostensibly, she is concerned about his health, and no one can argue with this. But why all the ugliness? Is she also concerned with the days and nights of nursing care he would require if he came down with some serious illness? She knows that the likelihood of that is slim. He will probably go on getting the usual colds and children's infections, regardless of how many pieces of dirty paper he picks up. I'm not denying Mother's right to forbid her child to pick up candy wrappers. The point is *how* she does it and not that she chooses to do so.

Youngsters tend to view adults' evaluation of their behavior as either good or bad, liked or disliked. They tend not to see evaluation on a spectrum—from one end, good, to the other end, bad. Adults will argue that offspring behavior is sometimes excellent, very good, not so good, fair, all the way to poor and impossible.

Yet if you ask a parent point-blank about any one piece of behavior, "How do you feel about it, good or bad?" at first there will be equivocation, generalization, and a series of "ifs." "If I feel tired," or "If I feel rushed." "No, no," you insist, "good or bad?" Finally, if they can be honest, they will say one or the other. All the rest is a lot of intellectualization for the most part. The child's ability to cut through all the complex embellishments to the good or bad of the evaluation is a common characteristic of little folk.

Clearly, the mother above is sending out the message that the child is "bad." Bad to pick up a piece of paper on the sidewalk? How can that be bad? What is good, then? Not picking it up? Why does Mother become so anxious and pounce upon him with such desperation?

Why Does Mommy Get *So* Angry?

Well, there are all kinds of reasons why Mommy gets so angry when her child does something she considers wrong. First, she is angry because she believes she has not trained her child properly. He shouldn't go around picking up garbage from the street, should he? What kind of a Mommy are you that your child picks up garbage?

Whether or not there is anyone else to observe all this is immaterial. You don't need anyone else to tell you that somehow you have failed if your child doesn't know any better. Then, there's the making-more-work thing. If the paper is sticky and dirty, his hands will get sticky and dirty. He might wipe them on his jacket. The stickiness will pick up more dirt and you'll have to wash it off. If you're going anywhere, he'll arrive dirty.

So when the child does anything that can set such events in motion, Mommy gets so angry because of all these possibilities and not because the child has done something terribly wrong or wrong at all. It's because, in her mind, she has done something terribly wrong. And it's terrible only in relation to an image she has of what a good parent should be. Her belief is that a "really good mother" would have a child who never did anything wrong. That he does, she feels, is a reflection of her own shortcomings for the world to see. She cannot tolerate that. She cannot yell at herself or slap herself. She doesn't even know what is motivating her feeling and behavior. So the little one "gets it." He's the bad one, not she. Sorry though it is, that is more tolerable for her.

The fact is that neither one is "bad." This badness exists only in relation to an inner, unrealistic standard of goodness. If this woman's image of mothering could be analyzed, we would find that in her fantasy view of motherhood a "good" mother has a "good" child, not just occasionally but in every single instance. Anything short of such a model isn't just a human lapse from perfection—it's a severe deficiency in *her.* You may say, "Fiddlesticks to that!" But if you do, then try to answer the question—"Why does Mommy get *so* angry when I do something wrong?"

Choices

Are you the kind of Mommy who sweetly asks her bright-eyed little daughter, "What do you want for breakfast, Honey?" "Cold cereal," Honey sweetly answers. "Wouldn't you like some nice scrambled eggs?" you reply, thinking that a hard morning in the kindergarten really requires a more substantial breakfast than cold cereal. You can write the rest of the script on this one. All I can say is that if you don't want to respect her choice, don't ask her to make one. Most children are quite happy to eat what is placed in front of them. In fact, many people are happy to eat what is placed in front of them, especially when they don't have to bother with its preparation.

Eating is a very primitive, necessary activity. Because it is so essential to our survival, and because it is so primitive, no big deal should be made about it in childhood. There is a whole lifetime to learn to be discriminating, to learn to make choices between this food or that, to make a big thing out of dining, which is very much more than mere eating.

In the early years, a parent's concern need not be with these issues. If you are concerned about teaching your child how to make decisions, let him practice on other things where he can make choices that make little difference to you. Does he want the blue or the yellow dish? Will he go out now or in fifteen minutes? Does he want to call Jane or John to play with? Will it be the brown or black shoes, the green or red shirt? And so on.

There is a world of opportunity for decision making, even during the early years. Why Mommy has to spoil for herself, as well as her child, a nice, easy, comfortable, pleasurable experience like eating whatever she puts on the plate is something she should ask herself. After all, she usually knows what foods her child dislikes, so she doesn't have to serve them. Also, she's not about to poison her child, so what she serves isn't going to hurt the child. Why not take the easy way?

Often in families, the cook (mother) asks what everyone wants for lunch or dinner. This is great for the mother who really likes running a noncommercial restaurant. It might be easier, though, if you write out a menu, because then there would be some limit to what they could order. As I said, this is very nice. And maybe it's your thing. But I have yet to talk with a woman who did not feel that her family was taking advantage of her good nature by asking for different things. So if you don't like running a restaurant, don't ask your family what each one wants. Just lay it on. This does not preclude taking a vote, upon occasion, when you feel like offering a choice.

Besides eating, other basic essentials of life are sleep, urination, defecation, clothing, and shelter. The latter is rarely a problem. With clothing, however, parents often judge their child's tastes or needs by their own, as illustrated by the three-year-old who asked her mother, "Mommy, can I take off my sweater when you feel warm?"

With sleeping, urinating, and defecating, I would say the same thing as with eating. These activities are with us always, and we have a lifetime in which to complicate them if we must. To the extent, then, that parents can simplify these activities, keep them free of tension, and place no undue emphasis upon them, children will, in most cases, learn to deal with these functions without fuss and everlasting distress to parents.

Eyes, Ears, and Mind

One kind of parent is overconcerned with children's needs and emits large numbers of anxiety vibes regarding the basic and simple necessities of life that I was just discussing. These parents are largely unaware of their overconcern. If it is brought to their attention, they justify their outputs and inputs on the basis of their child's needs (i.e., sensitivity, illness, weakness). They develop a remarkable anticipatory sensitivity to their children as a result of an ever-ready watchfulness.

Their alertness resembles that of the parent with a newborn. You remember how all-consuming that alertness can be. Unless the child is sound asleep, all senses are attuned for baby's signals. The parents I am discussing here continue that alertness throughout their offspring's childhood.

These parents often wear a perpetual, mildly worried look. They seem to be continually expecting danger and must therefore remain vigilant at all times. Even when baby is sleeping, they may check every half hour. Of course, children have to be checked—we know all about sudden illnesses, accidents, and crib deaths. But I'm speaking of excesses in that direction.

As the children of such a parent grow, they continue to be watched intently. Every piece of food ingested is registered, every bowel movement checked, every item of clothing hand-selected. This is necessary and reasonable in the early years. After such a time, however, minute attentiveness becomes less and less necessary.

Now here's the point of departure. Some parents gradually relinquish such guardedness, as they see it is no longer required. But some parents continue to exercise a kind of vigilance over everything their child does, thinks, says, wants. Some of them are very astute about it. Recognizing that they can be criticized for such vigilance, they are quiet about it. They recognize intellectually that such parenting may not be conducive to a spontaneously developing independence; but they find all manner of "good" reasons for continuing their protectiveness. The talking, checking, advising, deciding go on endlessly.

Checking, Always Checking

That parent does not know it, but the vibes of the constant checking are reaching out and touching the child all the time. I'm not emphasizing that they are necessarily harmful vibes in and of themselves. That's one reason why they can be so easily rationalized. They may be quite benevolent. But there are just too many vibes, too often and too soon. The child doesn't have the opportunity to do for himself. He senses that your ears are picking up every noise, your eyes taking in every move, your concern smothering every activity and relationship. It's just too, too much. It's too much for the child and too much for the parent.

Even though such behavior is destructive to both parent and child, the parent cannot give it up. It is a kind of addiction. No matter what anyone says concerning the close and protective involvement, it is usually of no avail. For that parent to give up such a preoccupation would be to leave himself devoid of purpose to justify an otherwise empty existence.

Repeating: Most parents do some of this some of the time throughout childhood and adolescence. And much of it is essential. I needn't go into the thousands of occasions where you must be alert to your children's basic requirements for growth. I've been talking about that all the time—how sensitive, how interested, how involved you must be with your child. But remember, too much ice cream can make you sick.

Can you imagine yourself working someplace with a supervisor watching you and listening to your every word the whole day long? Even if that supervisor were kind and helpful, how would it feel to have him there every minute? Maybe you're the kind of person who would like that. But for most people it would be too inhibiting, too crowding. And what if the supervisor were critical? You'd probably last about two days.

I want to give you some idea how it might feel. If you worked in an office, you could go home at the end of the day. Where can your child go at the end of the day? The kind of vibes I'm describing here, when excessive and harmful, are sometimes responsible when teenagers cannot seem to stand being at home and will roam about anywhere else to avoid being subjected to a continuous, disapproving scrutiny.

Furthermore, the child raised with such close, benevolent surveillance is so used to having someone at hand to assist that he does not have the opportunity to develop the resourcefulness required to meet various contingencies. In addition, such a child may develop a completely false notion of his own importance, and of people's interest in him. For it is highly possible that he will encounter such intense interest and care *nowhere else* in life. That could leave him puzzled, confused, and perhaps feeling unloved, if he cannot learn that love comes in many forms besides the sticky kind provided by Mommy and Daddy.

Such intense, benevolent surveillance of children is clearly a common characteristic of the overprotective parent. It is difficult to rebel actively against such parents, because their care may often be so reasonable, so soft and gentle, that the child finds nothing to fight against in rebelling. Also, because such surveillance appears to be harmless evidence of parental love, the child may feel guilty about trying to protect himself from its smothering effects. He responds with a sense of impotence for it is difficult to accept it and impossible to fight it.

In their dilemma, such children may become immobilized. These may be some of the passive youth we see about us today who seem unable to direct themselves to any purpose nor feel enthusiastic about any opportunity. They are neither incapable nor unintelligent. But they are not motivated, for their sense of exploration, adventure, and excitement has been somehow stifled.

Is Your Child Obnoxious?

The kind of parental attentiveness I've just described may lead to a form of egocentricity in a child that may make him feel superior to other children in some respects. This is especially true in the area of academics, and when children are highly intelligent.

Such children can become obnoxious because of the parent's power to make them that way. Parents of bright children often think that their child is exceptional. They don't know that there are many, many other children who are just as bright. They come to believe that they have to be special parents for a special child. This means some form of "enrichment of his experiences."

Now I am not against enriching anything that can be enriched. But unfortunately some parents tend to overdo. They become so tense over their role of special-parent-to-special-child that the child senses their tension and is made uncomfortable by it. *Tension and spontaneity are incompatible.* The parent thus loses his spontaneity, which is the most wholesome gift to offer a child.

In later life, most people are spontaneous in direct proportion to their parents' ability to be spontaneous. Often, in trying to "enrich" or "teach" everything imaginable to the child, paradise is lost. What do you have, then, with a well-informed, unspontaneous, tense child who thinks his ideas and actions are special?

"Special" as used here usually means a child superior to those around him. This kind of "special" child makes no bones about advertising his specialness. After all, haven't the parents been pushing it for years—to him, to anyone else who will listen? What else can he think? What else can he say? This is one of the ways he may become an obnoxious child.

If you have enjoyed and been light-hearted and easy-handed with any of your child's natural gifts, he will also. He will take his intelligence and ability to learn for granted and not feel compelled to inform peers and others about how much he knows, nor congratulate himself on his prowess. He will expend that energy on being more observant of the world around him, thereby adding to a fund of knowledge and experience. That is enrichment, and he does not have to be force-fed to accomplish it. This doesn't mean that materials and opportunities should not be given to enrich his growing experiences; but they should be provided with essential directions only, minimal expectations (or none), and a firmly closed mouth.

Twelve-Word Rule

Which brings us to a discussion of the *closed mouth policy* for parents. I think it's already clear to you that many parents probably talk too much but don't say enough. Too often, their words are not thoughtful, not in keeping with the matter at hand. I've described how this occurs when parents are not aware of the need for such thoughtfulness in their encounters with their children, especially teen-agers.

What can I tell you now?—don't talk? You will anyway. But I'll tell you anyway. Maybe it will at least reduce the volume of words. Don't think I'm singling out parents, though. Most people everywhere seem to talk too much without saying much of anything. So we're all in crowded company.

In parent groups, whenever we come to the point of talking too much, I make a kind of facetious suggestion. I call it the *twelve-word rule*. (I'll talk about it again in another section.) "Try to keep your sentences to twelve words or under," I say, "especially your answers to questions." Most questions can often be answered in two to four words. Try it. If you haven't said enough to satisfy your youngsters, don't worry; they'll keep asking. That way, they won't get the idea that you're flooding them with advice, guidance, and parenting just because they asked a little old question.

Button Your Lip

So try the twelve-word limit and then *button your lip,* as they used to say in the old movies. It's kind of fun to try and you'll find yourself much more interested in what your child is saying, in what you're saying, and how you're saying it. If you find yourself going way over the limit, don't feel bad, for you've probably cut it down a great deal anyway. And that's the point.

Is Mommy Happy?

Are you the kind of mother who is generally healthy, optimistic and responsive? If so, you are a relatively contented parent. That is basic to your family's well-being, for it's a well-known fact that if the mother in the home is not well or is disturbed in any way, the well-being of the rest of the family is in jeopardy. It may be that in future years, as fathers assume a greater share in the task of child rearing, this phenomenon may not be so prevalent. But for the present, it seems to be so, for mothers have borne and are still bearing the greater responsibility for child rearing.

There is, then, a direct relationship between the state of Mother's physical and mental health and the well-being of her children. Father's well-being depends also to some extent on Mother's position, but not nearly as much as does the children's well-being. He can find many factors outside the home with which to satisfy or harass himself, and he is not dependent upon her as are the children. This is not to say that his physical and mental state does not influence his children. Of course it does. But in the day-to-day relations, Mother has more impact than Father.

An example of an extreme case could be the addictive parent (drugs, alcohol, gambling, etc.). Where Mother is the addict, there is often chaos in the home. But where Father is the addict, to the extent that he keeps himself detached from daily routines, and to the extent that Mother can maintain some optimism and stability, the children have a better chance for healthy development. Where an addictive father is cruel and abusive to children and spouse, however, the children's health is more in jeopardy. But my premise holds true, for Mother could hardly maintain her sense of well-being in such circumstances. Then, the children would suffer from *double mal-parenting*.

Furthermore, it is unlikely that the healthy wife of an abusive addict would remain with him if she and her children were repeatedly mistreated. Only the morbidly dependent woman would remain in such a situation, and she could not be regarded as a healthy or a happy person. In remaining with an abusive addict, she would not be looking to her own welfare, and could therefore not provide her children with the *happy mother* we are talking about.

Overwork Is Out

It's not necessary to take such an extreme example to make the point. A more mundane example makes the same point. Contrary to common opinion, overworked, conscientious mothers are not usually the best mothers. How could they be? If a woman is overworked, it follows that she will be tired and feel drained, and she cannot have the patience or interest that children require. The more relaxed and rested a woman is, the better she will probably function in any capacity.

Overworked, conscientious mothers may look very good to an observer, or even to themselves. But do they look very good to the child? Are they very good for the child? Human beings have their limits, and overwork makes dangerous inroads into energy and emotional reserves.

Can you be *under*worked and conscientious? If so, being conscientious, you would want to do the best thing for your child. And being a little underworked, you have the energy to implement what you think your child needs from you.

"Underworked" doesn't mean inactive, lazy, or indifferent. I use it only in contrast to *over*worked, a state which is not healthy for anyone —parent, child, or beast of burden. I refer to a state where work is done in reasonable quantity, consistent with all other determining factors, such as age, strength, interest, stamina, need. As soon as you move into the overwork sphere, the quality of interest declines, and fatigue, resentment, and anger increase.

So Mommy should not be encouraged to overwork. While some fathers give lip service to requests for Mother to take more rest, their hearts are not in it. In fact, they may be happy that Mommy takes so much on herself. This is especially true of some of those men who are overworking themselves and would feel resentful if their wives were doing any less. In either case, the children are the losers, as well as the parents. While parenting is a demanding job, it doesn't have to be that hard.

On the other hand, children, until they are older, are not in a position to judge if their mothers are overworked. When they are in their pre-teens, they may begin to wonder why Mommy seems angrier than some other mothers; why she doesn't look and smell as nice (she doesn't have the time!); why she doesn't have fun and is not fun to be with.

Dad Can Help

But fathers can help a great deal in teaching their children not to be so demanding, so that mothers don't have so much to do and can take a rest once in a while. Fathers can be of tremendous help to mothers, if they will instruct—yes, instruct—their young children of three or four to put soiled clothes in the hamper, toys away, clear the table, get through baths and bedtime routines without interminable dawdling, and to perform dozens of other routine activities.

Mothers who assume all the responsibility for such activities often become nags, and everyone knows how children (and fathers!) respond to nags. So Dad comes in, fresh and crisp, with no anger aforethought, and spells out these duties clearly and seriously. I say seriously, because this is not fun and games. This is learning how to live with others. All the while, he is showing them what is to be done. Try it, Dad. It's really no big deal, as long as your heart is in it. If your heart doesn't seem to be in it, try harder. But don't become nag number two. And you'd better ask yourself why your heart isn't in it. Which comes first for you—your convenience, or your children's mother's feeling that you want to help, and that you care enough for your family to pitch in? She'll probably love you forever if you do.

Surprises Are Fun

That is only one example of how to make Mommy happy. It can be done in all the ways that you can find, and there are many. Besides relieving her of some of the routine work, it can also be done in nice little extras that she doesn't expect. "Let's all get ready quickly and surprise Mommy with a picnic," and so forth. Children of all ages are at their best when doing something they think is fun for someone else. And they usually like to prepare surprises for others. It's easy if only the steps are taken. Don't think this has to be done every day. Twice a year would be great. Once a month would be a veritable feast! But keep the number down unless you enjoy it so much that you cannot restrain yourself from doing it more often.

Another thing about happy mommies. While Father has to be the leader of the gang in a sense, Mother has to make her contribution also. It consists of two principal parts: 1) *Graciously* accepting the little gifts of joy and love that she is given by her family, without using her *critical eye;* and 2) seeing to her own happiness in not making it dependent only upon husband and children. This can be terribly difficult when one is out of practice. It includes care for her physical self (that's the easiest part), as well as for her intellectual, emotional, and social self. Even the intellectual part isn't so difficult to get started. Any woman who reads a newspaper *regularly* from thirty to sixty minutes a day will feel "in the know," and will be able to express opinions and converse with anyone.

The Mommy Trap

Neglected women are often the greatest contributors to that neglect. Other family members simply follow suit. Children know what they see, hear, and experience around them. Mothers who train their children to expect every glass of milk to be poured for them, every piece of puzzle to be put where it belongs, every bit of clothing laid out, every homework assignment gone over, every blouse and shirt ironed and hung up, have children who will continue to expect all such services indefinitely—unless Mommy does something to put a stop to such expectations. Should Mother be late getting home, such children will not prepare a simple meal for themselves even though food has only to be moved from refrigerator to table. They will not bathe or get to bed, but fall asleep in chairs or on sofas. In order to accomplish the interminable tasks of child rearing, mothers must necessarily neglect themselves in order to have the time to indulge their children.

Wives are also partly responsible for the so-called "helpless husband syndrome." (Husbands' mothers contribute largely also.) If this is the way a woman chooses to run her home and family, and is truly satisfied with it, there is no argument or discussion. These words are directed only toward those mothers who find themselves in a particular *mommy trap* without ever having chosen it, and who are feeling abused, neglected, and put upon, all the while taking no steps to extricate themselves.

So look to yourselves, mothers! The welfare of both your husband and children is directly proportional to your own sense of well-being. If you believe this, you will do whatever is necessary to make yourself the tension-free person you can be. Try to find out what kind of parent you are, what kind you want to be, and what kind you feel most comfortable being. If there are discrepancies among your findings, try to pull them together a bit. But remember that comfort and compatibility with any method you choose is important because the comfortable mother is the relaxed mother. And the relaxed mother is far more conducive to family harmony than one who is tense. Seek your level, Mom, and don't let anyone intimidate you when you find it.

CHAPTER XII

Supermom

A RE YOU TRYING to be a *supermom?* If so, don't, because I don't think you'll make it. I'll try to tell you why. While you may appear a supermom to everyone else, in your heart you won't feel that you are really succeeding. With energy, intelligence, drive, and barrels of effort, any healthy woman can appear a supermom to her peers. We've all known some. They cook, clean, shop, chauffeur; entertain, go to the theater, organize Brownies and Cubs, play the piano, tennis; sew, knit, garden, decorate their homes; go in for politics, write letters to senators; are concerned with population explosions, women's rights, drugs, crime, ecology. But in their secret self-view, they haven't achieved the inner goal only they know about. So even with all that, they still feel that they have fallen short.

There are many kinds of supermoms. That's why a supermom really can't be identified on any absolute scale. *Supermomism* is not so much related to the things a woman does as to an attitude she has about herself. I devote a separate section to supermom because so much can be said about her. She has already been described in bits, here and there. There are elements of supermom in the "checker," the "over-worker," the mother "who gets so angry" when her child does something wrong. (See Chapter XI.) Now I want to focus on supermom.

What Supermom Is Not

Before I go any further, let me say that I'm not in any way deprecating the kind of woman described in the first paragraph. There are many such women. But I have to divide them into two groups because of their differing basic motivations. One kind of woman has certain compulsive needs which drive her toward supermomism, needs over which she has no conscious control. The other kind never thinks of herself as supermom, nor does she strive toward that goal.

The latter may have a fine family and a good marital relationship. Such women do what they do because they want to, or need to, or whatever. When things turn out well, they are more pleased than anyone else. When things don't turn out, they may feel disappointed, but they take it in stride. For them, there is little time for self-flagellation and despair. There's too much that they want to do. Not a day is wasted.

These women know what their limits are and can accept them. They have no relentless inner time clock setting up irrevocable schedules, no inner council setting up standards, no inner judge waiting to deliver sentence. What they can do, they can do. What they cannot do, they cannot. They are impressive in what they accomplish because they are not burdened and impeded by those inner features which rob one of energy, wisdom, and spontaneity. To the extent that any woman—indeed any person—is free of such inner features, she will seem to have endless resources of energy, ideas, and desire to realize whatever time and space permit.

Such a woman has no traffic with the idea of supermom. She isn't being what she is to prove herself to anyone, to compete with anyone, or to avoid feeling bored. She is what she is because her being is always expressed through her feelings, thoughts, and deeds. She does what comes naturally. Of course, she has reasons for doing what she does, reasons that give her pleasure. Or, she may be motivated by what she believes to be her obligations, or whatever. But she feels neither compelled nor coerced into doing what she does. She obviously works harder than many other women. But she does it with no sense of coercion. If she decides not to do something, it is her decision and it doesn't gnaw at her. She doesn't worry about what some person will think or say about her. She feels no need to justify a change of mind, or any aspect of her personality, for that matter.

If there can be one distinguishing characteristic between this kind of natural, fully alive woman and the woman I am describing as supermom, it is that the *natural woman is not compelled to be what she is.* She is free to choose to be what she likes, whereas *supermom is compelled to be what she appears.* She has no freedom of choice. She feels she must be whatever it is that she has set up in her mind that she *should be,* whatever it is that she expects of herself, whatever it is that she believes others expect of her.

Supermomism

All these standards, internal and external expectations, are of the supermom's own making. They are her own beliefs. It's true that society certainly contributes to the quality, style, and content of those beliefs. But each individual suffers from the pressure of such beliefs only to the extent that she internalizes them and designates them irrevocably as the director of her existence. In psychoanalysis, we refer to what I've tried to describe, briefly as *intrapsychic* phenomena. When I say that one internalizes these beliefs and makes them directors, I mean that this is done unconsciously. In other words, supermomism, as presented here, is largely an intrapsychic phenomenon.

Everything I've said thus far refers to fathers as well as mothers. Only the content varies. Some fathers are no less "hung up" on an image of fatherhood than women are on supermomism. Generally though, most fathers are motivated more toward the goal of "success" than toward a rigid view of fatherhood. I hope I have clarified the main difference between what I call the natural mother and the supermom. Now I'll continue to address myself to the concept of supermom.

As I said, there are all kinds of supermoms. Each makes her own list of qualifications and requirements. That list is gradually compiled as a result of cultural, social, economic, political, educational, and familial traditions. To the extent that those are felt as *compelling pressures* upon the developing young woman, she grows with a sense of restriction of freedom regarding her own attitude toward them. A young woman may develop in such a way that she can choose at any given moment which tradition and which pressure she'll submit to, compatible with her well-being. Or, as with supermom, she develops choicelessness. She has no choice but to follow these internalized directives, whether or not they contribute to her welfare.

I do not mean to imply that such a woman is rendered choiceless in all areas of her life, or even in one area all the time. She may have some areas relatively free of such restrictions. Rarely are psychological aspects of men and women found in extreme positions, either all one way or all the opposite way. There is always an admixture of characteristics. As one example of this principle, I can say that the most severely ill psychiatric patient always has some *islands of health.* Similarly, the healthiest person has some islands of pathology.

Referring to the woman whose mind, ears, and eyes seem constantly centered upon her child, one can say that her inner list of requirements demands that she give her child this kind of care. Her inner view of herself as a supermom demands that she behave in that way. Her list consists of all the protective maneuvers she uses in her parenting. In her own way of looking at things, this is the supreme form of motherhood. That view is clearly a conglomeration of all sorts of attitudes, ideas, and experiences absorbed during her lifetime. Somehow, she has arrived at a fixed formula for mothering. She believes in it implicitly. No matter what anyone tells her, she knows better. She has a secret feeling of superiority, open to question though it may be. She cannot see the distortions she has evolved in her elaboration of that view. Such a view makes her feel "good." With it, she remains *sure* (as sure as such a woman can ever feel) of her position. She knows who she is. She must keep herself blind, therefore, to whatever destructiveness her position visits upon her child.

It is this good feeling, the feeling of sureness, that she cannot and will not relinquish. If she did, she would become uncertain, conflict-ridden and anxious. Then where would she be? She might be lost among her feelings of not knowing how to proceed, her sense of incompetence, unwillingness, resentment, all feelings at odds with the accepted standard of the loving mother. And doesn't society say all mothers should be loving and self-sacrificing?

If she leaves her self-image of supermom, she'll find that she is far from that standard. She can only despise herself for not reaching the standard—and that she could not bear. So she cannot permit herself to move, or to be persuaded to move, one inch from her rigid stance. To take one step away would be to plunge into an abyss holding untold horrors. No one could expect a woman to do that to herself. After all, it's a matter of survival, isn't it? Who, in her right mind, would be so stupid as to do that and jeopardize a secure, correct position? With such spurious justifications, this woman "sacrifices" herself to a grotesque realization of an unreal yet fixed concept of supermom, at whose altar she dedicates her life. Perhaps you think I'm being too melodramatic. I wish that were so.

Menopause

Supermomism is one reason *some* so-called "menopausal women" have such a hard time. Not only are the hormones of such a woman acting up (acting down would be more accurate), but by the time her children have matured and moved off into their own lives, she is deprived of an occupation, perhaps a compulsive preoccupation which had given her a facsimile sense of aliveness. To refer patronizingly to "the empty nest" syndrome is meaningless, unless one appreciates the cataclysmic deprivation of a lifetime of living through others (i.e., husband and children). This concept goes far beyond that of a home depleted of children.

I use the term 'facsimile aliveness' because any woman (person) with true aliveness cannot be made to feel so bereft, so anxious, so depressed, when that nest becomes empty through the passage of time. Such a woman has so many interests to occupy her that there is little opportunity, or certainly interest, to dwell morbidly on her "lonely and discarded state." She may feel lonely for a time, but she does not feel discarded. As for her hormones, their lower levels may produce fatigue and irritability; but that is treatable and cannot be blamed for all the problems that seem to beset menopausal women.

More Supermoms

Then there is the supermom who sets up her ideal as a dedicated cook. No matter what the circumstances, what the inconveniences, what the inpropriety, she prepares full-course meals for her family at any hour. I am reminded of a woman who had to rise every morning at 7 A.M. with her children, and who was busy with them all day. Her husband worked until 3 A.M. She rose at 2 A.M., cooked him a full meal, ate it with him, cleaned up, went to bed, had sex, and got up again at seven. In her view, she was a superwife and a supermom. Again, please remember that if she did all this without resentment, and of her own free choice, and if her health could stand it, there is nothing else to be said about it.

Then there is the woman with a large family, who spends all day with careful marketing, fine housekeeping, cooking, baking, sewing, who is always there when children return home, who helps with homework—and who is miserable. She cannot take time to do the things she wants to do for herself, and she cries whenever she sits down to write to her sister because she is too tired to write.

Perfection

Through an extraordinarily complex, lifelong process, each person builds his own sets of standards, ideals, or self-images, which he feels compelled to substantiate in some way. I would have to detail the evolution of the entire neurotic development in a person, as I see it, in order to outline the process to which I refer. Since I cannot do that here, I want to talk a bit about another side of those secret, internalized images I keep referring to. Because they evolve from both real and fancied attitudes, traditions and experiences, they have many unreal qualities.

Perfection is an idea which can be approached but not achieved. People caught in this particular trap, however, do not see what is real and what is unreal and they strive to achieve perfection itself, whatever their imagination tells them it is.

Not only do they strive to achieve it, but they *insist* upon reaching it. That insistence irrevocably precludes their satisfaction, for to insist that an ocean fit into a pail must inevitably make for continuous frustration and a strong sense of failure. No achievement is enough; no success suffices. One fraction of one inch away from perfection is not perfection. Therefore it is nothing.

It isn't that these standards are necessarily so high from an observer's viewpoint. The observer may not be at all impressed with them. But their creators make them the be-all and the end-all, and are driven to achieve them. That's why supermom works so hard to achieve. Although she doesn't ever get there, she sometimes manages successfully to deny her deplorable (to her) shortcomings, and transiently and fleetingly believes she has "made it." It is her only respite. Otherwise, she is subjected to an unmitigated rage (for her failures) which she is incapable of tolerating.

Anger

If I have succeeded in making this process clear to you, you can understand where the deep well of anger comes from. Women who attempt supermom status are secretly and continuously dissatisfied and disgruntled with themselves, their families, their lives. This can result in bitterness and disgust. (Both are forms of anger.) Sometimes the slightest spark can cause the anger to explode with full force.

There are two kinds of anger one can talk about—cold anger and warm anger. (See *The Angry Book* by T. I. Rubin, M.D.) Warm anger is part of everyone's life. It may have a cleansing, restorative quality. Occasionally we all become angry, suddenly or slowly, to a greater or lesser degree. You get angry with family members, friends, or others. Sometimes a grievance is stated as the reason for the anger; this may be followed by a brief explanation or apology. That gives the recipient of your anger something tangible to which he can respond, in order to restore a sense of pride. For it is often pride that is damaged when one is the object of another's anger.

I'm not implying that restoration of pride is a particularly worthy objective, in and of itself. But it seems to be essential, in our culture, to the maintenance of ongoing human relationships. It is useful in circumstances where hurt feelings (i.e., temporarily lost pride) have to be salvaged before progress can be made in the matter at hand. Such restoration seems to be operational not only between individuals but between nations as well. It has been implemented by the so-called need to "save face," a phenomenon Westerners identify with Eastern cultures, but which is as forcibly operative in their own.

Cold anger commonly occurs in two forms. It may be set off by something acute that happens suddenly. The initial angry response is called warm anger. Then, after the precipitating factor is no longer present, after one has left the field of action and moved on to something else, anger may be maintained. Such anger is cold anger.

On the other hand, cold anger may not require any acute precipitating factor. This anger is a kind of smoldering, omnipresent anger, requiring the least spark to set it off. Such continuous anger is often punctuated by large outbursts of hot anger. Yet there is a marked distinction between the sudden flare-up of warm anger and the flare-up of cold anger. Where the first might have qualities of humor, forbearance and intense aliveness, cold anger never does. It is humorless, grim, deadly, and ugly. No man ever tells a woman she is beautiful when she is coldly angry because she is not. Cold anger is the kind that grinds between you and your child, or between you and your partner, and can eventually destroy the healthy features of any relationship.

Parent Anger and Children

Should children be exposed to their parents' anger and quarreling? That question often arises in a group discussion. Whether they should or should not doesn't seem to be the primary issue. Sooner or later, most children are exposed to it. A more pertinent question might be: How can you deal with the situation when it has already arisen? So much of marital squabbling occurs over inane trifles that it is almost impossible to predict or prevent it. Before you know it, it's there. Little ears are flapping with the vibrations in the air. Eyes are big as saucers. Teen-agers are sneering, "There they go again!"

First, I want to say something about parents who "never fight." I believe that to be untrue. They do fight, maybe infrequently, maybe quietly, maybe nonverbally. Such parents may think that they have succeeded in kidding the children into believing that they do not fight.

Ordinary parents who fight fairly regularly provide their children with a natural, unavoidable slice of life. Children will not have to wonder and guess if Mom and Dad are "mad or glad." They can tell. When they are "mad," children keep out of the way. Unless the arguments are too frequent, or are of the ugly, cold variety, most children get used to them without undue harm being done.

If you are the type of person who really never fights in any way, then it might be well to "stage" a fight. That way, your child can have an important experience. He can learn that a fight is not a shattering event to home, parent, or child. He can learn that it has a place in the ordinary course of family living. He can learn that it has a *beginning,* a *middle,* and an *end,* and that it is a fact of life, in and out of families. It is one way to find out how the other person is feeling. It has the potential of leading to greater understanding and closeness. "Oh, I didn't know you felt *that* way!" It is a worthwhile experience for older children as well as little ones, in case you think your teen-agers are made too anxious by your bickerings. If that is the case, there's probably much too much bickering unrelieved by warmth or humor.

Whenever I make an unorthodox suggestion, I always feel it necessary to add that I'm not saying this is the best way or the only way to do something. It's just a *suggestion* that *might* be useful to you sometime, someplace—maybe only once, if at all. I don't say one *should* do this or that. A particular kind of suggestion may be complete anathema to your way of thinking and living. So be it. You will have no traffic with it in that case. Don't give it any place in your thoughts or time.

The point I'm making holds for anything I've said in these pages. All the ideas and suggestions I've presented are only for you to consider, to play around with, to let roll about in your mind, and to put to the test in every case. At least you'll get your money's worth that way. Discard any one of them, or all, as unrealistic, untenable, or frivolous, if that suits you. I want least of all to be the agent responsible for adding yet another compulsion to your list of "should dos" for your children.

Finish It

So when parents have a difference which results in angry outbursts, this is only the beginning. A fight is fine as long as it is clearly finished fairly soon after its onset. Parents must also show that they "make up." Anger is part of the continuum of living, as is any feeling or emotion. If someone tells you a joke, you laugh. You don't keep on laughing indefinitely, or laugh later on without some reference to the joke. If you continue to laugh over the same joke, something is amiss. This rarely occurs, and the child learns that one laughs in response to humor but that the laughter subsides eventually and one goes on to other matters, adolescent girls' giggling notwithstanding. However, if your youngster sees you become angry and go to bed angry, he might assume that that is what one does with anger, that it's quite all right to go to bed angry. Those of you who have done so, however, know better.

Is that what you want your child to learn? Do you want your children to learn, so young, that *indefinitely sustained anger* is a way of life? Unfortunately, one may indeed go to bed angry, and it is often unavoidable. But the child ought to have the experience of seeing you finish with your anger, at least once in a while. If children do see parents have a good fight, and later see them joke with each other, or show other evidence of diminished anger, or just start talking in a natural manner, they learn that one becomes angry and fights, then gets over one's anger and the fight is over. That's all there is to it. Is that a lesson worth demonstrating? You decide.

Connections

But we were talking about supermoms. What is the connection between anger and supermom? I've already made many allusions to that connection. What I call supermomism is a state of compulsiveness. It is not an evolving, by-choice form of behavior which rests upon convenience, suitability and preference. It is a way of life which a woman imposes upon herself because her inner directives have pressured her to do so. Those directives are culturally, familially, and individually induced.

Supermom's behavior may or may not be relevant to her life goals. When it is, she can live more easily with herself, for she will not be criticized too much by her peers and spouse for "going beyond the call of duty." When her behavior is not relevant to her goals, her suffering can become quite agonizing, for she has no external, reinforcing features with which to support herself.

Men also can impose such a compulsive form of living upon themselves. It often looks quite different because the content may be widely divergent. Sets of standards, which again may or may not be acceptable by society at large, are nevertheless as stringent as any of supermom's, and they exert just as much pressure on a father.

As I have already emphasized, the standards that supermom imposes upon herself are unattainable. She therefore feels angry with her failure to achieve the impossible. That the standards are impossible to attain is not consciously recognized by this kind of person.

Supermom's anger is usually a persistent, cold form, and can be extremely well hidden at times. It comes forth in sharp outbursts of temper which often seem entirely unrelated to cause, or seem exaggerated and inappropriate. Her anger may also come out against friends or spouse in quiet but continuous spurts of complaints, whines, and criticisms which are almost impossible to live with. Or, it may come out in forceful, demanding, and continuous complaints, criticisms and puttings-down of the "tyrant."

How anger is expressed depends upon the personality of an individual and his or her background and development. Such behavior is largely imitative and often bears, with variations, a strong resemblance to parental behavior modes. The person who needs to be approved and loved all the time is often the whiner who can never work up quite enough froth to really tell anyone off. As I said, it comes out in small spurts. However, these people may be pleasant, smiling, and helpful. But their voices may register their feelings (of which they themselves may be unaware) in a wheedling, supplicating tone.

The loud-mouthed tyrant is the one who doesn't care whose toes he treads upon. That person is self-indulgent with his mountain of anger and lets the chips fall where they may. When such a person is in a position of power, he is the one most feared, obeyed, and avoided. If not in that position, he has a lot of trouble throughout life with family and work relationships, because no one wants to put up with such unpleasant importunity.

The occasional outburst is more likely to occur in the person who keeps things under wraps by not becoming too involved in anything or with anyone. A quality of intimate closeness is often lacking in relationships. He maintains his equilibrium by keeping somewhat apart from others and trying very hard to be tolerant of others' shortcomings. This works for a time, but when the pressure becomes too great, there is an outburst.

I have described these personality types in somewhat exaggerated forms. All people are a little of this and a little of that. But some people seem to be a little more of one kind than another, so that they can be fairly readily identified. However, when one feels that a particular type has been established, one is confronted by puzzling contradictions. These cannot be regarded as mutually exclusive, however, for they are clearly present, whatever the contradiction.

Occasionally, one finds a tyrant who seems to possess a mixed bag of characteristics. Such a person may sometimes be continuously whining, complaining, and criticizing over little nothings, *and* other times forcefully angry and demanding. Each ethnic group has its own idiomatic labels for such people.

Such people can be lived with—but it takes strength and forbearance. In the best of such worlds, a great deal of *persistent kindness* (in the face of regular criticism and rejection) can often undermine, through the years, both the inner-directed and outer-directed destructiveness of such a personality.

It is well to remember, however, that tyrants, as well as any other kind of person, come in many forms. There are good-natured tyrants, choleric tyrants, whining tyrants. But a tyrant by any other name smells as bad. Lest we heap too much scorn upon the head of the tyrant, who in his own way suffers as much as anyone, let us be aware that *it takes two to establish a dictatorship.* No tyrant is possible without someone who will be tyrannized. No dictator exists without a dictatee.

Home

One final point has to be emphasized again. If supermoms are so industrious, so competent, so driving, intelligent, energetic and idealistic, why do they keep themselves in the bind I have been describing? Why don't they put their talents, resources, and efforts to use in leaving their shoddy anger behind them? Just think of the satisfactions they could achieve. And they could indeed, with all that potential.

Yet they cling tenaciously to their anger. I've said it's unconscious, unintentional. But one does not have to consciously rid oneself of a destructive inner force. Such an exodus may also occur as an unconscious phenomenon. But why, oh why, does supermom cling so?

Because she's afraid to let go. You see, her dedicated, all-consuming drive toward supermomism cost her a high price. That price was her naturally developing selfhood, her spontaneity. True, she paid unknowingly, while she was too young to know the price. Now, when she could know better, she keeps her dues up to date. The day she refuses to pay those dues and is willing to take the risks entailed, her cure has begun.

But for now, she's programmed for supermomism, and she's afraid the machinery will break if she upsets the program. (Remember, I'm speaking in absolutes.) With a loss of selfhood, of spontaneity, one lives in a semi-dead state.

"Alive" human beings cannot stand to be dead—even half-dead. It doesn't feel good. And anyway, it's obviously antithetical to life. So they will work hard to find ways to overcome that sense of deadness, and to achieve a sense of aliveness. Those ways are found in excitement of any form: games, hunts, wars, all kinds of spectator activities. Humans have been inventing forms of excitement throughout history. Violence is certainly one of those forms. Strong emotions like anger can be exciting. Anger? Yes, anger. If one can feel angry enough, long enough, one doesn't feel dead, or sad, or empty, or frightened, or even sexy—sometimes. (Could this be what frigidity is all about?)

Sophisticated workers with people in crisis have always known that one of the ways to keep indecisive, timid, terrified people mobilized is to keep them angry. Anger is potent busywork and can overcome other immobilizing feelings.

Thus supermom, who is always hovering on the edge of success as well as failure, remains angry for two reasons. The first I have already described: Sensing her failures, she remains angry with herself and with her world. Since success is unattainable, her anger inevitably remains.

But suppose she achieves a success—just suppose. Now she's at the top. She's arrived at her goal of perfection. So what else is there? Where can she go? A great computer with no new worlds to conquer. But wait and harken. What's that hollow sound—that rattling noise? There's something rattling around inside a beautifully decorated but empty cardboard box. Having paid the price of admission, she gave up her most singularly human characteristic—her selfhood. Nothing for nothing! Now she has nothing to feel angry about anymore. What's left to her? Feelings of emptiness, of hollowness, of deadness, that had previously been covered up by the alive feeling of anger? Which is worse? Which is better? Feelings of emptiness are anxiety-provoking; and anxiety, unless relieved in some way, is the most intolerable of all feelings. Ask someone who's experienced a few intolerable anxieties.

Having organized her life about seeking and striving, with all of its benefits of facsimile aliveness, she cannot enter into a new form of living. Her safety, her sense of security, rests with what she knows. Newness is unknown to her and would be too anxiety-provoking. Unconsciously, she guards herself from such anxiety by staying where she is, where she knows the territory, with all her old, comfortable, familiar complaints, frustrations, and agonizings. It's hell. But at least it's home.

CHAPTER XIII

"And a Little Child Shall Lead Them"

I F YOU HAVE NOT BEEN to parenting school, you had only your experience in your primary family to go by when you became a parent. If that was not very conducive to the development of mental health in you and your siblings, then you have almost nothing that would help you to be the kind of parent you want to be. I'm hoping that the few parent education programs in schools today will multiply within the next few years so that parents can be helped *before* they run into difficulty with their children. But unless parent education programs stress *prevention,* I believe the service they can render will be seriously limited. So we have the task here to find all and any possible sources and kinds of help.

In Chapters I to IV, I outlined a method for parenting that I think is useful. But there are many ways to learn parenting; and even after one learns any given set of principles, it is always difficult to apply them.

The best way I can talk about this is to ask first, "How do you learn to be a good friend?" Or I might ask, "How do you learn to be a good teacher, or a good spouse, or a good traveling companion?" You can't do it by yourself. You have to consider the other person always and learn from that person. What will make the relationship a smooth one, as well as a satisfying and rewarding one? But that doesn't mean that you do not consider yourself also. Because you won't like your friend very long if you find yourself always putting his needs ahead of your own. There has to be some compromise, some give-and-take.

You have to be willing to find out what your friend needs, wants, likes, dislikes, can contribute, can understand, can tolerate. You have to find out what his limitations are, what resources there are and how you can relate to both. You have to let him know precisely the same things about yourself. You have to be willing to exchange all appropriate information at every step of the relationship, for it will change in one or all of these respects as time goes on. Unless you are willing to keep all this information up to date, confusions can occur and misunderstandings can arise with resultant hurt feelings and suffering. Surely, I could make the same statements regarding a spouse. In marriage, however, when misunderstandings arise and hurt feelings ensue, suffering may be at its most intense.

If these principles of learning apply to friends, to spouses, or to any other significant persons, why should they not apply to your child? Let me repeat the question. "How do you learn to be a good parent?" "Well," you ask, "how can I exchange information with my baby? How can he understand what I am saying?" I reply at this point, "It's more important that you understand what *he* is saying. Let's leave Baby's understanding for later."

Listening

So what is Baby saying? How does the newborn talk to you? He cries and whimpers, gurgles and yells, and you learn very quickly and directly what Baby's needs are. You meet them as best you can and often with good humor. When you are tired, your good humor wanes. Things go fairly well in infancy if Baby is well. You are learning every day, mainly from your Baby, how to be an effective parent.

As Baby gets older, you learn other things. You learn what foods are preferred, when he's no longer hungry, when he has a diaperful, and so on. When you can put baby in the highchair, you learn that he loves to make noise by banging something on the tray. You learn, hopefully, that he's not doing this just to annoy you, but because activity and noise are fun. After all, Baby is limited at this stage to simple repetitious motions which help him learn how hands and arms can be used.

If you can't stand the noise, don't give Baby a hard object. You find out that Baby loves to throw things on the floor and then wait for you to retrieve them—thirty-eight times in succession. If your back or pride won't stand this, tie the object to the side of the chair with a stout string and teach Baby to pull it up.

With this act, you are beginning to teach Baby what your needs are. If you don't mind picking up objects thirty-eight times successively, fine! But if you do mind, he'd better know this, or he will have to deal with your irritation for "making" you pick up so much. This would not be fair because he has no intention of distressing you. He does it only because he doesn't know that this action distresses you.

You learn instantly when Baby is ready to eat—he grabs the spoon and starts. Now this is a moment when you have many decisions to make. You must first realize that he can't feed himself as effectively or neatly as you can. If you are worried about Baby's nourishment (which in most cases you needn't be), you can get another spoon and slip in a few quick ones while he's busy getting something on his own spoon.

If you are worried about a mess, all I can say is stop worrying— he *will* make a mess. I do believe, though, that if not too much is made of this mess, within days or weeks he may have learned to control his movements well enough so that his food doesn't get all over the walls as well as the floor. But you can put newspapers on the floor. (I don't know what you can use on the walls, unless you tape newspapers to them.) You can pull the chair away from the wall and place it in the middle of the kitchen. In this case, only the floor can get it. But don't be too surprised if the ceiling gets an occasional spoonful.

Teachable Moment

This is, of course, the *precious teachable moment.* If you let Baby go ahead with his own feeding, you have a golden opportunity to assist in your child's spontaneous, healthy development. When it's feeding time, you can ask if he wants to be fed or wants to do it himself. Even if Baby isn't talking yet, I'm sure this communication can be made.

So he has the chance to make a decision. Since he's changed from feeding to eating, he's made a stride away from Mommy. Now eager to manipulate a spoon, Baby can be shown how to hold it, scoop up, how to get it to his mouth, and so on.

Here, Baby is exercising choice and independence, and he is improving his skills. Perhaps most important, however, will be his feelings toward you, and yours toward him while all this is going on. As you know, whenever anyone succeeds in teaching you something you want to learn, you feel affectionate or at least positive toward that person. Well, here is your little darling. He's having the experience of a parent who loves him enough to teach or *let* him learn something he wants to do. I think Baby will always love you dearly for that opportunity.

If you are the kind of parent, however, who absolutely cannot stand the mess and uncertainty, it might be better for you to continue the feeding yourself. Baby may give you a little trouble if he prefers to feed himself. You have to decide which is the lesser of two evils for you. It would seem that to the extent that Baby can care for these primitive needs himself, you will be freed of some of your chores.

The parent who can tolerate the chaos of Baby's first efforts to feed himself can, for many peaceful years to come, sit at the table with Baby and the rest of the family and not have to be bothered with feeding or worry about how much Baby is eating. Not all, but many, babies who are allowed to feed themselves at an early stage are good, trouble-free eaters throughout childhood. One of the great hurdles of early childhood is thus easily and successfully coped with, all because you listened to your child when he said, "I can do it. Let me do it."

This approach applies throughout early development, when Baby is ready to move about, to walk, to climb, etc. He is constantly giving you eloquent messages, indicating to you what he needs, wants, likes. You can learn as long as you are watching and listening and are completely willing to heed the messages. You see how easy it can be.

It gets harder, though, not because the messages are not coming through loud and clear, but because the messages begin to conflict with your own needs. As in a friendship or marital relationship, compromises have to be made, turns have to be taken—now Baby, now you. You won't be able to reason with him. You'll just have to state your position. Often he won't like it and will say so in no

uncertain terms. If you have decided that it's your turn, then it is wise
to stand firm. It won't hurt. You can always change your mind if there
is really a good reason. If you are at all fair, he'll accept that you want
your turn. As early as the second year, little children will do no more
than look with great round eyes when Mommy states unequivocally,
but not angrily, "No, I don't want to do that." And that's all there
is to it. When children give you a hard time, it's usually because of
your own inner indecisiveness and wishy-washiness. But there's much
more about that elsewhere in this book.

Trust Baby

What can be done with your fears when your child decides he's
ready for a tricycle at three and you feel that he'll break his neck?
Well, you have to decide whether or not you're going to continue with
your schooling. If you decide to continue your parent education
course, with your child as instructor, then you'll pocket your fear and
trust his readiness. I'm not saying you won't continue to be afraid.
You will. Very much. But you won't be the first parent to let a child
do something that *you* weren't ready for.

This method works all the way. As the child grows older and
verbalizes better, he can tell you more, perhaps. Sometimes you'll ask.
But the procedure is the same. You have to be watching and listening,
willing to observe, hear, and learn. When misunderstandings occur,
you can admit (without abject apologies) that you didn't know something. As he gets older, advise your child to make sure that you do
understand. Remember all the while that you are letting your child
know what your limits are, how much you are willing to go along
with. You are establishing family rules and regulations and doing all
the things that are described here and in other works on family living.

The key issue here is watching for the message, receiving the message and responding to it. The lesson itself, or the message, originates
with the child. But you have to be alert to your child's temperament,
personality, and the way he conveys messages. If you are expecting
a particular kind of child with a particular kind of message, you may
miss obvious signs.

Temperament

Some people believe that all children are born the same and that after birth, their temperaments begin to develop immediately in response to their parents. While you influence your children greatly, I do not believe that you are the initiator of your child's temperament.

Workers have demonstrated differences in the temperament of newborn children. A casual visit to the newborn nursery reveals quiet babies, loud babies, contented and discontented babies. The differences are evident even before you have made any impact.

But things change when baby is brought home. Suppose you or your spouse like to be quiet. You like to read and do not feel comfortable when "waves" are made. Let us suppose that a strong, vigorous, noisy little boy is introduced into this family unit. This child makes some pretty big waves. He shatters the peace and quiet of your home. He serves as a forceful intrusion into your lives. Whether you like to admit it or not, he's an irritant on occasion. You love him, but nevertheless he irritates you sometimes. But that's not all he does: he jars the tranquil order of your life. He can do no other, for he is alive and needs a new kind of attention on your part.

Back and Forth

When you approach this child at a moment of your irritation, he can often sense it and respond to it. But he has already influenced you with his basic nature, or temperament. In this case, his way of being seems to initiate the exchange. Then you respond, and after that, the child reacts to your response. It is in these second and third steps that the most destructive parent-child interplay initially takes place. Where parents' first response to a baby's temperament is of a positive nature, baby's response will probably also be positive. If that occurs, the parent-child interplay gets off to a constructive beginning.

Suppose you and your spouse are two outgoing people who like to be very active, who like excitement and activity. Let us suppose that you have a very quiet, contented little baby who eats when he's "supposed to," sleeps when he's "supposed to," and makes no commotion whatsoever. Instead of saying, "Thank God! We have a good baby who will not interfere too much with our own way of living," you look at the baby and wonder what's wrong with him. You may feel you have to "stimulate" the child. Because of your doubts you are already tense, and you approach the child with unfounded anxiety.

In this case, the quiet child induces anxiety in the parent. Such tension is felt by the child and he then responds to that rather than to the soft, warm regard of the two people upon whom he is totally dependent.

Parents as Pussycats

Newborn babies need little to grow well and to be content. Parents often do not know that there is plenty of time for extensive playing with, talking to. I sometimes think that young mothers should watch a cat or dog with her newborn litter. They are a study in precise function and contentment. These animals do all that is necessary for their young and no more. The mother is with her young most of the time, poking or proding them into position for nursing. When they have found the teat, she leaves them alone and lets them feed. When their little bellies are full, she strokes them with her tongue, and they usually drop off to sleep. She is the epitome of relaxation. It is almost hypnotic to watch this for any length of time. It is so quiet, so soft, so gentle, so caring, so free of unnecessary activity. The mother doesn't fuss over them needlessly. If necessary, she will transfer them from place to place. As they grow, there is greater interchange among littermates and finally the curious venturing forth to explore the outside world.

All Baby Wants Is Caring

What parallels can be drawn? First, perhaps, is the desirability of complete relaxation on the part of the parent who is caring for the child. (She doesn't have to be a nursing mother.) It may be a father, a grandmother, a nurse—anyone. While we cannot ask the newborn how he feels about it, I don't believe that he cares one whit who this caring person is, as long as it is someone without a high level of tension, who will hold him comfortably, and feed, change, and tend him. For Baby finds parental tension very discomforting. He receives it with a most delicate sensory apparatus and responds to it as he sees fit. We assume this on the basis of differing responses of the same baby to different persons handling the baby; he will fuss and be irritable with one, and relaxed and content with another only minutes later.

While it is desirable, it is almost an impossibility for new parents to be as relaxed as animals, especially with the firstborn. New parents are often tense and doubtful of their ability to raise this firstborn child as they feel they are expected to raise him. Their tension prevents them from enjoying the baby and they begin to view him (often unconsciously) as an intruder and a burden.

In later years other features of their child's temperament, behavior, personality, or appearance may be found to be intrusive, irritating or annoying. Many parents merely overlook these and in many instances the rejected characteristic disappears, or merely loses its significance. At times, however, parents become uptight about certain characteristics and thereby help to establish lifelong negative self-views in their child.

Appearance

When a child has a physical feature that is unattractive, parents often call attention to it and thereby magnify its importance. A parent told her twelve-year-old daughter that she had "fat arms" in order to motivate her to do exercises to slim them. Inherited heavy arms or legs, with a slim body, will probably not respond easily to exercises, which ought to be done for general health.

Since there isn't very much one can do about unattractive physical features, it is not a kindness to call attention to them before the youngster notices them. When she does, suggestions can be offered as to how they may be made to look slimmer, without ever referring to their fatness. Certain styles of dress can help. Emphasis can be placed on what to do for improvement, not upon the unattractiveness itself. For example: "This base will make your complexion look rosy," rather than, "You need this rose base to cover the yellow sallowness of your skin." Let's trust the girl to notice the difference for herself and thus be motivated to improve her appearance without having her parent imply that she is unattractive.

Mistakes

Parents often want to know if "mistakes" can be corrected and if so, how. While it is a problem requiring much attention, patience and perseverance, the outlook is not entirely grim. If a parent-child relationship has been poor and the parent wants to improve it, a beginning can be made at any time in childhood, adolescence, or adulthood. It's never too late. A woman of forty was tearfully grateful when she found that her sixty-five-year-old mother had loved her all along but had never shown it because she thought the daughter would reject any show of affection. The daughter, in her teens, had rejected her mother's offers of affection and the elder woman had never dared to show them again!

The important thing is to know what is going on, to be aware of the need to effect some change. Having arrived at this awareness, you must focus on one particular point and identify the troublesome feature. If, for example, your back hurts because your shoes are too tight, attention to the back will not constitute a cure. You must identify the source of the difficulty before you can make the next move effective. With some adolescent children, parents find that they cannot hold a conversation without an argument. Here, it is necessary to identify the fact of arguing, when the intention was merely to converse.

Once the point is identified, you must consult with yourself about it. This means literally that you must sit down and think about it. This is best accomplished when you are alone and will not be interrupted. Such a problem requires thoughtful attentiveness and cannot be reflected upon in the midst of an argument or ordinary family turmoil and activity. Parents do not often afford themselves the luxury of a few quiet moments to contemplate some of the difficulties they are having with their children. The question, "What can I do to change this pattern of behavior?" is rarely asked.

Patterns

You will find that by the time your child is five, six, or seven, patterns of behavior are well established by both parent and child—patterns that may lead to unhappiness and dissatisfaction. While you may say to the child, in effect, "You have to change your ways," you must be prepared to change yours also. If your way remains the same, chances are that your offspring will respond with the same familiar behavior pattern.

First, then, it is necessary for you to know that you want to change your ways and to identify what you are willing to do to change them. You cannot proceed until you do so. You can use whatever help you can get in your attempt to change. You can talk to friends, your spouse, neighbors, anyone. They can help with the dozens of daily routine issues which can cause repeated unpleasantness and stress in the family. If it's a serious problem, I recommend that you talk with a person who has the training to help you with that specific problem. All of this, however, has already been illustrated and described earlier in the book.

In many cases, you must be willing to alter something. If you keep putting the same ingredients into the hopper, the child will keep putting in the same ingredients also, and you'll both have the same old stew. So something has to change, and this can happen at any age. When you try something new with teen-agers, they're shocked, but often pleased. I must warn you, however, don't hold your breath waiting for thanks. Just have faith.

CHAPTER XIV

Double Message: Yes/No

P ARENTS OFTEN ASK, "How do you get your child to listen to you and do what you want?" One parent described an incident in Woolworth's where her five-year-old girl wanted a toy and was refused. The child kept nagging and Mother kept refusing, becoming more and more annoyed. This woman said that she did not think her daughter should have a toy every time they went into that store. Then she added, "But she's only a child, and I can really afford a small toy each time." Clearly, she was of two minds and was saying, in effect, "Yes, you can have it, and no, you can't."

The child, upon receiving this *double message,* of which both mother and child were unaware, apparently placed emphasis on the *yes* part of the message because of her own desire for a toy. She "kept after" her mother, hoping that she might follow through on the *yes.* In many instances, the parent does capitulate, explaining, "I just couldn't stand to listen to her!"—an honest reaction, to some extent. It also provides an excuse for the parent to follow through on the *yes* without losing face, or without feeling guilty about being an overindulgent parent.

Double Trouble

You can see, then, how the original double message of *yes/no* arises from this parent's conflict regarding indulgence, teaching her child the "value of money," and other confusions with which she is laboring. No definite parental decision can be made under such conditions. In addition, the parent transfers her confusion to the child, who is left with the burden of decision. Quite often, the child decides to pursue a particular desire, and is able to tip the scale in his own favor. If this happens repeatedly, the child sets up a pattern of response which may be difficult to alter, even when the parent is able to give only one straight message without conscious or unconscious seesawing. It requires persistent patience to stick with the principle of one message until your child responds to it. Even when you recognize that you are using a double message, and are willing to make a change, you have to keep from becoming discouraged when your efforts meet with failure.

Parents' Rights

Another woman gave a double message to a teen-age son when she asked him to go the market for her. (She was angry with him before she asked because she anticipated his refusal.) Her double message was: 1) I want you to do this; 2) I don't expect you to do it. Her son heard the second message more loudly than the first, and willingly fulfilled her expectation. He found her anger irritating and insulting, and he felt no desire to please her.

What drives this parent to address her son so equivocally? Certainly, anyone's view of himself is revealed in the way he relates to those most closely associated with him. In business or with her friends, this woman sees herself as a successful, adequate person. She has no difficulty telling those she supervises what to do. And they do it. With her own supervisor, she can also state her position, and accept or reject suggestions as she sees fit.

At home, she finds that she cannot assert herself. She conveys an apologetic manner when she makes requests of her family. In a sense, she fears her power. She feels that she can be loved by her children only if she remains a self-effacing, "permissive" parent. Her rule book says that children should make their own decisions. She doesn't question which ones they may make and which ones are her responsibility. She thinks firmness is meanness, so she meekly says, "Why don't you go see the dentist?" when her teen-age son's teeth are rotting in his head, knowing that he'll go only when she makes the appointment.

Should she let him wait until his teeth fall out? How many of you could stand letting that happen? So speak up. Say what you want to say. You have that right. Your child is not so fragile that he'll break if you confront him directly, honestly, and without malice.

The classic example of the double or multimessage is the saccharine-sweet question, "Don't you want to go to bed now?" It really says: 1) It's time for bed; 2) I hope you won't give me any trouble tonight; 3) I don't expect you to go without the usual hassle; 4) I wish I didn't have to go through this every night; 5) I think I'm kidding you as well as myself by asking you, because we both know I'm not asking; 6) I'm trying to tell you to go to bed, but I can't do it; 7) I want you to take the responsibility and say you'll do it.

Of course, the child in this kind of a bind with a parent is not able to assume such responsibility.

Hearing Mother's voice, seeing her face, sensing her equivocal attitude, all routines familiar to him, Junior goes through his own familiar routines of not wanting to go and of not getting ready. When he's eventually in bed, the charade continues with his getting out of bed for the dozens of reasons children find and to which some parents acquiesce.

Will You Love Me?

Double messages are the mark of the person who cannot state a position clearly. Such persons often don't know what their position is. That is because they are busy trying to please all the time. They try desperately to avoid offending. While stating a position is not necessarily in the realm of offense, these people are afraid that they will incur displeasure by being too "pushy." Displeasure can lead to anger, anger to vindictiveness, vindictiveness to hurtfulness.

In the case of parents and children, many parents have a free-floating fear that their children will not "love" them if they impose their will upon them—anytime. It may be that a child will be angry with a parent for making a demand. But parents have to run such risks. The chances are good that the child's anger will blow over, sooner or later.

Firm Is Not Mean

Rather than run the risk of losing love, these parents avoid making flat statements or taking a firm stand when that is clearly required on an important issue or even on the most routine matter. Such parents confuse firmness with meanness or regard taking a stand with rigidity as authoritarian. Yet they *want* the child to get proper rest. They *want* to fulfill all of the ordinary needs that a child has. They are driven to satisfy these needs. But they do it in such a way as to confuse their children, who sense true meanings but want to indulge their desires.

The point is that you, as well as your child, are entitled to say *no* if in your judgment *no* is indicated. *No's* should be based on the given conditions of the situation. Among them might be intensity of desire, factors of appropriateness such as time, place, age, health, etc., parental factors such as fatigue, irritability, anxiety, and convenience. Don't underestimate the last—convenience. Parents are often annoyed with children because they are involved with them in ways that are not only inconvenient for them but unnecessary for their children.

The Unequivocal No

Regarding intensity of desire, you might decide to withhold a reasonable and unequivocal *no* if your child wants something urgently. While inconvenient or inconsistent with your general policy, you might permit it anyway. For example, your five-year-old girl is sitting with older siblings watching "Peter Pan" on TV and it's past her bedtime. If getting to bed is of crucial importance on that night (which it probably isn't), she gets an *unequivocal no* when she asks to stay up to see the rest of the movie, which will run till 10:30. But if she really wants to be with the family and see the rest of the movie, that *no* might be withheld that one time.

Don't worry that she'll nag you to stay up again and again; she very well may. If she reminds you that you let her stay up to 10:30 last week, you can *briefly* explain to her that that was a special circumstance and a special program. If you add that there might be other programs she may watch in the future, for instance in three months, she may be quite satisfied. Your success will depend on your unequivocal attitude. You must believe what you say. Your decision for the *moment* must be unequivocal even though in your heart you may be vacillating. This is not easy to do when you've been a frequent user of double messages and the equivocal *no*. But practice. Think about it. Plan for occasions when you can use it. Then go ahead and act.

A Majority of One

As far as other factors are concerned, such as convenience or appropriateness, you are entitled to use them in making your decisions. If you have been traveling with your family and everyone is tired and cranky, and the children want to go to just one more place, consider the consequences. It may seem very easy to just stop in because you are so near. But if it will take another two hours, and your spouse has a headache, and everyone is hungry, then a firm *no* is the answer, regardless of the dissenting voices. Mean? Possibly. But it's not *mean* mean. It's really only human. And that's all you are, after all.

One, and Straight

In order to be able to convey one message at a time, you have to recognize first that two or more messages are being given. If you want to convey double messages, fine. But if you think double messages are single messages, you must understand that they are not. Here the process of identification may take place. "What am I saying that makes my child buck me? What am I doing that creates such a gap? How am I feeling when I ask my child a question? Am I feeling afraid? If so, why? What do I think will happen if I come out and say, No, your Mother and I don't want you to go to that place at that time—period?"

Answering these questions helps to identify the problem. Then you can decide if you want to, are able to, have the courage to give your offspring one straight message—unequivocally yet not unkindly, seriously yet not grimly, responsibly yet not rigidly.

Listening and Responding

How you listen and respond to your child when he talks with you can also contain double messages. So much is touted about "communication" with children, especially teen-agers. Very often, though, when they are expressing a wish to talk, parents don't listen or respond, and parents don't know it. But their children do.

There are five common ways parents listen and respond. The first way is not at all. This may be due to parental indifference or preoccupation. The second is absentmindedly; this too may be due to indifference or preoccupation and to boredom and disinterest in the subject. A third way is by not permitting your youngster to finish talking before you interrupt with whatever you have to say. These may be regarded as examples of one kind of double message wherein, for example, the message of disinterest is conveyed by an irrelevant response.

A fourth response is overenthusiastic. Middle-class, educated parents often fall into this group because they are so grateful to be "communicating" with their teen-agers. But it turns the youngsters off, for parents go all-out trying to make the most of each opportunity. Such parents rarely do this with others. When they do, it also serves to turn off.

A fifth way is used by parents who listen and respond directly to the information received or questions answered. No double responses here. The essence of any good conversation is to listen, respond, and wait—listen, respond, wait. If a teen-ager feels that he doesn't have to compete with you to get a word in, or doesn't doubt that you are listening, he will have more interest in talking with you, listening to you, and responding to you. It works both ways. Once they start talking and sense that there's an open field before them, they'll go on and on.

The Ubiquitous *What?*

Even the ubiquitous *what?* can be a double message whether it's used by you or any other family member. Most often, however, it's merely evidence of daydreaming or some other distraction. When children or spouse are three feet away from you, with hearing intact, having actually heard your voice, and come back with "What?

What?" you can believe that your words didn't register. It's not your fault. Nor are they out to annoy you, even though it may seem so. They are involved with some other thought at that moment. Furthermore, they may not be able to tell you what it is.

But at other times, the *what?* may serve as a double message: 1) I can't believe what you said; 2) You're not saying what I want to hear; 3) I don't want to be involved with you just now; 4) I don't know what you mean; 5) I don't know what to say; and 6) I need time to think.

If you accept these possibilities, you can see that they all have to do with something related to your child, not to you. It is unlikely that you are being maliciously rejected, ignored, or frustrated. Adults are more likely to intend such outcomes than children. Your youngster is trying to come to terms with what you are saying. He sometimes has to wrench himself away from some inner world of which you have no knowledge. That takes time. Give him a few seconds. Let him have a few *whats?* What does it take—twenty seconds? It can save you a great deal of irritation, elevation of blood pressure, and the sorry worry that your child is rude and impossible. He's neither. Just a kid being a kid. He'll change sometime. Wait and see.

Yes or Nes, No or Yo

Even when you are aware of your double messages, you may still be compelled to use them. It's something like the alcoholic who knows he's one yet can't keep away from liquor. Perhaps a new vocabulary could be devised to help identify the double message. Thus both parent and child might know what was going on.

Then, when parents come on with an equivocal *no* or *yes* or some other double message, they might coin a handy new word or two to use instead. Perhaps they would feel better. Such a word would certainly give them the feeling that they were trying. And youngsters might not feel that someone was trying to pull wool over their eyes. Everything would be clear and aboveboard. A parent could then know if he were being indecisive, uncertain, and double message-y.

Depending upon the *manifest message* being conveyed—that is, the message the parent thinks he is conveying, either no or yes—your youngster could say, "There goes Mom again with her No/Yes message." But perhaps a better combination of No and Yes might be Nes, that is, NO + YES = NES. Could Mom say Nes-nes when she wanted to say No-no, but there was Yes-yes in her eyes? Of if she wanted to say Yes-yes, with a No-no in her heart, she could say Yo-yo, that is, YES + NO = YO. If Father were double messaging, perhaps your youngster could say, "Oh, oh. There goes Dad again with his Yo-yo." That way, the whole family could know whose double messages were showing. Silly, you say? Maybe not.

Surely double messages are a significant enough feature in family communications to be accorded the distinction of a special vocabulary. Indeed, double messages abound in all areas of living—between marital partners, business and professional associates, casual acquaintances, perhaps least among friends. They are clearly in evidence in national politics and international relations where they are, for the most part, intentionally produced. In political circles double messages have always enjoyed a high degree of respectability. Recently, that respectability has been enhanced by an augmented vocabulary which, while seemingly obscure to the untutored, quickly becomes perfectly clear to the willing learner. Even more recently, however, that very respectability has become somewhat tarnished about the edges, and some of the associated vocabulary has fallen into disrepute.

And so it goes, back and forth, just like parent-child relationships with their backs and forths, ups and downs. But remember, there's a positive side to almost everything. For many essential human exchanges would not be possible without some use of the double message.

CHAPTER XV

The Indifferent Parent

B EING ALIVE, CURIOUS, INTELLIGENT, and needing other people as frames of reference to feel themselves against, children react strongly to their parents' vibes. Very early, children must have someone as a sounding board, or they cannot learn who they are, what they are, what they stand for. The child left alone too much may develop in strange ways. There is no measuring what too much is. All that can be said is that the child is too much alone where there is not enough human contact for him to develop a sense of self and a place in the world.

A "Nothing" Child

An indifferent parent is perhaps the most difficult for a child to deal with, whether he is one, ten, or sixteen years old. With an indifferent parent, the frame of reference, the sounding board, is absent. The child has and feels nothing against which to evolve his identity. He doesn't know where he stands—he doesn't know how he affects others. As no interest is taken in him, he cannot feel any interest in himself. Such children are often anxious children. They may be quiet,

176

depressed, pathetic children, or active, disruptive ones demanding that they be noticed in any way, good or bad, just so they may feel less anxious and know better what they are. For them, it's far better to feel, "I am a bad child," than to feel, "I'm am a nothing child."

The indifferent parent sometimes has a shadowy quality. He (or she) is a difficult person to identify, for he doesn't go around saying, "I am an indifferent parent." He doesn't even know that he is one. He may see himself in many guises and believe them to be what he is. Such a parent may well have had an indifferent parent also. We need not go into the polemics of where did it all start. However, we need to identify some of the signs of indifference so that such parents might at least begin to have a glimmering as to where they stand—if they're interested. Whether or not they want to do anything about their discovery is their choice to make. I do believe, however, that most parents who actually discover a shortcoming of this kind in their child-parent relationship have already made a move toward diminishing the extent of the disorder.

The indifferent parent may see himself as the permissive parent. In some circles, this is supposed to be "good." Therefore, he believes himself to be a good parent because he doesn't intrude upon the development of the child. Nowadays parents are reaping the fruit of this kind of permissiveness when they hear their children complain, "They let us do whatever we wanted because they didn't really care!" Yet these same children might have made things very difficult for parents who imposed rules and regulations. I say "might" because it would depend entirely upon the way the rules were imposed. A reasonable rule, fairly imposed, has probably never hurt a child, nor is the child likely to make much of a fuss over it.

The indifferent parent may go through motions of caring. This would include physical care, proper toys, equipment, exposure to varying experiences, good academic planning, spending of money. Sometimes it may be one of these, sometimes all. How, then, you ask, does the seemingly devoted parent neglect his child in such a way as to give the child the feeling that no one cares?

Here again, the indifferent parent often has no intention of coming across that way to the child. He has no intention of being disinterested. He just is, and it can't be helped unless some awareness of the condition is aroused. As far as that parent knows, common parental motions and noises establish parenthood, and nothing more need be done.

Some intentionally indifferent parents know it and act it out. Their guilt level about it is usually quite low. If guilt is present at all, they justify their attitude on the basis of duty. "Yes, I let my child do his own thing because it's my job to see that he makes his own mistakes and learns to take care of himself." That's difficult for some people to argue against unless one remembers the "too much" principle. I'll say a bit more about such parents a little later.

But unconsciously indifferent parents are so often puzzled when their youngsters are rejecting and full of derision for family members and traditions. It is so that rejection is not as damaging for parents as for children. Nevertheless, when rejection is "on the other foot" it is just as painful for the caring parent. Children's rejection of their parents is not so much a new phenomenon as it is a more open one in these times. At some time in their young lives, adolescents have rejected their parents' attitudes and beliefs; but until recent times they have been neither so obvious nor outspoken about it. Today, it has become as fashionable to talk about parental "hangups" as any of the other popular subjects which seem to flash and fade with the seasons.

The indifferent parent is also puzzled when children get into serious difficulty with health, learning, or the law. Questions uppermost in their minds are, "How did it happen? What did I do to bring this about? Why doesn't my child seem to care about us? What is the matter?" Many "experts" have attempted to answer these questions.

Answers are sometimes helpful and sometimes not. They are probably all valid to some extent. Yet the questions persist, indicating that parents do not find the answers useful. So new questions arise.

Information abounds. Answers abound. The *what* has been abundantly answered, if not helpfully. So the problem now is the *how*. How does one get a parent to use all this information to improve the quality of the relationship with the youngster? The crux of the matter seems to be how the information is put to use—or perhaps more pertinently, how the information is not put to use.

Although some parents remain ignorant of the simplest basics leading to satisfying human relationships, many are fully aware of them. Yet they are not able to apply what they know. It doesn't take very much to know that patience, kindness, courtesy, and respect are essential in dealing with all persons, including children. But it seems to take a great deal to convey the idea that patience, kindness, courtesy, and respect are not the same as endless indulgence, overprotection, saccharine and obsequious deference.

Quality Attention

I think that caring can best be measured not by what a parent does for a child, but by a quality of attentiveness. While shopping, a mother asks, "Which dress would you like to have?" The child replies, "I want the red one." "Oh, why don't you take the blue one? It's so much prettier. The red one makes your skin look so pale." This kind of response does many things in one fell swoop: It 1) reveals that no question is really being asked, because a real question implies the consideration of an answer; 2) imputes poor judgment regarding ability to choose a dress; 3) spoils the pleasure of having the red one (if she should finally select it) because the child will not forget that her mother doesn't like the dress; 4) places the child in the position of being disobedient; 5) spoils the fun of shopping with Mother, if this happens frequently; 6) may leave the child feeling that it isn't worth all the fuss and cause her to lose interest in her appearance.

No mother has to ask the child which dress she prefers if she has already decided on the blue one. Mothers may say, matter-of-factly, "We'll do this" or "We'll do that." And there are many, many other opportunities for a child to have a choice. But to ask a question and then ignore the response, or deprecate it, is a cardinal sign of disrespect. Whether toward a child or an adult, disrespect is a bitter pill to swallow. As a basic characteristic in a relationship, it can play havoc with parent-child relationships. Furthermore, inattentiveness is a sign of disrespect.

Understand that it would be impossible for a parent to be attending to a child constantly in a detailed, sensitive way; there are just too many distractions, too many hardships parents must cope with. The only requirement for the kind of attentiveness needed is that it be evident once in a while—and not very often at that.

As I've said, parents who are having difficulty with their children have no idea that they can improve conditions by making one or two small moves. They do not understand that the quality of their attentiveness is less than heart-warming. They do not believe that the relationship can really be any different. Such pessimism is very painful, however, and is not well tolerated. In a move to protect themselves against such continuing pain, they admit defeat, give up. Little do they know that giving up may not only be difficult, but may also be searingly and persistently heartbreaking.

Giving Up

Have you ever lain awake in the middle of the night, after a particularly difficult hassle with your teen-ager, and thought what an utter and abysmal failure you have been as a parent?—that your son or daughter is not only unappreciative and ungrateful, not only resentful, sullen and contrary, but that he hates you as well? All this effort, all this anguish—and you get hate! Here you are getting older and weaker, and you have to put up with such shenanigans. As if the world were going to end if they can't go there or can't have that or can't do this. As if a refusal on your part or some act of insensitivity were a knife stab to them.

It's too much. You can't stand it. You'll get old before your time. You'll get sick. The marriage can't stand such tension. Your spouse will divorce you. Besides, you're not getting anyplace, anyway. You never will. Because a child who would put you in this position, after all you've done, must be a pretty stupid, ungrateful kid.

So you say to yourself that you've done it all and you've had it. *You have had it!* Let the stupid kids go their own way; let them go and get into trouble. Let them take all those silly, unnecessary risks. Let them go where, with whom, and how they want. Maybe one of several things will happen. Either they'll learn the hard way that they can get into trouble, or that you were right in so many respects. Or that home, Mom, and Dad weren't so impossible after all. Maybe you'll even be liked a little. Maybe they'll even love you again by the time they're twenty-five. But you don't care if they do or not. All you want at this point is a little peace.

Peace

A little peace? From what? From an insidious belief that you've been a pretty "stupid" parent? What, with all your education and good intentions? Worse yet. If you didn't have an education, you'd at least have an excuse: you wouldn't know any better. But even if you don't have an education, you still feel pretty bad. You feel that maybe you didn't try hard enough. Maybe you didn't love enough. Maybe, maybe. Wherever there's an *if,* there's usually guilt. So it's probably peace from guilt, peace from feeling incompetent, peace from feeling disliked by the one you don't even like very much anymore.

So give yourself a little peace. You not only deserve it; you absolutely need it. You cannot go on the same way. You're not going to do or say anymore. Let them do what they want. Anything you do is all wasted anyway. A parent dropout, that's what you're going to be. Everybody else can drop out, so why can't you? After all, you only pass through here once, and other such clichés. How many good years have you got left anyway?

You feel sad and cry a little. Well, you would have liked it to be different. But that's it. If there were another time around, you'd know better and do differently. The death of a beautiful idea is taking place. To worry, to do, to sacrifice for the little ones, and to have their undying love was a great idea; but somehow it didn't work out. What went wrong? It was never easy, but as they got older, your efforts seemed less and less fruitful.

Too Much

Was it too much? Maybe you put too great an investment into them. Maybe you didn't look out enough for yourself. Maybe there was too much emphasis on their needs. Was yours a child-centered home? If so, what a fat nuisance for them, to be the center all the time. To be listened to so pointedly. To be responded to so deliberately. To be taken dead-seriously all the time. To be deprived of a delicious privacy because *you* always knew everything that was going on. A nuisance for them and a nuisance for you because you would much rather have been doing something else. Maybe they felt this. Maybe they felt you weren't as interested or thrilled as you appeared to be, which would have been perfectly all right with them. But you always felt you had to be so pleased with them. It would hurt them if you weren't, you thought. It would be irrevocably damaging to them if you let them know you preferred your peers' company to theirs—and all the rest of it.

Can't you just see the vibes floating all over the place?

Is Giving Up Good?

So you're giving up. You don't like it, but there's nothing else to do. But wait—maybe there's something worthwhile here. Are you giving up trying to be a superparent at the expense of your own integrity? Are you giving up that silly kind of voice and face you put on when you're supposed to be pleased with a particular bit of behavior that you couldn't really care less about, and when you're wanting everyone else to look and sound silly too, and are hurt if they don't? If you are giving up some of these things, good! You'll be more honest and therefore more relaxed, and therefore more open and sensitive, and therefore a lot of good things, and therefore a happier parent.

But there is such a person as a real parent dropout, and I'll go into that a little later. For the most part, the parent who decides unequivocally to give up in the middle of a feeling of profound despair usually finds himself giving up over and over. This frequently happens in the middle of the night, when certain conditions seem unresolved. But most often, one does not stick with a resolve to abandon one's child. So you need not feel guilty when you have such thoughts of child-abandonment. You will undoubtedly get over it. What often happens is that you do undergo some change. There is, or may be, some shifting of position, some slight increase in flexibility, some relaxing from self-imposed standards and expectations neither you nor your children can meet. This is probably all to the good.

Perhaps you are really ready to get off your children's backs. Maybe now your youngsters can find out what they are about and try to conduct their own lives (within reasonable limits, of course). But you might remember that they still need your interest and concern, and certainly your kindness (not shoved down their throats in large doses, but present if they want it).

But now we run into another trouble. Having decided to give up and shut yourself off from repeated hurt and disappointment, you unknowingly may withdraw affection and any kind of approval. It's very hard to dismiss your child without being angry with him for "making" you do it. This kind of cold anger is difficult to camouflage; it can lead to a damaging, corrosive quality in the relationship. There might remain a surface congeniality, but the cold anger lurks just under the surface and spoils any hope for real peace, either for you or between you and your child.

Very often, giving up is a positive move toward a more satisfying relationship with your teen-agers, even though it may be heartrending when you initially make the decision. But any worthwhile outcomes of giving up have to be nurtured. Negatives, like cold anger, should not be permitted to stand in the way. Your cold anger will intrude and keep you from appreciating how you've perhaps helped your child and yourself by deciding to give up.

Consider your giving up only as a first step. Consider what is good and what is bad about it. Use it as a steppingstone to something else which will be more beneficial for your arteries than cold anger can ever be. Maybe you will actually find out that such anger is not good for arteries "and other living things."

Parent Dropout

There is a sort of person who is a real *parent dropout*. There are really different kinds: those who cannot tolerate the strain of parenthood; those who are overwhelmed by the responsibility from the start; those who dislike their children for any number of reasons; and those who never wanted a child and will not submit to *any* restrictions caused by the existence of a child.

So a real parent dropout is one who has irrevocably relinquished the position of a caring parent and has abandoned the child to his own resources, or one who never was a caring parent from the start. While it is desirable for parents to free children to explore and develop their resources as much as possible, there is a marked difference between that and abandonment. The abandoned youngster has no parent to turn to when he (or she) comes to the limit of his resourcefulness and needs advice to fill in for the wisdom he hasn't yet acquired. This accounts for the extreme dependence one encounters among the young members of haphazardly organized "family" groups. (I differentiate between these and ongoing, positive, communal-type groups.)

There is the parent dropout who, soon after the child's birth, senses

something of what it means to have another human being completely
dependent upon him and to be completely responsible for his welfare.
A decision is quickly reached: "Not for me!" While such a mother (or
father) may not permit the child to starve to death, she is able to
disengage herself from any positive attachment to it. She agrees to
undertake the *chore* of taking care of the child, but always with
reservations and resentment that her own existence is being interfered
with. Should the child die, there may be a transitory feeling of guilt,
but no real sense of loss. Should the child wish to live with someone
else, permission is granted with a profound sense of relief.

This parent cannot wait for the youngster to be old enough to fend
for himself. She is the parent most likely to repeat from the time that
the child can comprehend, "You're going to have to take care of
yourself. Nobody's going to give you anything. And don't think that
I'm going to do for you for the rest of my life." This is probably the
parent who never had anything done for her and who indeed had to
scratch for everything she had. It is a desolate tragedy that such
attitudes are handed from generation to generation. There is not a
great number of such parents around. But there are enough for us to
question how they might be helped to appreciate the wonder of rearing a child.

The Non-Engaged

One group of parent dropouts never intended to drop out, but felt
that they had no alternative. They put forth conscientious efforts and
did what they thought was conducive to proper child rearing. Exam-
ined closely, their efforts leave much to be desired, even when measured by the most rudimentary yardstick. This is the group that
permitted its children to make too many of their own decisions, even
in areas where they were not competent to do so. But the impression
left with the child was that not only could he make his own decisions,
but that he'd better make them because no one else would.

This is the group who would call themselves permissive parents but
who were actually *non-engaged parents*. I am not knocking permissiveness in child rearing. It has a place. But very few parents can be
truly permissive, even once in a while. Many parents go through the
motions and think they are permissive, but they are not really.

These non-engaged parents run into serious difficulty when their children become teen-agers and begin to be the cause of mounting pressure and tension in their well-intentioned parents. The tension is more than this group of parents can bear and they give up, drop out, shrug their shoulders and say, "Well, I've done my best. I can't help them anymore. They'll have to work it out for themselves." And they mean it! This group may or may not be affluent; they are involved in their own pursuits; when they can, they supply their children with funds and are relieved that the children are going their way, wherever it is, and relieved that not too much stress is placed upon them, the parents. It is the appeal of peace again, of lessening the pressure of tension, doubt, self-recrimination. Disengagement is essentially a protective act, for these parents could not tolerate the pressures exerted by a child whose "own thing" is not compatible with established family norms.

Such parents are aware of their position and can tell their children where they stand. Sometimes this is done quietly, resignedly. Most often it is done in anger, following long periods of repeated frustration, deep disappointment, and a feeling of hopelessness in their parental role. They feel that they might just as well occupy themselves with other concerns. And they do; for once this parent has divorced himself from his children, there is a large vacant space left into which he will collapse if he doesn't scurry around to fill it with something.

Another group of parent dropouts does pretty much what the previous group does, but is entirely unaware of having given up. This is perhaps a less honest position but unintentionally so. Yet, one cannot hold another responsible for something he doesn't even know. Remember that even legally, a person must first be shown to understand the difference between right and wrong before he can be convicted. And Christ certainly knew whereof he spoke when he said of his persecutors, "Forgive them, Father, for they know not what they do."

This unawareness creates very serious difficulties. The children in this situation, although never told that their parents have abdicated their responsibility toward them, seem to know it, consciously or not. They react to this knowledge by taking off, literally or figuratively, feeling that no one really cares for them or what they do. And, in a sense, they are right. Their parents would like to care for them. But they cannot. Teen-agers don't care very much that their parents *cannot* care for them. All they know is that they are not cared for. They respond with hurt, resentment, anger, and sometimes with vindictiveness to a parental output of indifference.

Met by all this, parents are shocked and cannot understand why their children are so sullen, so mean to them, so inconsiderate, so intractable. Anger is met with anger, unkindness with unkindness, vindictiveness with vindictiveness. It becomes a struggle to the death, symbolically speaking. For parents in this group are struggling to maintain the myth of parental caring, a myth which they cannot fulfill and which they have unconsciously abrogated; and the child is struggling to keep his parents' regard by worrying, dismaying and infuriating the parent, yet knowing those gestures are futile, for he has already lost the caring he wants and so desperately needs.

Is This All?

Is all this as hopeless as it seems? Does this mean that once a parent has really dropped out, consciously or not, that it is the end of everything? Yes, it does, but only if that's the way the parent is willing to leave it. If the parent wants to do something about a severely damaged relationship with an offspring, there is always hope. But I must say that the persistency, patience, fortitude, stamina and strength required must be no less than admirable; for the door must always be ready to open, the parent must be available, and he cannot indulge his pride.

No matter what the parent does it is unlikely that the child will accept it for a long while. He will be suspicious, rejecting, disbelieving, ridiculing and hateful in dozens of ways. The parent may need to find specialized help in this task, for he may very well not have the resources to undertake it alone. Besides having to cope with the tremendous societal, cultural, and economic pressures of the day, each person has his own inner limits in coping with each relationship in a family.

Very often, two parents cannot cope with each other in any constructive way. In this case, their ability to cope with their children will be impaired. Parental giving up is only one outcome of this impairment. It is perhaps one of the most malignant and most indicative of the hollowness of the marital relationship.

How to Meet It

How to meet this? First, you need to know that, out of an exasperated sense of failure (always associated with guilt and self-hatred), you have given up on your youngster and have thereby actually ousted him from your sphere of kindly concern and interest. Second, you need to know that you are, in all probability, deeply angry with him as well as with yourself and your spouse. Third, you need to know that your anger makes you feel guilty that you are capable of harboring such feelings toward your own child. I am not talking about the towering rage that parents may feel toward their offspring upon occasion. I am speaking of the persistent, pervasive, bitter, *cold* anger that stems from deep disappointment, frustration, and a sense of helplessness. Fourth, your attempts at expiation are an outcome of this feeling of guilt, and not a new, spontaneous interest in the child. Fifth, the self-harassment you visit upon yourself makes you so uncomfortable, despairing, and anxious that you have to remove yourself physically as well as emotionally, in order to obtain some respite. Sixth, this makes you feel even more self-depreciatory; and finally, when the child leaves home, a sense of relief is coupled with a sense of outraged despair, further guilt, but also sometimes a renewed intention to do something constructive to bring about a change in the situation.

When the parent comes to any appreciation of these factors, he is ready indeed to be of help to himself as a person, and to his child as a parent. Without these realizations, efforts are very often mere vigorous flappings about that further obscure an already obfuscated problem.

CHAPTER XVI

Permissiveness

PERMISSIVENESS IS A STATE OF BEING which must be a totality, even if just for a minute, or it is not true permissiveness. One either permits or one does not. There are no halfways. You can place limits on the duration of your permissiveness, but there can be no limit on the quality of permissiveness.

Part-Time Permissiveness

Theoretically, one could be permissive all the time. In practice, however, parents find constant permissiveness incompatible with realistic family living. Each parent has to establish an individual program with respect to time available and specific areas that can be dealt with permissively. Permissiveness makes sense, therefore, as a part-time feature of family living, determined largely by appropriateness, convenience, personality of parents, and time available for various activities.

You can be permissive one month at a time or during summer vacations. You can be permissive on Mondays and Fridays, weekends only, holidays only, three to five every day, five minutes before each meal—whenever you decide. Your children will quickly learn the regulations, or exceptions to them, as long as you know them yourself and do not equivocate.

A family with three very young children had moved to a country home where they kept a freezer in the barn. It was soon stocked with all kinds of goodies, including three gallons of ice cream. The children were told that, with prescribed boundaries, they had the run of the place. Coming upon the freezer, they ogled when they saw all that ice cream within easy grasp. Quivering with anticipation, they ran to their mother, shouting, "Mommy, Mommy! What are the rules for the ice cream?"

What is more important than *when* you are permissive is *how* you are permissive. Ideally, your permissiveness should be a total commitment when you feel that you want to be permissive, even for a few minutes. Parents who want to be and who consider themselves permissive get into a bind when they think that, to be permissive at all, they must be so 100 percent of the time. That's being just as rigid as never being permissive. The essence of permissiveness is flexibility, for it is often impractical as well as impossible to be consistently permissive.

An element of permissiveness is freedom—freedom to be or not to be permissive. Put another way, each parent should be able to *permit* himself to decide the time, place, and extent of his permissiveness. Otherwise, one is bound by the rigidity of *having to be permissive at all times*, just as one is bound by any other compulsive act. The word itself does not make for the condition, for permissiveness is actually a feeling.

All the Way

Permissiveness is a state of being, then, combining heart, mind, and soul in a total commitment of feeling, principle, and practice. Often parents do not understand this. They believe that one can be permissive no matter how one feels. That is not so, for feeling and being are inseparable. However, one can *act* permissively no matter what one feels or is; and that's all it is, an act. That's all right too, for parents choose to act in many ways they believe conducive to family well-being. But they need to be aware that this particular act is a conscious one and that it may be inconsistent with how they feel. A typical example of such a discrepancy is the courteous manner of one toward another when in fact that person would like to punch the other's face.

A woman tells her child, "You can have eggs, cereal, or candy. Take your pick, I don't care which." If that parent is *feeling* permissive, she will accept any choice the child makes. If she is *acting* permissively, she may be annoyed if her child chooses candy. Nevertheless, she goes through the motions of permissiveness for her own reasons. That is her prerogative.

This is what I believe that permissiveness is in the context of family living. Test it for yourself. It requires careful self-examination and honesty to decide how able you are to be permissive. If you can accept unequivocally your child's response to an issue, you are being permissive on that one issue. It doesn't include any other issue. And remember that accepting does mean liking or approving.

If you are trying to be permissive, but feel some conflicts about it, you are not being permissive. I would consider this as *pseudo-permissiveness*. This too has to be recognized for what it is, for this is the form of permissiveness that causes parents so much trouble. They believe that they have been permissive all along and never recognize that their true feelings were opposed to what they were saying and doing.

Often this ambivalence makes for oversolicitous parents. They sense that they are feeling too directive. Believing that this is being a "bad" parent, they bend over backward to be good, kind, and permissive parents, mistakenly equating goodness and kindness with permissiveness. Yet their feelings cannot be adequately suppressed, so they are always at odds with themselves.

The fact is that the permissive parent is not necessarily the "good" parent—or the "bad" one. Similarly, the authoritarian parent is not necessarily the "bad" parent or the "good" one. Parenting cannot be evaluated by the degree of permissiveness involved. That is only one aspect of parental *style* with children. It is by no means the entire fact of parenting.

You can see why it is difficult to be really permissive, even on a single issue. A working mother who lived near a lake was permissive about letting her four-and-a-half-year-old son go swimming. As long as he wore his life jacket, it didn't matter to her which beach the child went to, what the weather was like, or how deep the water was. There was no checking on him, and there was no anxiety on anyone's part.

Whenever the boy was hungry, usually between eleven-thirty and one, he would come home, drink a glass of milk which he poured for himself, eat a sandwich and piece of cake his mother had left him, and return to the lake.

This, it seems, could be called permissiveness in the context of swimming activities at a particular period in this child's life. He was not a neglected child in any sense, for his mother's interest in him was a deep and affectionate one. I must add, however, that it is highly unusual to find such trust and total commitment to an agreed-upon arrangement. Most parents would find it impossible to make this kind of commitment. Perhaps this woman's necessity drove her to extend the boundaries of what she could permit without a sense of conflict or guilt.

I'm trying to demonstrate what permissiveness may be, as practiced in *one* family, and why most of the permissiveness as practiced in many families is really pseudo-permissiveness. Real permissiveness is a commitment to freedom of choice at any given moment within a particular context. It does not have to pervade every aspect of your parenting.

A set of parents had two-year-old twins and lived in a fine apartment building. They had divided their large living room with a three-foot-high divider and gate. Children, furniture, toys, tricycles, etc., were kept behind the divider, as were two comfortable old chairs for the parents. The children used them for climbing. No attempt was made to keep the area looking attractive. These parents gave their children to understand that "anything went" in that area. There were no rules or regulations. They had decided to follow this plan for several years, after which they would decorate their living room as they wished and do away with the free space. As long as these parents felt no resentment or anger toward their children, this form of permissiveness fulfilled the requirement of an unequivocal commitment to a plan of action.

Pseudo-Permissiveness

Where there is a discrepancy between deed and feeling, severe tension may arise. An eighteen-month-old child, Carrie, is being taught by her parents, who regard themselves as permissive, to sit at the table "like a big girl." She is put on a chair with several telephone books. (Have you ever sat on several telephone books?) She wriggles around until one book slips to the floor. She shifts to her knees and rests her elbows on the table. "Isn't that cute?" her parents say. She smiles in response, and, encouraged by their approval of her new position, continues to explore. Previously she had only been in a high chair or on her parents' laps.

She touches everything within reach, knocking things over in the process. Permissiveness still reigns, but not in Mommy's heart. She's getting a little uptight—there are glasses of wine on the table. One little foot is drawn up and planted on the telephone book. As Carrie balances herself on the table, up goes that tiny rump, quickly followed by little feet. Now she's on all fours. Isn't she adorable? If you are being a totally permissive parent at that moment, you will think so.

But if you feel a flash of annoyance, that's the signal (identification) you are no longer feeling totally permissive. You are no longer permitting Carrie freedom of action at the dinner table which, of course, you don't have to. Your permissive feeling has come to an abrupt end. If you can identify your feelings accurately at this moment, Carrie may be tucked under one arm and installed in her old high chair. This may be accomplished without any commotion, depending on your approach. With an unequivocal and nondisapproving attitude, your shift may be made without psychological injury to Carrie.

Having started something, however, some parents feel they must finish it. They feel they might "lose face" in the eyes of their children, especially older ones, if they don't follow through. But Carrie has no way of knowing when your experiment was supposed to end. She doesn't know you were hoping she'd stay on the chair during the whole meal. For her, the experiment can end anytime, as long as you don't let her feel she's been a "bad girl" when you decide to end it. If you are angry and sweep her off the table with an angry gesture or angry tone and facial expression, she may become frightened and cry. You think she's crying because you removed her. Perhaps so. But it's more likely that she's frightened by something in your attitude.

Some parents may disagree. "Don't you think she should be put in her high chair now?" "Oh no, she's OK. Let her stay. She's enjoying herself." Carrie looks from one to the other. What's this? Mommy looks strange and Daddy's still smiling. She heaves a fat little knee onto the table, then another, and then crawls across the table to him.

Mommy is having a fit. "Oh, look at what she's done now!" "Leave her alone, can't you? She's having a good time. Here's Daddy's little girl. What did she do? Climb across the table to Daddy? No, no (smile, smile), she mustn't climb on the table."

This is another example of the double message. Smiling means approval, or yes. No means no. So this little girl is already having to translate her parents' double message. What is it? No/yes? Tables are for climbing. Tables are not for climbing. Mommy says it's bad to climb on tables. What can she make of that? She has to make a decision. If climbing is more fun, that will be her decision. Now try to keep her off.

Another couple may permit her to climb, crawl, sit, eat, and play among the havoc she has wrought on the tabletop. If you can really permit this and not feel angry with your child, that is an example of permissiveness. Remember, no one says you have to like that approach, only that you can permit it unequivocally if you expect to be actually permissive with the decision you have made.

Another couple may let her sit on the table and say how cute she is, and think how permissive they are. Yet an angry tension arises and will at one point come out—perhaps not in an angry burst, but as a quiet, "Now's the time to get off the table," as if everything is great. The discrepancy between an angry feeling and letting her stay invalidates the permissive stance.

A woman tells us, "I don't expect my children to help clean up. I prefer to have them spend the time on their homework. Anyway, they're more of a hindrance than a help." Then that parent turns to someone else and adds, "You'd think they'd help me once in a while. I don't mind doing it, but what do they think this is—a hotel?"

Some young teen-agers often speak rudely to their parents, who seem not to be bothered by it. They try to espouse the principle of free speech and all that, and are worried that their children will become inhibited if they tell them to "knock it off." Such parents consider themselves permissive parents.

I heard of a teen-age boy who began to appear at dinner looking more and more unkempt and wearing fewer and fewer clothes. His mother urged the father to "speak to him." The father refused to be put in the role of disciplinarian, but agreed that the boy looked disgraceful.

They were unhappy about it and embarrassed whenever visitors came into the house. The condition lasted some time, until finally the mother decided to take steps. One evening she came to the table in bra and panties, with her hair hanging over her face. The boy was outraged and said so. She told him, "If you can come to the table in your undershorts, so can I. Maybe next time I'll come topless!"

That was a dramatic alternative she offered, but it proved effective. The boy knew they weren't enthralled with his appearance, but he had had no inkling of the intensity of their feelings about something so inconsequential to him.

One can argue that it makes no difference how a boy looks in his own home or even elsewhere. Some parents truly could not care less. Many do care, but feel compelled to go through their permissive "charade." Need I repeat that there is no feeling of permissiveness in the hearts of these parents?

Some parents of teen-agers have reluctantly said that they are willing to go along with the new social and sexual mores of young people in the interest of being permissive. But their reluctance gives away what they really feel. They are not permitting anything. They are putting up with something they feel helpless to do anything about. True permissiveness is a straightforward attitude. While one may not like something, one may permit it and lose no sleep over it.

The attitude of putting up with something causes resentment and it results in feelings of parental failure. Sleep *is* lost. I'm not saying you should or shouldn't be one or the other. I'm only campaigning for *knowing* your true feelings about the troublesome issues which arise in your family.

Consistency

Consistent permissiveness in making decisions is rare, and with good reason. There are too many other areas of need in families where children are not equipped for or interested in making decisions. And parents of young children do not want to wait around until a child decides how or when to eat, sleep, dress, bathe, etc.

A completely permissive household would have to be oriented about the children's wants, needs, and whims. Few parents could tolerate that for long without feeling put upon. Consistent permissiveness, then, is neither practical nor necessary. In addition, it would present the child with an utter distortion of what a broader world is. The child from the totally permissive home might have a hard time in school, with peers and others outside of his home. He might not be comfortable outside the home and might have to remain in it more of the time to feel safe.

You have read of unusual cases where a young man or woman stayed at home with parents for a number of years without going out of the house at all. Possibly one of the factors contributing to this inability to venture outside was the feeling that only parents could permit what the individual felt he needed to survive.

Parents may be completely permissive in circumscribed areas. Mother may have hers and Father may have his, and they do not have to coincide. Children quickly learn that Father permits certain things that Mother does not, and vice versa. When they are with Father, they can have hot dogs; when with Mother, it's hamburgers. There is no conflict in such discrepancies as long as Father and Mother don't wage relentless battles over them. Father's permissiveness does not have to be approved by Mother. She merely has to permit him to exercise his brand, while she has her own.

Each parent may grumble warmly and good-naturedly about the other. "I don't know why your mother lets you play in the rain. I certainly wouldn't allow it." Father is clearly accepting Mother's idiosyncrasy but not liking it very much. Children tolerate such differences well. What they cannot tolerate are bitter, ugly arguments that reveal their parents' mutual resentment.

Ideally, when neither can permit the other's permissiveness on particular issues, a compromise has to be reached. The children will be fine if the parents can arrive at some workable agreement. Children are able to respond well if a parent says, "You know, I don't care if you do that or not. But your mother has told you that she doesn't want you to, so I'll go along with her decision." Brief, clear, serious, simple, straight, unequivocal.

Responsible Love

The following is an account of a young woman, Anne, with whom I worked for some time, who had tried to follow a permissive approach in her child rearing. By the time her daughter Tara was three years old, the child was having frequent, severe anxiety attacks which she expressed in the form of tantrums.

Anne felt totally incompetent to deal with these attacks. In the interest of permissiveness, she had tried to go along, hoping that someday the tantrums would cease. She did not realize that she really was a pseudo-permissive parent, and could not understand why her child was reacting in this way.

Anne would stand by helplessly while her three-year-old threw herself down, screaming and banging her head on the floor. She knew that if she touched her, the child would scream all the louder. If she tried to pick her up, she would be kicked and scratched. She felt an anger, born of helplessness, rising. She knew that if she became angry enough, she might scream and strike also. She was in dread of this; how could a grown woman justify striking a child? She had never struck Tara. But the indignity of it—for both of them—carrying on like that!

This happened again and again. Lately it was happening more often, several times a day. According to the babysitter, it seemed to happen with greatest intensity when Anne or her husband was with Tara. The sitter remarked that Tara had had minor tantrums only a few times when she was alone with the child. Anne had spoken with her husband often about the problem. He kept saying that Tara would grow out of it. They often ended a discussion about it by screaming at each other, because Anne expected him to do something definitive, and he, poor man, didn't know what to do any more than she did. Later, she would think ruefully, "No wonder the baby has tantrums. The two of us have them!"

Whenever Tara stopped screaming, exhausted and perspiring, Anne would gather the child into her arms and they would sit quietly about ten minutes. She'd wipe Tara's tears, stroke her head, and coo to her, not referring to the episode. Sometimes Tara would put her chubby little arms around Anne's neck. When she did this, tears of sadness and frustration came to Anne's eyes. At some point, Tara would slip off her lap and go about her three-year-old business. It never ceased to amaze Anne how Tara seemed to turn it on and off.

It was always something very insignificant that turned the child on. The very least frustration and she was off. "But," Anne reasoned, "I can't watch every little thing I say and do." That would be impossible and make her tense beyond endurance. She knew the child was sensitive. But she didn't have to be *that* sensitive! How will she get along in the world if she can't tolerate the slightest frustration?

Anne's pediatrician knew of these tantrums because the baby had one each time Anne took her for a checkup. The doctor was used to such goings on, and, of course, here too the baby would eventually stop. In fact, Anne had noticed that the baby had a tantrum in almost any new situation, besides the daily ones at home. It embarrassed her, and she was ashamed to discuss it with her friends or neighbors.

Realizing that such behavior could become a more serious problem in later years, Anne came to believe that she would certainly be remiss as a parent if she didn't try to end the tantrums. She had visions of Tara as a recluse in fear of strangers. She shuddered at the idea of being an old woman with a forty-year-old daughter hiding whenever the doorbell rang. "What a horrible thought! I've *got* to do something," she told herself.

Gradually, Anne realized that it was up to her—not her pediatrician or her husband or her neighbors—to find a way of helping her child. She did not know how to do it; she only knew that the responsibility was hers. All the while she had been expecting someone to advise her, to "do" for her. Alone, she had not felt adequate to the task.

One day, as Anne watched Tara pounding her head on the floor, she discovered a new sense of responsibility. Without pausing to reflect on her actions, she picked Tara up, held her firmly so she couldn't strike or kick, and carried her into the bedroom. She felt the little arms and legs straining against her. How small Tara was, how really helpless. How could the child possibly hurt her mother? Anne realized how much stronger she was than the child. It wasn't true that little children could wriggle out of your arms, as long as you held them properly and purposefully. Only if you were afraid of being hurt and held them loosely were they sometimes unmanageable.

She had held Tara for some minutes when she felt the struggling subside. As the child relaxed, Anne loosened her hold. Within another minute or so, Tara was crying, spent, in her mother's arms, which were by this time cuddling the child. Surprised at this outcome, Anne said nothing, but swayed gently back and forth. Great! she thought. I actually stopped the tantrum! Pity and anger had vanished. She felt a rush of tenderness and a sense of accomplishment in helping Tara get over her panic.

It took Anne some time to discover why she had wept so many times. She had felt so sorry for Tara, for herself, for the mess she had apparently made of parenthood. Where was the joy of having children? The pleasure in watching them grow? She had played with Tara and they laughed and had fun. But so much of the time she had been tense and uncertain. After her first victory, Anne kept on with the same method. She noted that the time that Tara struggled against her grew shorter and shorter. One day, when Tara became upset and was about to start screaming, Anne said firmly, "Now Tara, please don't start anything. I'm too busy to bother with you just now." Tara's eyes grew large and teary as she looked at Anne in bewilderment. Anne had rarely used that tone; she had usually been more pleading. At this moment the phone rang and she went to answer it. That was all. There was no tantrum. This was a surprise indeed!

The next time a similar situation arose, Anne did the same thing, realizing that firmness had done the trick. Also, the ringing telephone had deprived her of the chance to relent. It then occurred to Anne that perhaps she was being more honest with Tara in conveying clearly that she didn't want to put up with a tantrum. Previously, she had always felt obliged to be relentlessly patient, and to behave as if the tantrum were acceptable. Now, Tara was more at ease with her mother's new, unequivocal attitude.

Anne was not miraculously relieved of the problem, however. Tara had occasional tantrums during the next few years, but they were within tolerable limits. Anne found that the sooner she disengaged herself from the child by leaving the room to use the telephone, etc., the sooner the tantrum subsided. For many years, she would speak very firmly to Tara on such occasions. Most of the time, the tantrum was replaced by a not completely unreasonable shouting back and forth. As Tara grew older, Anne learned better and better what some of Tara's fears were and how to deal with them. Years later, mother and daughter were good friends, with only the ordinary family arguments occurring now and then.

Anne's effort helped her to deal with her sense of parental incompetence. Having won that battle, she was freed of much of her own anger and guilt. But the quality of her love for her child had to change before she could succeed. It had to change from that of a parent who regarded her child as a toy that could easily break to a realization that Tara was not a fragile doll but a person who deserved the best her mother had to offer. Then Anne was able to deal with the child and love her in a new way, knowing that loving children without a sense of responsibility toward them and their development could do serious harm.

CHAPTER XVII

Who's Ready for What?

WHAT A LOT OF POPPYCOCK one hears about being *ready* to have children! Is anyone ready for the Olympics without ever having been in a contest?

No one is ever ready because no one knows what it is to have a child, care for it, and rear it until the child is born and you are there with the baby twenty-four hours a day, seven days a week. Sure, sure, you can always get a baby nurse or a babysitter and have your time off. But do you know how you will feel when you are off somewhere having a "good time"? If you call home, perhaps you're not really having such a good time. If you don't call, you think, What kind of a parent am I that I don't call home and find out if my baby is still alive?

You can only say in retrospect that you were or were not "ready" at the time you had a child. If parents were honest, many would probably answer that they were not ready, simply because it's not possible to be so. Would you be ready to play in a concert if you had never played before?

More pertinent questions to be asked of people who are contemplating having children are the following: Are you willing to have a child?

Are you willing to subject yourself for the rest of your "natural life" to the mysteries, complexities, vicissitudes, pleasures and satisfactions of having a child?

More Than One

Maybe a parent who has a first child is "ready" for a second. Yet many parents I have questioned could not possibly have been "ready" for the amazing series of events that are set into motion by the birth of a second child. Some parents believe a second child might require twice or even half (!) the effort of a first. Maybe. And if so—cheers! In my experience with young mothers, I find that they feel the second child is anywhere from four to twelve times the work of the first. I don't mean that they are complaining—I'm only pointing out that the involvements with more than one child tend to snowball.

Parents who have had two or three children may be "ready" to have a fourth, fifth, or sixth, because such parents, assuming that they have been even minimally successful, have acquired such experience and such wisdom that anything they said on the subject would be important. I must admit that I have had little experience with such parents; they rarely come to my attention. Either there aren't very many around anymore (which I really don't believe) or they have little need to come to my attention either as discussion group members or as psychiatric patients. The few with whom I have spoken have impressed me with their practical good sense, attitude of calm authority, and sense of humor. I suspect, however, that such parents would have these same qualities whether they had one, two, or five children.

If couples cannot be "ready" for parenthood, should they then not have children? That would hardly be a solution. Besides, one can carry the readiness bit *ad absurdum*. Who can be said to be ready for marriage? Who is ready to be President? *Willing* seems the more pertinent word. Readiness for parenting, perhaps, can only be evaluated in retrospect.

Let's Face It

This line of reasoning may raise hackles. My purpose is to raise questions—for those who are satisfied with mere pronouncements of readiness. Such pronouncements run the real risk of leading to false expectations of oneself. "I was so ready. What ever happened that I have failed so miserably to fulfill my expectations?" Expectations born of mere pronouncements of readiness may lead to disappointment, to marital stress, and to parent-child frustration.

My wish is for a little more realism in approaching parenthood. No mother or father can know enough, before actually being there, to be ready for that job. If we can accept that we don't know something, we are in a better position to learn. We are more open to watching and listening to our little teachers who will tell us every day what needs must be known so that they can grow and show us, by their example, the wonders of life that we so readily forfeit.

With all due respect to the woman who raised eight younger brothers and sisters, with or without Mother's help, I say she is more experienced in the *mechanics* of mothering than in the totality of parenting. Even she would find enormous gaps in her knowledge and experience which she could never have predicted on the basis of her previous mothering experience. One can only grow into parenthood and keep growing and growing and growing. There is no end.

Not Ready

Years ago, couples used to wait until they could "afford" to get married. After marriage, they waited until they could "afford" to have children. Curiously enough, birthrates in the depression years were kept low, with only rhythm (poorly understood), interrupted coitus (chancey, at best), and the condom (every man's best friend). Birth control "pills" were unknown. I suppose that demonstrates that if you really want to do something, you just do it.

Then the "affluent society" came along, and money was no object in many families. Finally, one didn't have to wait for anything. Children were wonderful, adorable, and in the affluent family they would not be deprived of anything. Everyone loved them and wanted them. Everyone was ready for children. What a myth that was!

For all that material readiness, we have seen that the great enthusiasms and expectations of those years did not produce children that gave parents unbounded joy. With all that money, other problems began to offset the apparent benefits of affluence. Gradually, a constellation of negative outcomes gave rise to the questions: What went wrong? Why aren't parents and children, with all the material benefits at hand, delighted with one another?

The Affluent Syndrome

With toys and other objects, parents have provided the means for the gradual separation of their offspring from themselves. Objects have literally been placed between parent and child. The pile has become so high that neither can see the other over it. Seeing the pile instead of the person, each has come to know the other through it. In a sense, the pile of objects has come to symbolize a person, much as the wire monkey mothers in psychological experiments come to be regarded as real mothers by the baby monkeys.

With greater affluence, a room for each child and for each function came into existence. (I believe in separate rooms for children!) Then it was a transistor radio for each child. They were held at the ear, as one strolled along, obliterating casual conversation, other sounds, and a good many sights. Then came stereo. Fifteen-year-olds suddenly needed two large boxes to listen to a rock record. Other equipment and accouterments followed. With all this abundance in each child's room, he could easily entertain all day there. No one was left to occupy the family room. And then the really "super" touch—one's own telephone. A completely self-sufficient unit, requiring only occasional foragings for food and drink.

Repercussions

Now start the complaints, questions, and doubts. Should friends of the opposite sex be entertained in your child's bedroom? Everything is there for this purpose. Should your child be using the phone at 2 A.M., keeping some other teen-ager up who also has a bedside telephone? If you are in no quandary over these questions, there is no problem. But if you are, what is to be done? Sometimes very little. Sometimes a great deal, if one is willing to alter one's life-style to some extent.

The most reasonable way to handle such problems, if indeed they are problems, is to avoid them in the first place. (See Prevention, Chapter I.) Here are a few suggestions for doing so.

1) Small but separate rooms for children, rooms which are cozy and delightful but not big enough to contain everything the child needs for such a degree of self-sufficiency and entertainment.

2) A living room for *living,* with some of that equipment in it.

3) A kitchen children can use. Youngsters enjoy being in and about the kitchen.

4) One good radio. One TV set. One telephone with some outlets judiciously placed.

5) If possible, a small playroom (family room) for entertaining peers.

6) Not so much housekeeping assistance that children have no opportunity to share the chores.

7) Occasional conversations (planned if necessary) with children for purposes of guidance. *Not* long lectures. (See Chapters II, III, IV.)

8) Establishing boundaries and limits, if possible, before an issue becomes a point of contention or a play for power.

9) Family meetings, in keeping with the family's life-style, to discuss matters of family concern.

10) Providing children with a certain amount of repetitiousness and predictability.

11) Reserving decisions for parents that are reasonably in their province. Using appropriate opportunities for youngsters to make decisions.

Separateness Is Up

Affluence is only one factor causing a loss of a sense of family, in that it has made isolation of family members an actuality. Money for babysitters made it possible for adults to enjoy themselves regularly, unhampered by their children. No doubt it's more fun that way for some parents. Money for housekeepers made possible frequent vacations for adults. Well-equipped rooms made it easy to send children there when they got on elders' nerves, or were just in the way. Exotic teen-age summer vacations took children off for weeks at a time.

I am not saying that adults should not play, talk, and relate to their peers without their children around all the time. But I am saying that too many children must have gotten the message that parents did not want them around at all. Children are often difficult to take, it is true. But because it was so convenient to send them off, many parents missed the opportunity of watching their children grow in a daily, hour-by-hour, intimate fashion.

By the time children are ten years old, they have their own world, and should to some extent. But Mommy and Daddy may very well not play an important part in that world anymore. This is especially true as children become more complex personalities and require even greater sensitivity and understanding than when they were younger. Parents who feel they cannot cope often make no attempt to do so. Children are the losers; but they try to learn to be emotionally self-sufficient. To them, this seems to be what Mommy and Daddy want. And it may be true. True or not, however, teen-agers need some person to feel close to. Another teen-ager in the same position may be sought. Together they form a mutually dependent, iron-clad unit which some parents find so exasperating.

The point is that too much physical separation, in addition to other factors, gives neither child nor parent the opportunity to learn to live with each other. As the years pass, it becomes more difficult, and they try less. The time is reached in late adolescence when family members seem to be strangers living in the same house, resigned to a bloodless status quo, because no one had sufficient awareness to try to make something richer of their shared existence.

Together or Not Together

On the other hand, people cannot always be with others; this is true also for parents and their children. At times, most of us need absolute solitude, when we are not being depended upon by anyone or anything —where there is no responsibility requirement; where we are, in a sense, completely isolated. Parents who do not offer themselves this respite develop an insidious sense of being intruded upon, and an ensuing irritation. When the intrusive factor is the child, unbeknownst to the parent, resentment builds up slowly over the years. It is one (only one) of the factors responsible for an inexplicable feeling of outrage in response to some of the small absurdities of our children's behavior.

Parents sometimes feel that they are "selfish" if they indulge themselves this need, unaware that it is as essential to their well-being as fresh air and food. The parent who sees to such basic needs can be more relaxed with a child and be in a better position to attend to him.

Every good thing in the world can be exaggerated. Then it may become toxic. This is true of drugs, which may be lifesaving or death dealing, according to how they are used. It is true of alcohol, with its helpfully relaxing qualities, but which may cause family disintegration, psychoses, and many social and economic ills.

Family togetherness is a beautiful concept, if judiciously entertained. If, for example, once a month a family were to do something together with attendant pleasure, it would probably give children a feeling of belonging to a cozy family unit, of being wanted by Mother and Father, and of having a sense of security. When families really enjoy frequent and regular family outings, that is all to the good.

But where parents feel that every day should be family day, yet do not truly enjoy it, tensions resulting from *obligatory togetherness* are bound to arise. Tension is caused by irritation, impatience, annoyance, pains and aches, fatigue, all contributing to common irrational responses, clearly inappropriate to inconsequential child demands.

Parents must find out where they stand on togetherness. Then it is necessary to feel free to indulge that position to the extent that it is compatible with family harmony. If you feel that you want to have nothing to do with your family, you are obliged to raise some questions for yourself. Why did you have children in the first place? If you have no interest in children—and only the most honest and courageous of parents can admit this—you are obligated to find a way to deal with the matter.

If that is your dilemma to a greater or lesser degree, it must be discussed with your spouse, unless he (or she) is completely unsympathetic. (Surprisingly, mothers are found among this group as well as fathers.) A *modus operandi* must be found. If family togetherness is an utter bore or chore, the partner deserves to know it. Plans can then be made to spare the parent who suffers most. Remember, however, that one partner never suffers alone. When one suffers, the rest of the family catches the flak.

But that is only the first step. The bored parent cannot expect to be entirely relieved of responsibility. Free choice or not, parenthood is yours, and unless you decide to leave the family, a compromise has to be made. Some steps have to be taken to maintain the most health-ful possible level of family integrity. The bored parent must review personal needs for his composure, and be willing to fit into a weekly or monthly routine time that will be relegated as family time.

Family togetherness often fails because only the motions are gone through. The body is there, but mind, heart, and spirit are elsewhere. This is not only a waste of time; it can have destructive outcomes. While it might be better than nothing in some instances, your physical presence is not enough. Your child needs more of you. No great demand is being made on your time. The only demand is that when you decide to be together, you try to be as wholehearted about it as possible.

The actual activity must be carefully planned. If it is dull, look for something that is fun. It may be just poking around the house. Don't worry about your children's response. Children are delightful in that they are so adaptable. Many children can be counted on to enjoy most things you do, as long as you are really enjoying them in a recogniz-able way. Unfortunately, this does not work both ways. But children seem to enjoy their parents' genuine pleasure, whether it's reading, fishing, sports, dancing, talking, sightseeing, or whatever. Although we do not often enough take enough cues from them, they generally take all cues we give them.

So find your own level of pleasure that can be shared with your youngsters. If you enjoy nothing, experiment. The chances are good that you will discover a way that will bring mutual pleasure, if you try. Freed of the obligation to believe that you must be an enthusiastic parent so much of your time, you may find yourself a more relaxed one. Then—who knows?—something nice might happen!

CHAPTER XVIII

Sex Education
for the Under Six

NO MATTER HOW EFFECTIVE sex education programs are in the school system, you still have the responsibility of dispensing some kind of information to your child before he begins school. But many parents find this age group more difficult to inform than older groups.

The Easy Way

There is, however, an easy way to inform children on sex matters *in which they are interested.* I emphasize that phrase because that is what makes it so easy. You don't have to be an anatomist, or know all the proper terms to satisfy the average young child's curiosity. The *easy way* can be used by the least informed, naïve parent, or by the most sophisticated, educated one.

If you are uninformed or very young and don't want to be bothered reading the manuals, this could be an easy way out. It may surprise you to know that many parents feel no great pressure to inform themselves in order to teach their children.

Short, Straight, Now

First, there are five basic principles which must be adhered to in using the easy way. They are brevity, honesty, directness, pertinence and immediacy. In other words, *short, straight, and now.* Maybe we can call this the SSN technique—everything nowadays seems to be designated by letters. Incidentally, this technique is great for almost any form of initial communication with youngsters of all ages. I stress initial because if your child shows a willingness to discuss, then, of course, you can be much more long-winded if you feel like it.

Twelve-Word Rule

By short, I mean exactly that. Questions from children under six can often be answered with three, six, or twelve words, unless the subject matter absolutely demands more. Anything beyond twelve words is often an indulgence on your part. Many people like to talk and will *overtalk* when given the opportunity.

If you have a child who talks a great deal and it bothers you sometimes, it's more than likely that you are the kind of parent who talks to him a great deal. That talking is usually done to inform about the cow, the daffodil, the chipmunk, and other encyclopedic subjects. These too are examples of *parental input.*

I am not suggesting that parents should not talk to or educate their youngsters. Talking to them is essential for their development as articulate persons. But I am pointing out something about the quantity of your input, and your reaction when you feel that they never shut up. Possibly you talk a great deal and they are merely imitating.

Straight

The concept of honesty is a difficult one for many parents. They may feel that only informed, elaborate answers to important questions are honest ones. I know that *you* know better. But I'm talking about feelings. You are sometimes not satisfied with a short, straight answer. I'll illustrate presently.

An honest answer can be given with one word, or with "I don't know," or "I don't want to tell you—I can't explain it—let's ask Daddy—let's look it up—I'll tell you later," and so on. If you disagree that these can be called honest answers, can you call them dishonest? As I've said, this matter of honesty and dishonesty can be sticky. You have to square your answers with yourself. Insofar as you can say what you think is honest, or straight, to that extent you will probably feel comfortable with what you are saying.

Straightness includes being direct, or to the point. In this context, I am reminded of the old story where five-year-old Jimmy asked his mother where he came from and she gave him a long spiel about the birds and bees. After she finished, he said, "OK, Mommy, but John comes from Cincinnati. Where do I come from?"

When your child asks you a specific question, answer that question *only.* This makes it possible for you to be brief. If you answer the question and then try to elaborate, you cannot do it under twelve words. The more you say, the more trouble you get into, especially if you're not well informed. You need no apology to yourself for knowing no more, nor for saying more than is necessary.

Now

If you follow the principles of brevity, directness, pertinence, and honesty, the *now* is the easiest part. If you feel that a dissertation is required, then you have to prepare yourself, so you cannot answer now. But if you decide to meet your child's question with a twelve-word answer or less, you can hardly use the excuse that you don't have the time to answer now. Stretching it, one word takes less than a second. So it would take roughly twelve seconds for an answer. Even if you used a hundred words, that would be something like one and one-half minutes plus maybe another thirty seconds for pauses and for thinking. When don't you have two minutes to answer your children's question? Any question?

The way to test these principles is to try them. See for yourself if you can use them, and if your child can be satisfied. Young children are usually not nearly as long-winded as their parents. I have found them to be satisfied with the briefest of answers as long as the answer refers to their question and they don't have to wait for it. If they want more information, they will ask the next question and the next. Each one may be answered in the same way—briefly, honestly, directly, pertinently, and immediately. If you have answered one or more questions already and don't want to answer any more, your child can usually accept something like, "That's enough questions for now." Most children are more reasonable than parents expect. Even teenagers and young adults are, as long as you are reasonable yourself and don't get hysterical when you are frightened, angry, or anxious.

Wait

I have left pertinence to the last, because all the other principles are predicated upon this one. By pertinence I mean giving the information asked for. *Wait for the question.* This relieves you of the responsibility of seizing opportunities for educating, or of manufacturing these opportunities. The chances are excellent that your child will someday ask you where he came from or how babies are born. You can relax until then. If he doesn't ask, it probably hasn't occurred to the child yet.

I don't really believe that healthy development will be impaired if a child doesn't have these answers before going to school—unless, of course, there are other factors impairing that development. There may very well be better methods for disseminating sex education to the under-six group. But I haven't promised the best; only one easy way. Let me add, however, that it has been demonstrated to be effective, and parents seem to be very comfortable with it.

Easy Attitudes

Perhaps the most important point in the entire matter of sex education for youngsters of any age is your *attitude* regarding 1) the information; 2) your delivery; and 3) your child's reception. As the provider of sex information, some parents are immediately embarrassed. This embarrassment may not be identified as such by an under-six child, but he senses something unusual and may be puzzled. Puzzled or not, don't think that he is not registering something about your feeling. That's all part of your output. If he is puzzled, it may be because your embarrassment is so irrelevant as far as he is concerned. If you can recognize its irrelevance yourself, you may be able to avoid beginning an association of embarrassment and sex in your child's mind.

Some parents feel a little silly when giving such information and convey this with inappropriate smiles or giggles or wisecracks. This silliness may or may not be a manifestation of embarrassment. In any event, this too is irrelevant to the child. If he were to ask, "Is it going to rain?" and you responded with a silly attitude, it would hardly be appropriate. Again, if silliness is your response, your child may be apt to associate that feeling with sex. It's certainly possible that in the context of discussing sex with peers later on, he'll get silly with them. You don't have to be the one to initiate that in him.

Some parents respond with delight to their children's questions regarding sex. These are often well-educated parents who respond joyfully to their children's curiosity about anything. (Not all well-educated parents do this.) Whether the child asks, "How do men get to the moon?" or "How do babies get born?" these parents revel in the child's curiosity.

That's fine—but how much delight is necessary? Don't feel put down. If you are really and truly delighted with something your child does, and express it, I don't see how it can hurt him. But I have often observed a put-on delight which is neither necessary nor useful. Furthermore, it provides your child with a model for the expression of insincere feelings. Here again we may have the problem of a double message. To act and sound as if something is delighting you, when you don't care all that much, presents your child with false premises for your words. Don't accept this idea if you don't like it. But please consider it.

Most children's questions do not require a celebration. An acknowledgment and an appropriate response are usually sufficient. Would you want them to feel special in asking a question that several million children ask every year? Consider this carefully if your answer is yes. If your child feels that he can get a rise out of you by asking questions about sex (and needs, for whatever reasons, that special rise) then he might just develop a morbid curiosity about the subject. That isn't going to do him much good at that or any other stage.

Perhaps the most common parental response to questions about sex, until a few years back, was mild panic. This was often caused by thoughts of "Now what do I do? What do I say? How am I going to get out of this?" This reaction occurred because parents 1) didn't have any information at all (they thought), and 2) they weren't sure whether or not they should answer such questions. Such a reaction is not so common now; but it isn't uncommon either. If you fall into that group, don't despair. Use the *easy way.*

No matter what method of sex education you use, or what you finally say or don't say, your attitude and feelings (inputs and outputs) are perhaps the most important messages you convey to your child. If you can be relaxed while giving the information, your child will probably be relaxed about receiving it. This will set the stage for easier participation in the more sophisticated exchanges that will take place later. Both you and your child will come to these better prepared if you've had an easy beginning in such discussions.

The easy way I am suggesting is especially designed for the tense parent who, if he (or she) tries the method, may find tension diminishing. There is also the reward of satisfaction in doing a job you may consider important.

Repetitious

Before I illustrate, by means of dialogue, how you might answer your child's questions, I want to prepare you for the repetitiousness of your child's questions. Not all, but many children will ask the same question over and over. Ten times. A hundred times. This applies to all questions, not just those about sex. You remember all the times he wants to hear the same book read, the same record played. Maybe you feel that you will go out of your mind, but he doesn't feel that way.

Repetition is one way children learn. When your child asks you the same question again and again, you can give the same answer. He is not asking it again because he expects a different answer, or because he is dissatisfied with your previous answer, or because he wants to annoy you. He is asking it again because he wants to hear the answer again. He wouldn't bother asking if he didn't want the answer *now.* And remember, we're talking about the easy way for the parent.

Does the child ask because he doesn't remember? I don't know. Ask. If you find that he does remember, you might wonder why he wants to know again. But it doesn't really matter why. If you find that he doesn't remember, you might also wonder why. Is it because he's stupid? Or is it because he didn't listen in the first place? I doubt it. When he asked before, his interest had been aroused at that moment, for some reason. Whatever the reason, the fact is that the child became interested and asked. Then he lost interest. Then he became interested again, and he asked again.

Who says a child has to remember all the things he's told once or a dozen times? How many times have you told him how to eat at the table, to wear clothing, etc.? They forget over and over, perhaps because they are simply not interested in these directions. I suspect most children just couldn't care less about good table manners. I'm not saying they are unimportant. I'm only trying to describe what a child's feelings might be.

Similarly, the child may have no interest, between questions, in your answers on sex matters (remember, he has little reason for consistent interest unless a big thing has been made of it), and a time lapse may cause forgetfulness. So I hope that you will not become irritated with your child (because you think he's so stupid), or with yourself (because you think if you had given an adequate answer, he wouldn't be asking again), and snap back impatiently, "I've already told you that! Don't you remember?"

The Dialogue

When your child is two or two and a half, or three, four, etc., he asks what are called "questions on sex." *We* call them that, not the child. He's just asking questions which have aroused curiosity and which are related to himself. At this age, a child is egocentric because his world is very small, and everything in it is important and precious. That's how *you* get in on this. And that, incidentally, is why he loves you so much—because you are precious to his sense of well-being.

If you do not contribute to his sense of well-being, or if you make your child feel tense, he has less reason to love you. If your child is afraid of you, he can sometimes believe that he loves you because it is advantageous to do so. After all, what can a six-year-old do with a belief that he does not love a parent? That would be pretty difficult to accept. Even some young adults have a terrible time with it.

The first question may be asked when he's noticed Aunt Jane is "fat." Little children often may not notice their own mother's "fatness," perhaps because it's so gradual. They are more likely to notice the woman they have not seen in some time.

Child: Mommy, Aunt Jane is so fat!

Mom: *Yes, she is.* (Three words.) This dialogue may end right here if the child does not ask a question. You are not obligated to say, "Yes, because she's having a baby." In fact, no question was asked at all. She didn't ask, "*Why* is Aunt Jane so fat?" Merely a fact is being stated. This conversation may continue.

Child: Mommy, why is Aunt Jane so fat?

Mom: *Because she's going to have a baby.* (Seven words.)

Again, it might stop here. Now let's test this response according to the principles previously stated. 1) It's pertinent; 2) it's under twelve words; 3) it's honest; 4) it's a direct response to the question; 5) it's answered immediately. I repeat, nothing else is required unless another question is asked. This might be the following:

Child: Why? (Why is she going to have a baby.)

Mom: *Because she wants one.* (Four words.)

Now this might be an out-and-out lie. It is altogether possible that Aunt Jane didn't want this pregnancy at all, but was careless. So she has decided to have the baby and let's hope that, having made that decision, she can welcome it when it comes. If you know the facts, but also know that the baby will be accepted with good grace, you may not be altogether dishonest when you say she wants to have the baby. (Of course, it is not necessary to go all through this background material for your under-six child.)

These vignettes of dialogue might occur all together. But they are more likely to occur with a few, or many days or weeks, in between. As I said, each question may be asked many times before your child goes on to the next question.

Child: When is Aunt Jane having her baby?

Mom: *In the summer.* (Three words.)

Child: When is that?

Mom: *A pretty long time away. When you are through with nursery school.* (Just made it—twelve words.)

This answer could be confusing. For what has nursery school to do with Jane's baby? And when is nursery school over? So let him ask.

Child: When will that be?

Mom: *When it's warm weather. Here, I'll show you on the calendar.* (Eleven words.)

He still might have no concept of when it is, but it may not matter. It doesn't seem imminent. But he can have a fine conversation with a friend and say that when it's summertime, Aunt Jane is going to have a baby because she wants to.

If the oncoming baby is the child's mother's and will be a sibling, he might be more interested. But if birth is far off, he might very well forget about it. Remember, a child doesn't know as much as you do. He doesn't know anything about being displaced (unless there's already a younger sibling), about sibling rivalry, or about how tired and impatient Mommy may be when she has been up with the baby all night. He doesn't need to be reassured that Mommy and Daddy are going to continue to love him, because the possibility that they will not never crosses his mind.

There may be some anxiety if he knows of a peer who's had trouble with a younger sibling, or someone plants the idea, or he senses some anxiety in the parent over the oncoming birth. Although he doesn't know the reason for the anxiety, it can make him uncomfortable and he may associate it with the oncoming event. But, I repeat, this discomfort will occur only because it was put there from the outside by parental or other outputs. I believe that it is unlikely—not impossible, but unlikely—that a young child will originate the idea of rivalry or feel apprehension regarding the birth of a younger sibling, without some unfortunate outputs and inputs.

I shall now run quickly through other possible questions and answers. Remember the time lapses and repetitions.

Child: Are you going to have a baby?

Mom: *Yes, I am.*

Child: When?

Mom: *Next year.*

Child: Why don't you have it now?

Mom: *Because it's not ready to be born.*

Child: Where is it?

Mom: *Inside here* (patting abdomen).

Child: Where?

Mom: *There is a special baby place inside my tummy.* (It's perfectly all right to use a simple vocabulary if you choose. The term uterus is fine if you know it and if you want to explain further what it is, because he'll probably ask. He doesn't care whether it's a uterus or not. It's enough that it's in Mommy's tummy.)

Child: How will the baby get out of your tummy?

Mom: *Through the baby hole.*

Child: Where is that? (This question sometimes stymies mothers. They think they have to lift up their leg and show where it is.)

Mom: *Between the sissy hole and the BM hole.* (Here again any familiar family idiom is useful. Both parent and child will feel more comfortable with these terms.)

Child: Can I see the baby hole?

Mom: *No.*

Child: Why not?

Mom: *Because I don't want to show it.*

Child: Do I have one?

Mom: *Yes (or no).*

Child: Does Daddy have a baby hole?

Mom: *No.*

Child: Why not?

Mom: *Because daddies don't need baby holes.*

Child: Why don't they need them?

Mom: *Because they don't have babies. Only mommies have babies.*

This last statement is gratuitous because no question was asked about it.

This is a small sample of common questions asked in many different forms and in different sequence. The five principles still apply to the answers. Later questions might be the following:

Child: How does the baby grow in your tummy?

Mom: *Daddy plants a seed there.*

Child: How?

Mom: *With his penis* (or whatever term is used).

Child: Where does Daddy get the seed?

Mom: *He has a special place in his body where he keeps the seed* (or egg).

Child: How does he get the seed into your tummy?

Mom: *He puts it in the baby hole.*
Child: How does he do that?
Mom: *With his penis.*
Child: How does he get it out of his body?
Mom: *Just like the sissy.*

I want to emphasize that many terms may be used and much other information can be given. Such a dialogue might occur over a period of several years, with many related questions being asked. Material from many excellent manuals can be used if you feel you want to give your child more information. You may find one you like more than others. Select whichever makes you most comfortable.

But most important is that you *are hearing* your child, *are acknowledging* his existence, *are giving* the questions due consideration, and *are responding.* This is what he wants and needs more than anything else. The accuracy or extent of your answers at this age isn't that important. He can't know how accurate the answers are anyway. But he can know that you are not amazed or annoyed at being asked. He can know that you think he's stupid or not stupid for asking, and he can know whether or not you regard him as an individual worthy of response. All these are sensed through all your vibes. Your child's "antennae" will receive accurately the information those vibes convey.

So you see that we are talking not only about a dialogue on sex, but about a dialogue between any two persons who can be respectful of each other's position. A discussion on sex with your under-six is only another opportunity to enhance the relationship between you and your child with child-affirming inputs and outputs.

CHAPTER XIX

——

What Does It Take?

P ARENTS HAVE WISDOM; but because they are often quite alien-
ated from it, they cannot avail themselves of their wisdom. For
example, most parents are well aware of the need for patience, kindness, courtesy, and respect in dealing with their children. But they
often act as if they had never heard of those words as living principles
for human exchanges.

If I had to choose only one of these characteristics in my quest for
deepening human relations, I would choose to explore kindness because it's so inclusive. Isn't the kind person also the patient one when
someone else can't do, can't think, doesn't know? Isn't the kind person
usually courteous in his encounters with all people, not just those who
are older or more prestigious than himself? Isn't the truly kind person
respectful of all human beings, regardless of race, creed, sex, or age?

People often interpret words or concepts inaccurately, or to an
extreme. A definition of kindness might be limited to "a property of
being kind, of good nature, favorable." Patience, as the "state of being
patient" or "having the power to continue a course or task undis-
turbed (or not duly disturbed) by obstacles, disappointments, doings,
or the like," or, "free from excitements, discontent, or *free from undue*

eagerness in awaiting a delayed event or uncertain outcome." (Definitions from Webster's.)

This last should be embroidered and hung on the wall! Think of all the parents who cannot "await" the maturity of their children, and of those who have the fortitude to persist with what they consider worthwhile parental efforts in the face of seemingly repeated failure. Even without the "failures," is the "worrying" that parents do about the outcome of their children's development not evidence of gross impatience in "awaiting" a delayed event or uncertain outcome? Is it this "uncertain outcome" which lies at the heart of so much parental anguish?—and do parents await the event of development with "undue eagerness"? How does one "await" in the process of developing? How does one know that this awaiting is not waiting for some fantasy future to unfold, but a waiting on the present as it is uncovered by your child's every glance, smile, or tear?

What Do They Need?

Most young people cannot be alone and not remain dependent in some respects. They are certainly dependent upon their families for some consistency of affection and a sense of rootedness. No peer can provide consistency in these needs. When a peer does seem to provide that consistency, however, he will be irresistible to your youngster. This need accounts for the sixteen-year-old girl who risks pregnancy or venereal disease because she hungers for a sense of being liked, wanted, approved, needed by some boy who hungers for precisely the same thing. Needing it so badly, each will at some point be unable to provide it to the other. Each then is bereft of a basic need, and that is the dependability of relationship. This dependability of relationship is one reason for the appeal of communal living to young people with this particular need. If one peer proves disappointing, there are others to fill the gap.

The power of the peer group lies in the fact that it replaces, for the youngster, the sense of belonging and of being wanted that the family has traditionally provided. This sense of consistent belonging and rootedness which people need is perhaps the basic raison d'etre for marriage and family. This is perhaps why the organization of the family, as we have known it, has lasted so long. This basic need is probably as essential to one's well-being as food and shelter. Where the family fails to provide it, the youngster seeks it elsewhere.

In previous years, it could not be sought elsewhere, because young people didn't know where to seek it, nor did they have the means at their disposal. In addition, there were neither the opportunities nor the provocations that exist today. But now, with instant information as to "where the action is" and with the means to get there, youngsters are no longer hesitating to seek their brand of the "holy grail." However, many young people involved in such migrations, because of their high level of anxiety and self-contempt, have sought to relieve themselves with drugs. It is almost as if the ticket to relationship must be paid for by *addiction* to drugs, sex, or other form of self-destructiveness. Where self-destructive payment for belonging is not extracted, the group of young people may be finding out about the beauty of human relatedness—or to put it simply, that people are more fun than anything.

What Is Important?

Parents have a lot of trouble deciding what thing is more important than another. While many things that you expect of your youngsters may all be desirable and worthwhile, you often have to decide what your priorities are in order to live in some peace with your children. If you want your twelve-year-old son to cut his hair, keep his face clean (so he doesn't get pimples), wear his boots when it's wet, his hat when it's cold, do his homework, finish his jobs, pick up his room, and do well in school, you'd better decide which of these are most important. Because, unless he's very different from many other sons, he won't do them all—and not, mind you, because he can't. He's perfectly capable of them all and of many more. You might even be able to get him to do all of them if you remind him often enough—which is really most of what nagging is all about. But the chances are that, at twelve, he will resent the nagging, whereas at eight or ten he didn't seem to mind being told every time he went out, between November and April, to wear his hat, coat, or whatever.

But if he begins to huff and puff when you remind him, it's time to sit down and do a little thinking. At stake is: 1) The amount of resentment he can build up; 2) the quality of relationship; 3) how he will respond to really important issues with you; 4) how he regards you as a separate person, as well as a parent. The way he relates to you on these picayune little issues may very well be the way he will relate to you on other issues as he grows older. How he regards you now at the beginning of his adolescence may influence how he regards you later, either as lifelong friend or as something of a nuisance to be tolerated as graciously as possible. Recall your own feelings and attitudes toward your own parents or in-laws.

While it is true that young adults and their parents can hardly stand each other sometimes, it is also possible that they may be the greatest of friends after the children have matured a little more or have their own children. But this thought is small comfort when you are right in there with the hair, the hat, the sneakers, and the dirt.

As you are sitting and thinking it might be well if you ask the question: Now do I want to be on good terms with my son some of the time? (forget *all* of the time; you won't make it!)—or do I want to be nagging and annoyed with him most of the time? If your answer is that you *must* teach him how to care for himself in all respects, and that anything else would mean that you were a rotten parent, then you will have to put up with the consequences. One of them is that you will probably be annoyed with him most of the time. And lest we forget that old two-way street, he will undoubtedly be annoyed with you. But remember, you started it. This is sad, because God knows there will be plenty of things you will both find to be annoyed about that neither of you will have anything to say about.

If your answer is that you would like to be on good terms with him at least some of the time, your next step is to decide which issue on the required list is dispensable. Is hair and face more important to you than homework and boots—or vice versa? Once you have whittled down your list, you have yet another question to ask yourself. Let's say you've decided to throw out picking up room, hat, boots, and finishing up things. That leaves you hair, face, and homework. Now you have to ask yourself if you have a chance of success. You might decide that you won't stand a chance with the hair, but maybe with the face. So choose the face. It's foolish to put yourself in the position of probable failure and increased tension on the other issues.

While these concerns may not coincide with any of those you have with your son or daughter, raising this question can often lead to a relaxing of many lines of tension, whatever their causes. What is more important?

Is Your Sofa More Important Than Your Child?

The old battle about the young child's feet on the furniture is a case in point. First, let me say that if you don't want your young son's feet on your new sofa, it's quite possible to teach him this. However, if you have been unable to do so and still insist upon it, the question is pertinent. If you cannot stand to see your child's feet on the sofa, you will constantly nag, scold, and punish for the transgression. Parents are capable of building up feelings of tremendous anger over such an issue. They will burst out with all kinds of variations on "How many times must I tell you not to put your feet on the sofa? Are you stupid or just deaf?" This is often screamed at the child in a shrill voice, with an ugly facial expression. If you've ever done this, you know what I mean. If you haven't, then this isn't meant for you.

There is more at stake here than the sofa, however. The parent in this position feels that inability to get a child to obey is a reflection upon competency as a parent. If he (or she) were an adequate parent, he feels, the child would obey. Since the child doesn't obey, then he is *ipso facto* a poor parent. Of course, this evaluation can be arrived at only from the point of view of the particular expectation you have for yourself as a parent. If your expectation is that you should be able to get your child to obey, then you have no alternative but to be very annoyed with yourself when you fail at this.

Now we are in more trouble. The parent who considers himself a poor parent doesn't like himself very much. This is one of the most uncomfortable of all human feelings. People will do almost anything to rid themselves of such a feeling. Since the feeling is so uncomfortable and guilt-producing, the parent turns on the child because, after all, it was that little snip who started the whole thing by not obeying. But here we are in the old cycle again. How can you blame a poor little child for this? What a truly terrible parent you must be. Actually, this confirms that fact. You are then so enraged at yourself that your anger is used to siphon off that feeling each time you bark, *"Will you get your feet off that sofa!"*

It's difficult for a parent to feel that his job as teacher is not important. I agree that it *is* important. But at this point, can you ask, "Really now, is keeping that sofa clean so much more important to me than my relations with my child?"

Can the Rule Bend?

A story comes to mind of the parents with the timid, withdrawn teen-age daughter who seemed to be in a world of her own. The parents could not tolerate her estrangement, and were constantly picking on her to talk with them and to "get involved." She was finally seen by a therapist who began to work with both child and parents. The therapist gently insinuated that the parents might try to get off the child's back with the involvement bit and try to be more patient. They were able to hold their fire to some extent. But one day the child came to the therapist in utter despair and related that a terrible scene had taken place at home. It was a rule in the family that the one who used the last of the toilet tissue was to put in a fresh roll. The girl had neglected to do so, and all hell had broken loose when her father saw the empty spool. So I ask again: In that circumstance, which was more important, father's inconvenience, or his child's state of mental health for that day and perhaps many days to come?

Sometimes Kids Aren't Much Fun

Honesty. That's one of the things it takes, because sometimes kids aren't much fun. Parents are often troubled because they find that they don't want to play with their little children, or if they do, they don't enjoy it. They don't know that this is quite natural and they feel guilty that they can't play with the children for an hour or two without getting cranky, irritable, or just plain bored.

It's true that it's fun to watch a child grow. But this isn't done for long stretches of time, or all at one time. You notice now and then some little thing your child does and you think, Isn't that great! or Isn't that darling! or, How fast he's growing!—and so on. The little encounters that elicit these responses in you are usually short-lived, aren't they? Maybe a few seconds? A few minutes?

When you play peekaboo with your baby, or run around the table and catch him and he shrieks with delight, how long can you keep it up? Five times? Fifteen times? Each time takes maybe ten seconds. That, with five seconds between, multiplied by fifteen, makes about five minutes. You can get pretty tired running around the table five solid minutes, even though he can run around a hundred times. So you stop. He coaxes you to do it again. Enough! The books say, "Find a quiet toy and distract your child with it." But do you do that? Maybe. If you don't, you say, "Now don't bother me anymore." If you say that unequivocally, he'll probably leave you alone. But if you think you should be playing with him some more, you won't be very convincing (the double message again). Then the tug of war starts and, whether you play again or not, you probably become angry and speak sharply.

He can tell you're angry and can tell it's on his account. As he grows older, he may begin to feel that he is a "bad" child if you are angry. He's not sure what's bad, but something is—and this can undermine his self-confidence.

Why do you feel you should go on playing with your child? Some parents really like this kind of play. Many do not. They'll put up with it for a few minutes. And it's fun to see and hear the child respond with glee. But the actual game may not be much fun. Depending upon the age of the child and the activity, how many adults really enjoy cards, board games, or other games with children after fifteen or thirty minutes? How do you enjoy playing cards with your child when, if you play honestly, you win every time? If you don't win, you're probably playing dishonestly. Some people can become very hung up over this issue. But honest or dishonest, is that the kind of game you enjoy? How long would you play that kind of game with your spouse or your friends? If you feel your spouse requires that kind of playing, and you've made up your mind that this is how you're going to do it, fine. But don't expect to enjoy it very much for very long.

Go Out and Play With Your Son

When you go out to play catch with a five-year-old son, can you just stand there and throw the ball gently so the little fellow can catch it sometimes? Do you expect him to catch it even though you've thrown it twenty times? Do you get impatient and find yourself saying rather sharply, "Come on now, hold your hands closer together so the ball doesn't fall through?" Or can you patiently throw a few times and spend the rest of the time walking and looking at the trees and the bugs crawling on the walk? You don't *have* to teach him how to catch the ball perfectly each time you go out. Remember, you're supposed to be playing with him, not training him. He'll learn faster if you play rather than train. If you have a goal, you will be disappointed if he doesn't live up to your expectations. And if you are disappointed in him, you won't be fun for him. How would you like to play a game with someone who repeatedly told you that you were some kind of klutz?

This goes for his throwing the ball as well. Some children can't learn to throw a ball properly. Now I ask you, what fun is it for a grown man or woman to play ball with a little boy who can't even throw a ball in the right direction? And there is great big Daddy running like a fool all over the lot to retrieve the ball. Well! You're going to teach that son to throw it straight if it takes all afternoon! And you might succeed. But you'll pay. You'll pay.

You can make it easier for yourself by waiting until he's older and can better control his muscles. Then you'll have many *teachable moments,* for he will be more ready at that time. He'll appreciate your teaching, but not before. If you've been too early with this, and he keeps failing and disappointing you, he can only dislike you for showing your displeasure.

Parent Boredom

Many parents are just plain bored by long periods of their children's company. They don't mind taking care of their children's concrete needs, taking them places, entertaining them with shows, parties, companions, and so forth. But just to be with a little child for a long period of time is something that drives some parents up the wall. I consider a long period to be anywhere from one hour and up. I think most parents can stand about half an hour fairly comfortably. Yet they persist because they think it's their duty. So what the child has to cope with is an increasingly irritable and tense parent, who is not liking himself nor the child very much. What a drag for both of them!

After all, what can you say to a three-year-old for two hours? He can say plenty to you, but do you want to hear it all? Fine, if you do.

But really, if you had a choice, would you choose a three-year-old companion? Or would you choose a peer with whom you had some interest in common? If you can accept the truth—that you don't really like to play with your child longer than thirty minutes—the chances are you'll find something else or someone else he can pass the time with. This is nothing to be ashamed of; you are not doing your child a service by inflicting yourself, as an irritable parent, upon him. He's better off with only fifteen or thirty minutes of good fun with you, if you are more relaxed knowing that the time will be limited, than with two hours of irritation.

Don't compare yourself with the babysitter who may sit for four hours and never seem bored or irritated. That's her area of expertise. She's devised all kinds of ways for doing this. How many other things do you have to do when you are sitting with baby? Shall we count them? It might be a good idea, though, to watch the babysitter once in a while so that you can use her techniques when needed. But I don't think you'll enjoy it.

The problem of being bored with baby diminishes in intensity as he grows older. There are many reasons for this. He becomes more interesting to be with. Skill at games, or whatever, increases so that you really have someone to contend with. He develops many other interests, so he isn't so dependent upon you for company. His expansion into the world is exciting to witness and to hear about. And then, as he gets even older, and you begin to encounter the vicissitudes of adolescence, I can almost guarantee that, while you may be miserable, you won't be bored.

Epilogue

I mentioned earlier that reference material here has been derived from parent discussion groups, private practice, and from other professional and social associations in educational and psychiatric milieux. But in addition to that, my most significant and steadfast point of reference has been the works of Dr. Karen Horney.

As a student of Freud, Dr. Horney received her psychiatric and psychoanalytic training in Europe during the early part of this century. Unable to reconcile many of the features of orthodox analytic theory with her clinical findings, she began independent study of the impact of the culture upon the development of individual neuroses.

Especially troubling to her was the discrepancy between views on feminine psychology current at the time and evidence provided by her patients. She felt that the opinions of a small group of analysts, largely men working with limited numbers of severely neurotic young men and women, could hardly establish valid criteria for a definitive psychology of millions of women in Western cultures. As a brilliant, perceptive clinician, and as a woman, she argued that a valid theory of feminine psychology should apply generally to all women, including herself.

Dr. Horney's papers on feminine psychology were well received because of her sound position and prudent tone. But increasing political pressures in Europe, plus an attractive invitation to lecture in America, led to her decision, in 1932, to come to the United States to live and work.

Her theories were set forth in a series of writings which continued until her death in 1952. She drew upon literary and philosophic writings and the works of her colleagues, but mostly upon her own clinical findings. Her material kaleidoscoped into the evolution of a theory of neurosis containing unique and previously undefined features.

Her books have been and are used as texts in colleges and universities, both here and abroad, by students in the psychological, educational, and sociological disciplines. Because of such broad exposure and a subsequent large following, Karen Horney's ideas have filtered through much current thinking on the human condition, often without the awareness of those whose very work rests upon her premises. Teachers, for example, have found her concepts useful in understanding their own reactions in the classroom and in dealing with all youngsters, especially disturbed and disruptive children. Perhaps the introduction of Horney's works into teacher training courses might contribute to greater understanding of the dynamics of learning and behavior in the classroom.

My own first contact with Dr. Horney's works was in the 1940s, when I was studying for a master's degree at Columbia University. I studied her comprehensive theory of neurosis later when I was in analytic training in New York City, at the American Institute for Psychoanalysis, which was founded by Dr. Horney in 1941. I learned then that the depth of her understanding of intrapsychic processes reached previously unexplored dimensions. Intensive study, coupled with extensive clinical experience, was required to grasp the scope of her theories.

Perhaps Karen Horney's greatest current appeal is to those women who have felt inner strivings for greater autonomy. While Dr. Horney insisted upon exposing the myths of feminine psychology of her day, she did not, however, promote the welfare of any one group at the expense of another. She believed in the potential for constructive growth in *all* human beings. Nevertheless, she could certainly be called one of the *first women liberationists* to have gained any stature.

My own deep belief in the incredibly broad, and for the most part unrealized, potential of any person motivates me to make efforts to help people see blockages to their growth, obstacles that they have unwittingly established within themselves. These blockages often keep them from realizing even the most modest aspirations. It is these blockages in your relations with your children that I have tried, by two means, to help you overcome. One is by presenting some of the destructive exchanges which actually take place in the family. The other is by describing a method which may serve to overcome the blockages. If I have succeeded in any small measure, your increased sense of well-being will reward us both.

INDEX

Index

action phase. *See* solution testing

addiction, 140, 221

adolescence and adolescents, 22–6, 31–3, 49–50, 51, 81, 99, 106, 114–15, 119–20, 122–7, 183, 222; and affection, 125–6; and communication, 125; and disapproval, 127; and kindness, 124–5; and sincerity, 122–4

American Institute for Psychoanalysis, 229

anger reactions, 10, 131–2, 150–7, 186–7; as crisis resolutions, 156; and parental failure, 186–7; and personality types, 154–5

The Angry Book (Rubin), 150

anxiety, 53–4, 63–5, 71–2, 81–4, 85–8, 118–19, 135; and parental permissiveness, 195–9

babies, 159–67; and anxiety, 96–7; communication with, 159–67; needs of, 164–5; and parent development, 116–17; reactions to stress, 82; and tension, 82

bedtime problems, 37–9; and 'double message,' 37–8; and permissiveness, 38; solutions to, 38–9

bed-wetting, 7

child-centered homes, 103–4

child-parent relationship. *See* parent-child relationship

233